Tortured Confessions

Prisons and Public Recantations in Modern Iran

Ervand Abrahamian

UNIVERSITY OF CALIFORNIA PRESS

BERKELEY LOS ANGELES LONDON

University of California Press
Berkeley and Los Angeles, California

University of California Press, Ltd.
London, England

© 1999 by the Regents of the University of California

Library of Congress Cataloging-in-Publication Data

Abrahamian, Ervand, 1940–
    Tortured confessions : prisons and public
recantations in modern Iran / Ervand Abrahamian.
        p.   cm.
    Includes bibliographical references and index.
    ISBN 0-520-21623-7 (alk. paper).—
    ISBN 0-520-21866-3 (alk. paper)
    1. Torture—Iran.   2. Political prisoners—Iran.
    3. Confession (Law)—Iran.   4. Punishment—
Iran.   5. Iran—Politics and government.   I. Title.
HV8599.I7A37   1999
365'.64—dc21   98-42989
                                                CIP

Manufactured in the United States of America

9 8 7 6 5 4 3 2 1

The paper used in this publication is both acid-free and
totally chlorine-free (TCF). It meets the minimum
requirements of American Standard for Information
Sciences—Permanence of Paper for Printed Library
Materials, ANSI Z39.48-1984.

Contents

Acknowledgments

This book, like most, is a joint effort by many. I would like to thank first and foremost the many refugees at the Archiv für Forschung und Dokumentation Iran in Berlin who gave me unlimited help and openhanded hospitality. Without them this study would not have been undertaken. I would also like to thank the National Endowment for Humanities for an annual fellowship; Baruch College in the City University of New York for a sabbatical leave; the Research Committee at the City University of New York for a travel grant to Europe; and the Baruch College Research Committee for lightening my teaching responsibilities. Thanks also go to those who commented on earlier drafts of the manuscript—especially Hamid Ahmadi, Ali Gheissari, Dr. Morteza Mohit, E.A., Evan and Minou Seigal, Mohammad Reza Afshari, and Mansour Farhang. Further thanks to Hamid Ahmadi for providing me with videotapes from his Iranian Left History Project. Finally, I would like to thank Lynne Withey, Rose Anne White, Suzanne Samuel, and Sheila Berg for guiding the manuscript through the editorial process. Obviously, the above individuals and institutions are in no way responsible for the errors in judgment and facts found in these pages.

Introduction

Torture has ceased to exist.
Victor Hugo

Return of Torture

Sixty years ago Iranian lawyers would have readily agreed with Victor Hugo's famous pronouncement, "Torture has ceased to exist."[1] Iran had followed Europe's example of banning torture from the whole judicial process. Policemen were prohibited from using brute force to extract information and confessions. Judges lost their age-old array of corporal punishments. Similarly, prison wardens no longer routinely inflicted physical chastisements—even though they were not averse to killing their wards if ordered to do so. They murdered—but observed the taboo against torture.

By the 1980s, however, torture had returned with a vengeance. Prisoners—especially political ones—were now routinely subjected to physical torments reminiscent of bygone centuries. The taboo had been broken. According to Amnesty International, the United Nations, and Human Rights Watch, in a world in which prison brutality was rampant, Iran outdid most other countries in its use of systematic physical torture.[2]

This return of torture obviously runs counter to Michel Foucault's *Discipline and Punish*.[3] According to Foucault's famous paradigm, societies inevitably replace physical with nonphysical punishments as they move from traditional to modern dis-

1

courses. In traditional societies, punishments came in the shape of corporal torments—on the public scaffold as well as in closed judicially supervised torture chambers. In modern societies, however, they come in the form of prolonged imprisonment—often under close surveillance. According to Foucault, the "theater of horror" gives way to penitentiary walls; the imprint on the body, to "remolding of the soul"; the street scaffold, to the carceral archipelago; and the medieval Inquisition, to Jeremy Bentham's Panopticon—at least in grand aspiration if not in actuality.

The return of torture to Iran has been accounted for in a number of ways.[4] Some claim the reemergence is not surprising because torture is deeply ingrained in all "Asiatic" cultures. Others argue the reemergence is to be expected because the Islamic Republic, being a "throwback to the dark ages," has reverted to all things medieval. Yet others argue that the return does not invalidate Foucault because its ultimate purpose is to establish social discipline by "making and then remaking the victim."[5] Meanwhile, apologists for the present regime have argued that Iran—like many other contemporary states—has no choice but to resort to emergency measures to counter heavily armed terrorist organizations. After all, even Jeremy Bentham, the champion crusader against torture, was ambivalent on the question of whether in emergencies the police could use force to obtain information that would directly save innocent lives.[6]

These explanations, however, do not bear close scrutiny. If torture was so ingrained in Iranian culture, why did it recede from the national scene for more than half a century—from the early 1920s until the early 1970s? In these five decades, prisoners often complained about *shekanjeh* (torture). But by this, they meant a slap on the face, verbal abuse, a withheld meal, or, at worst, a few days solitary confinement. Brute force was rarely used. "Shekanjeh"—like the English term "torture"—is a useful yardstick for measuring the prevalent "threshold of outrage." One generation's "torture" is another's inconvenience. In the words of one former prisoner, "In the 1930s we often complained of being tortured but our suffering was nothing compared to what prisoners have to bear nowadays."[7] Another former prisoner writes, "I begin my prison reminiscences with much humility fully cognizant of the fact that our hardships were nothing compared to those of later generations."[8]

If torture is intrinsically linked to the "traditional" nature of the present regime, why did its return predate the Islamic Republic? For it began to reemerge under the "modernizing" Pahlavi monarchy—half a decade before the revolution and the appearance of the clerical republic. As this book will show, the Shah in the early 1970s was beginning to resort to torture for reasons very similar to those of the subsequent Islamic Republic. These reasons had little to do with modernity and tradition but much to do with ideological warfare, political mobilization, and the need to win "hearts and minds."

Similarly, the desire for social discipline cannot explain the return of torture. If its main purpose is to create discipline in the wider society, why is it hidden behind closed doors and its existence vehemently denied? The public scaffold may possibly induce social conformity; torture behind closed doors cannot. Moreover, if discipline is the main purpose, why are prison wardens so oblivious to the whole issue of order, control, and regimentation? Prison memoirs are unanimous in reporting that the authorities invariably leave the administration of the wards to the inmates themselves. Ironically, this makes the prison the one place in the whole country where "grassroots democracy," including voting and direct participation, is practiced on a daily basis. Furthermore, torture, despite its physical damage, rarely "remakes" the personality. On the contrary, the victims—at least, those who survive—end up more alienated from the regime. As one prisoner notes, very few of her cellmates changed their views even in the worst days of ideological indoctrination. She adds that many lost their lives simply because they remained ideologically contemptuous of their interrogators.[9]

Finally, the search for security information cannot explain the return of torture to Iran. If the ultimate aim is to obtain such information, why then does torture invariably continue

until something far more important is obtained: the public
e'terafat, a term that means, significantly, not only confession
but also political and ideological recantation. Some modern
states—especially in Latin America—have used torture for information, intimidation, and self-incrimination. But Iran uses
it predominantly to obtain these ideological recantations.
Some states—again in Latin America—give their interrogators
free rein, thereby providing them with the opportunity to grat-
ify personal whims and sadistic instincts. But the clerical authorities in Iran keep close tabs on the interrogators and
invariably stop the torment once they have obtained the
sought-after recantation.

This gives the term "torture" a special poignancy as the victims themselves can end the pain by simply complying with
their interrogators' demands. It is torture in the true sense, distinct from inhumane punishment, gratuitous pain, and degrad-
ing treatment. According to its Latin derivation, "torture" is the
infliction—or the threat of the infliction—of intense physical
and psychological pain to extort from the victim what the authorities demand. Some recent works on torture have diluted
the term by minimizing its political poignancy and calculated
rationality and stretching it to encompass any form of pain,
including war suffering, plain brutality, domestic violence, religious flagellations, and even sadomasochistic pleasure. To
practice torture, states do not necessarily have to be sadistic
and primitive. On the contrary, they can be highly rational,
modern, and calculating.

Public Recantations

Public recantations in Iran come in various forms—in pretrial
testimonials; in chest-beating letters; in mea culpa memoirs; in
"press conferences," "debates," and "roundtable discussions";
and, most prevalent of all, in videotaped "interviews" and "conversations" aired on prime-time television. Under the Shah,
leftists had monopolized such television programs. Under the

Islamic Republic, television has become an equal-opportunity medium featuring prominent figures representing a wide spectrum of opinion—from monarchists, liberals, religious conservatives, and secular nationalists, to conventional Marxists, Maoists, and Trotskyists, all the way to radical Muslims and even ex-Khomeinists, who, for one reason or another, have fallen by the political wayside. Recantations from lesser figures often do not hit the airwaves. Instead, they are shown on closed-circuit television within prisons and then filed away for future court use. In fact, they become the essential component of the prisoner's *dosieh* (dossier). The chief warden of Evin, the main political prison in Tehran, has boasted that more than 95 percent of his "guests" eventually oblige him with his sought-after videotaped "interview."[10]

These tapes bear striking and eerie resemblance to recantations produced elsewhere—especially in Maoist China during the 1949–54 "brainwashing" campaign and the 1965–71 Cultural Revolution; in Stalinist Russia and Eastern Europe, first during the 1935–39 Moscow trials and later in 1951–54 during the so-called Slansky trials; and in early modern Europe, from the thirteenth to the seventeenth century, when both Catholic inquisitors and Protestant monarchs often extracted confessions from political as well as nonpolitical prisoners, notably from religious dissenters. Although other societies, such as the United States during McCarthyism, have also shown some interest in public recantations, none have outdone Iran, Stalinist Russia, Maoist China, and early modern Europe in their systematic use. These four can be considered to be in a league of their own.

Despite the wide gap in culture, time, and space, these four societies have produced recantations uncannily similar in format, language, imagery, and even metaphors. These recantations are replete with such potent terms as "redemption"; "repentance"; "forgiveness"; "second chance"; "open eyes"; "seeing the light"; "cautionary tales"; "reflection on past errors"; "return to the Community"; "treason"; "betrayal"; "deviation from the straight and narrow path"; "sin and pitfalls of utter damnation"; "devilish deeds"; "clandestine meetings"; "sinister conspiracies"; "hidden hands"; "richly deserved punishments"; "wolves in sheeps' clothing"; and, of course, "consorting with the enemy and his representatives." The same scriptwriter could have composed all the recantations—with, of course, some improvisations for the immediate circumstances. A recantation given in Iran could well have been presented by Nicolai Bukharin, Rudolf Slansky, a Chinese revisionist, Galileo, Thomas Cromwell, or a Templar knight.

Even witch trials in early modern Europe produced similar confessions—although their victims were "social" rather than "political" deviants. They were invariably dragged to court by neighbors rather than by the authorities. They were accused not of high treason but of *maleficium*—use of black magic against fellow villagers. They submitted themselves to punishment ostensibly to save their souls in the next world rather than to redeem themselves in this world. Despite these differences, their confessions repeated themes found in political recantations the world over: demonic meetings, crimes against fellow beings, choosing evil over the good, deviation from the correct path, the mortal danger posed to all by external forces, the naming of names, and the plea to be reintegrated into the Community. Not surprisingly, some consider witch trials in early modern Europe to be merely an extension of medieval heresy trials.

The recantations in these very different societies are similar precisely because they perform a similar function—that of grand theater staged by the authorities as positive propaganda for themselves and as negative propaganda against their real and imagined enemies. They are intended to destroy as well as to win over hearts and minds. The texts are similar precisely because they have comparable subtexts, pretexts, and even contexts.

As positive propaganda, the recanters praise on high the powers that be—whether Church, State, Crown, Party, or Leader. They submit to the authorities and recognize their legitimacy by meticulously citing their honorific titles, grand claims, and historic achievements. They reaffirm the official version of reality, of Truth, and of History. In short, they repeat the Gospel according to their Rulers. They also reconfirm the importance of ideological conformity and the pitfalls of non-conformity. This explains why such shows appear less in conventional autocracies and more in ideologically charged societies—whether modern or medieval, whether totalitarian or highly traditional. Some have mistakenly linked public recantations to modern totalitarianism, forgetting that such shows were pioneered by medieval inquisitors who lacked even rudimentary state institutions. In submitting, the recanters affirm not only the omnipotence and righteousness of the authorities but also, significantly, their intrinsic benevolence. This explains why they invariably absolve the authorities of any pain they may suffer and instead stress that punishment ultimately originates from God, the Community, the General Will, or the Irresistible Forces of History. Forgiveness comes from the authorities; retribution, from powers beyond.

As negative propaganda, the recanters proclaim on high their own and their colleagues' utter depravity. They come onto the stage to humiliate, dehumanize, and demonize themselves as well as their asssociates. Repeating official accusations, they depict themselves as criminals, saboteurs, conspirators, traitors, scoundrels, deviants, degenerates, vermin, mad dogs, and even the Devil's sexual partners. In short, they confess to having inverted and subverted society's positive values. The intention is to devastate the opposition through disillusionment, demoralization, and depoliticization. In fact, this negative propaganda against the enemy is as significant as the positive propaganda for the authorities. While the introduction and conclusion of the text sing loud praises for the authorities, its main content rants and raves against the enemy.

One's mere presence on the stage is itself a form of suicide, for it signifies the explicit rejection of oneself as well as the implicit betrayal of one's own friends, colleagues, and beliefs. One does not have to be a Christian to be repelled by the figure of Judas—by "traitors," "betrayers," "turncoats," "rats," "finks," "stool pigeons," "squealers," and those who name names to save their own skins. Not surprisingly, many Iranians in the 1980s equated recantations with suicide and total destruction of one's *aberu* (honor, reputation, self-respect, and even persona).

Recantations work best when their publics, especially the targeted audience, share two preconceptions. First, they feel that their society is mortally threatened by omnipotent external forces plotting incessantly with enemies well hidden in the very bowels of their community. This *mentalité* can be termed conspiratorial—even paranoid. Second, they are remarkably innocent of the stage preparations that precede the show. They associate confessions with truth, guilt, redemption, and moral conscience—not with torture, coercion, violence, and unbridled power. Consequently, the recantations stress the "voluntary" nature of the whole exercise as well as the sinister links between external and internal enemies. These two issues feature as prominently as propaganda for the authorities and against the opposition.

In all four cases, the enemy was omnipotent as well as omnipresent. In medieval and early modern Europe, it took the shape of the Devil, his well-concealed agents, and his equally well-concealed dupes—Jews masquerading as Christians, churchgoing peasants harboring Manichaean heresies, or witches pretending to be harmless old women. The Inquisition handbook *Malleus Maleficarum* (The Hammer of the Witches) spelled out how to identify, unmask, and convict such deadly women. Cool-headed scholars such as Thomas Moore and Jean Bodin, not to mention John Calvin and Martin Luther, were convinced that thousands—perhaps hundreds of thousands—of witches were running rampant and endangering the whole of Christendom. According to one leading historian of European witchcraft, many of those burned at the stake had aroused their neighbors' suspicions long before they were actually brought to trial.[11] Similarly, the charges brought against the Templars—however fantastic to the modern ear—struck a chord for their contemporaries as many already suspected this secretive order of practicing homosexuality, worshiping the

Devil, and aiding and abetting the Muslims in the Holy Land.[12] The confessions merely reinforced public suspicions and preconceptions.

In the communist world, the external enemy took the form of imperialism—especially German in the Moscow purges, British in the Slansky trials, and American in the Chinese Cultural Revolution. Imperialism was deemed extremely dangerous because it could recruit agents who to all outward appearances seemed to be militant communists—even veterans of the Bolshevik Revolution, of the Spanish Civil War, and of the Long March. In his *Short History of the Communist Party*, Stalin drastically revised dialectical materialism to argue that the class struggle would inevitably intensify—not wane—in the decades following the triumphant revolution. Thus, according to Stalin, the danger of conspiracies increased in the 1920s to peak in the 1930s. The Moscow trials were clearly pitched to two different audiences. For the party faithful, those in the dock had aided and abetted the German "fascist"—if not objectively, at least subjectively by not fully supporting the party leadership. For peasants who still believed in the supernatural, the defendants had sold their souls in exchange for the destruction of cattle and crops. This explains why Trotsky (Lev Bronstein), even though isolated in distant Mexico, was credited with demonic powers and accused of damaging the harvest as well as masterminding grand conspiracies with his archenemies—Kamenev, Zinoviev, and Bukharin.[13]

The "paranoid style" is equally prevalent in Iran.[14] The public—at least since the 1930s—has become increasingly convinced that foreign enemies are incessantly plotting to destroy the country with the help of a *seton-e panjom* (fifth column). This foreign term has gained currency not only among nationalists, royalists, leftists, and liberals but also among religious conservatives and even so-called fundamentalists, who supposedly reject all alien concepts. For some, the real enemy is capitalist America; for others, imperialist Britain; for yet others, communist Russia. In Khomeini's terminology, America is the "Great Satan," Russia the "Other Satan," and Britain the "Little

Satan." These satans are to be taken with the utmost serious-
ness because they have for years created their own fifth col-
umns by recruiting citizens who appear loyal in terms of birth,
upbringing, language, and even religion but, in fact, are dis-
loyal in their inner thoughts and ideological affinities. The ac-
cusation of being a "foreign agent" and a "fifth columnist"
invariably sticks simply because much of the public is convinced that foreign powers are pulling many of the strings
within the body politic. In fact, the accused themselves often
subscribe to the conspiratorial paradigm—although they
would make an exception of their own cases. In the same way
that European "witches" believed in the existence of the Devil
and his agents, self-confessed "foreign spies" in Iran subscribe
to the prevalent conspiratorial theory of politics.

The recantations become especially useful when the audience is predisposed to accept confessions at face value and is
innocent of the efforts that go into producing the show. The
recanters, not to mention the authorities, insist that the testimonials are the product of much self-examination, reflection,
and reconsideration, and that such confessions have nothing
to do with coercion but are genuine signs of guilt, penance, and
striving for redemption—either in this or in the next world. In
Iran, as in premodern Europe and the communist world, confessions are deemed to be the "proof of proofs," the "mother of
proofs," and the "best evidence of guilt." In the words of two
European historians, "common justice demanded that witches
should not be condemned to death unless convicted by their
own confession."[15] Had not Saint Augustine himself declared
that self-confession was the very best proof of heresy? As Bukharin cryptically noted in his final speech, "The confession of
the accused is a medieval principle of jurisprudence."[16]

Even the Inquisition minimized the role of torture—at least
before the public. It preferred the euphemism *quaestio*—"to
question." It reserved the term "torture" for the suffering borne
by the supposed victims of "black magic." It convened behind
closed doors, presenting to the public only the final testimo-

nials and the climactic auto-da-fé.[17] It restricted the circulation of handbooks on judicial torture—these books became well known centuries later when anticlerical historians cited them with much relish.[18] These books regulated the types of torture to be used, stipulated that blood should not be spilled, and required that the damning confession be repeated outside the torture chambers—this made them "voluntary."[19] Henry Lea, the leading authority on the Spanish Inquisition, argues that the court proceedings have "singularly few" references to torture simply because it was felt that its mere mention "would invalidate the force of the testimony."[20]

The Inquisition argued that this form of questioning was incidental to the final outcome. It also argued that the primary function of the procedure was to save souls; that the devious nature of the Devil made it impossible to obtain direct evidence; and that information gathered from "questioning" was as good as direct evidence so long as it came from those who were "probably guilty"—that is, those deemed suspect because of their social standing and individual behavior. Similar rationales are to be found in contemporary Iran.

The role of torture was also hidden during the Moscow show trials. The American ambassador reported to President Roosevelt that the confessions proved "beyond doubt that the defendants were guilty."[21] Why else, he insisted, would they present such damaging confessions against themselves? Similarly, British jurists observing the trials reported that the confessions "proved" beyond doubt that the defendants had conspired with the Gestapo.[22] A Russian scholar writes that "at the time it did not occur to people that a confession made in a public court had not necessarily been freely and voluntarily given."[23] One prison inmate relates how newcomers even in 1938 were shocked to discover the "methods of persuasion" used to prepare defendants for their trials.[24] Significantly, such trials lost their press coverage in 1939 as soon as the Soviet regime acknowledged that previous police chiefs had used brute force to obtain the 1935–38 confessions.[25] Once confession is linked to torture, its spell is broken. Once broken, the confession carries the danger of damaging the authorities as much as their intended targets.

This accounts for why public confessions raise eyebrows in the West—especially among those exposed to such potent works as Voltaire's *Candide*, Beccaria's *Crimes and Punishments*, Dostoevsky's *The Brothers Karamazov*, Poe's *The Pit and the Pendulum*, Orwell's *Nineteen Eighty-four*, Arthur Koestler's *Darkness at Noon*, Bertolt Brecht's *The Life of Galileo*, and Arthur Miller's *The Crucible*. Their readers inevitably see confessions through jaundiced eyes—even if the confession happens to be genuine. The terms "confession" and "Inquisition"—especially when the latter is accompanied by the adjective Spanish—automatically invalidate the whole procedure by conjuring up images of torture, intolerance, and medieval superstitions, for example, Goya's *Auto de Fe* and *The Holy Office*. This is one arena of modern life where art has left a deep imprint. Only deconstructionists continue to find redeeming features in the inquisitional process.[26] Once confessions are coupled with state torture and coercion—not with individual guilt and redemption—the macabre theater threatens to undermine the authorities rather than to bolster them.

It should be noted that those most instrumental in exposing the Moscow trials were from the left—Orwell, Koestler, Isaac Deutscher, and the now-forgotten Victor Serge. An anarchist who helped to found the Comintern, Serge fell afoul of Stalin but was saved from the gulag by his French literary friends. He influenced many others, especially through his autobiographical works *From Lenin to Stalin* (1937), *The Case of Comrade Tulayev* (1948), and *Memoirs of a Revolutionary* (1951). He was the very first to compare the Moscow trials to the Spanish Inquisition and political recantations to medieval confessions. Also, Deutscher suspects that Brecht wrote his *Life of Galileo* (1938) under the shadow of the Moscow trials.[27] Few Iranians before the late 1980s had read these potent works; and those who had tended to dismiss them as worthless pieces of Western cold war propaganda. They did not value them as useful prisms through which they could view their own contemporary arena—at least, not until the early 1990s.

The impact of public recantations was enhanced in Iran by the introduction of television—especially of the videotape in the late 1970s. This armed the Islamic Republic with a propaganda weapon unimagined by the likes of Stalin, Mao, and the Shah—not to mention the Tudors, the Spanish Inquisition, and the European witch-hunters. Prisoners could be tortured into giving confessions and recantations. These could be taped—with little effort and cost—then edited, polished, and, if necessary, remade from scratch. The final product could be aired on radio and television, reaching audiences far greater than those of newspapers and pamphlets. By the mid-1980s, most Iranians—including peasants—had easy access to radio and television. The video further enabled the regime to fully control the timing as well as the content of the eventual show. Some tapes were previewed by Khomeini himself before being aired to the nation. What is more, the most important recantations were given additional circulation through newspapers, pamphlets, and books. The Islamic Republic, often dismissed as "medieval," is highly creative in this realm. In fact, it has the dubious honor of being the world's premier producer of recantation shows.

As public texts carefully prepared by the state and its victims, these recantations reveal much about contemporary Iran. They place in the limelight the state's avowed ideals—in the ideological as well as in the political, social, and economic realms. They hold up the opposition as the inversion of these ideals. They cite moral issues that bolster and undermine those active in the public arena. They also provide an avenue into the psyche of the larger society—its hopes and fears, likes and dislikes, dreams and nightmares, values and taboos, aspirations and aversions, past grievances and future strivings, collective memories and selective histories. In short, recantations throw valuable light on the country's mentalité.

Prison Literature

Although few in Iran had read the potent Western works on tortured confessions, Iran has a rich genre of prison literature going back to the 1940s. The genre began in 1942 when Bozorg Alavi, a young Marxist writer just released from prison, published two best-sellers entitled *Prison Scrap Papers* and *The Fifty-three*. These works left a deep imprint on Persian literature as well as on modern Iranian politics.

Bozorg Alavi's books are unlike previous prison literature found either in Iran or in the West. Such Persian literature had been composed mostly by fallen court poets pleading clemency, bemoaning their plight, singing praises of those on high, and groveling in the hope of regaining royal favor.[28] They can be described as conventional court poetry—but composed in royal dungeons or in provincial banishment. Bozorg Alavi's writings are very different. Classic Western prison literature—Dostoevsky's *House of the Dead*, Oscar Wilde's *De Profundis*, Serge's *Men in Prison*, and Prince Kropotkin's *Memoirs of a Revolutionist*—is presented in a chronological narrative. Bozorg Alavi illustrates the human predicament in prison with poignant vignettes, vivid character sketches, composite events—part real, part fictional—and frugal brush strokes reminiscent of Ernest Hemingway, Franz Kafka, and John Steinbeck.

In a subtle and low-key manner, Bozorg Alavi depicts how ordinary individuals confined within narrow walls, often for indefinite periods, try to preserve their sanity, dignity, privacy, hopes, principles, political ideals, and humor (invariably of the black variety). Without moralizing, political sloganeering, and appeals to the transcendental powers of God, Justice, and History, Bozorg Alavi recounts how diverse individuals thrown together by force of circumstances—or rather, by force of the state—cope with such mundane problems as boredom, meddlesome guards, difficult cellmates, lack of cigarettes, and strained family relations. He often uses small events in prison to illustrate issues of social injustice in the larger world outside. The true heroes, in his eyes, are ordinary humans who survive prison by retaining their sanity, personality, and individuality. In a short story entitled "Waiting," he writes,

> The prisoner's greatest pain is not the separation from loved ones. Nor the lack of normal pleasures. Nor the kick on the behind from the guards. Like it or not, one has to put up with these. One gets used to them. No, one's worst pain is being locked up with others. The place, after all, is a prison. You are cooped up with people with whom you have nothing in common. You have to eat with them, talk to them, share a cell with them. How long can you talk to someone about your personal life? How many times can you tell them you are sick and tired of this existence—especially of looking at his torn underwear? How long can you sit and watch your cellmates gobble down their food into their gaping mouths? How long can you stand having loud nervous laughter rudely interrupt your daydreams about snow-covered mountains and green fields? This type of torment can go on endlessly.[29]

Some have noted that the historical novel came to Iran in the 1920s as an instrument for building modern national consciousness. Few have noted that the prison genre arrived in the 1940s—thanks to Bozorg Alavi—as a form of protest against the state, of resistance against the establishment, and of eyewitness account against the powers that be, including the condescending literati eager to relegate dissenting voices to oblivion. Much has been written on the Persian novel, but nothing on this genre of prison literature.

Hot on Bozorg Alavi's heels, two veteran communists—Ardashir Ovanessian and Jafar Pishevari—published their own prison memoirs. Others trickled out in the next ten years, until the 1953 coup put a temporary end to them. The genre, however, resumed as a torrent in the decade immediately after the 1979 revolution. Although most recent memoirs deal with the more immediate 1980s, some go back to the 1930s, some to the 1940s and 1950s, and some to the turbulent 1960s and 1970s. Many of the authors are women bearing witness to loved ones who did not survive prison. Most are written by leftists; some, by royalists, nationalists, and Islamists. But whether the authors are old or young, men or women, leftists or nonleftists, they are all influenced—explicitly or implicitly—by Bozorg Alavi.

Although these memoirs often lack Bozorg Alavi's subtlety and literary talent, they nevertheless provide a wealth of information on prison life. They—especially those written by women—throw light on daily life: on the relationships between classes, ethnic groups, young and old, rival political organizations, leaders and followers, sympathizers and true believers, Muslim and non-Muslim. They illustrate changing perceptions of shame, honor, justice, self-respect, individual rights, and the human body. They also illuminate the culture of resistance, especially attitudes toward violence, deprivation, torture, and corporal punishment. They contain some hints as to who does and does not survive the ordeal with body and mind intact. Even more important, they reveal the behind-the-stage preparations that went into the making of the famous, or rather notorious, television recantations. They do for Iran what Orwell, Koestler, Brecht, and Miller have done for the West.

1

Reza Shah

Qasr Prison was known as the
Iranian Bastille. In actual fact, it
did not deserve such a macabre
reputation.
Ardashir Ovanessian, Memoirs

Traditional Punishments

Nineteenth-century Iran—like most traditional societies—punished transgressions not with prolonged imprisonment but with various forms of physical torment and violent death. *Sharia* (religious) as well as *urf* (state) courts inflicted an array of corporal punishments—some of which were prescribed by the Koran and the *sunna* (religious traditions). They gouged out eyes. They amputated fingers, feet, and ears. They hanged, decapitated, strangled, impaled, disemboweled, crucified, hurled from cliffs, buried alive, and drew-and-quartered. Most common of all, they flogged the soles of the feet in a process known as *falak*. The English called this the bastinado—a Spanish-derived term. The Spanish themselves preferred the Persian-derived word *falanga*. The falak could also be inflicted by provincial governors, tribal chiefs, guild elders, and even village headmen.[1]

Iran, like traditional Europe, did not contain proper prisons in the sense of places for long-term posttrial incarceration. Instead, it had small jails and dungeons for those awaiting trial

17

or punishment. These were invariably in royal forts, citadels, and armories. Prominent figures were punished with physical retribution, internal exile—often to their villages—or banishment to bleak faraway fortresses. The best known were Maku in northern Azerbaijan, Kalat in northern Khorasan, and Khorramabad near the southwestern border. The last was notorious as the Falak al-Falak. It continued to be used until the 1950s.

In theory, urf and sharia courts had separate jurisdictions. The urf courts, headed by the Shah and his governors, adjudicated cases that directly concerned the state. They based their verdicts on unwritten traditions as well as on *maslahat* (political expediency). The sharia courts, manned by clerical *qazi*s and *shaykh al-islam*s, enforced the religious law on moral, civil, and criminal matters. In practice, the line was not so clear-cut. The Shah claimed ultimate authority over death sentences. He appointed the qazis and shaykh al-islams in the sharia courts. The urf courts themselves supposedly abided by the sharia. What is more, most capital crimes—for example, heresy, sedition, and even banditry—could be deemed offenses against the *dawlat* (state) as well as against the *ummat* (religious community). The most serious crime of all was *mofsad fey al-araz*— sowing "moral corruption" as well as "political sedition" on earth.

Both systems freely resorted to judicial torture even though the sharia in theory frowned on such practices. Had not the Prophet himself declared that "God shall torture in the next world those who have tortured others in this world?"[2] Had not the Prophet been outraged when Meccans had tormented his companion Bilal to renounce Islam? According to tradition, Bilal would have accepted anything as his true God, even a beetle, to stop the unbearable pain.[3] Had not the Prophet's immediate successors—the Rightly Guided Caliphs—explicitly outlawed even verbal intimidation on the grounds that such pressure could frighten the innocent to bear false witness?[4] What is more, the sharia—like medieval Roman canon law— developed stringent rules of evidence, especially for capital crimes. It categorically rejected circumstantial evidence. It stipulated that eyewitnesses had to be highly reliable, which was conventionally defined as at least two upright adult male Muslims. It also stipulated that confessions could not be accepted in court unless given freely, orally, and publicly.

These stringent rules led the sharia—again like Roman canon law—to rely heavily on self-incriminatory statements, all the while pretending such statements were entirely voluntary. Thus it accepted judicial torture under various guises: maslahat (expediency), protecting the state and the community; *towbeh* (repentance), because penance could alleviate punishment in this as well as the next world; and *ta'zir* (discretionary punishment)—a non-Koranic term—which permitted magistrates to mete out noncapital punishments to suspected criminals, including suspected perjurers. In short, despite the Prophet and the Rightly Guided Caliphs, magistrates freely resorted to judicial torture but acted as if the confession presented in open court was completely unrelated to the physical coercion exerted during the interrogation.

Although nineteenth-century Iran kept judicial torture behind closed doors, formal punishments were performed in full public view—often in the Maydan-e Falakeh (Flogging Square). They were carried out by the Mir Ghazabs (Masters of Wrath) and their *farrash* (footmen). The Masters of Wrath were also known as the Nasaqchis—literally, those who both "multilate the body" and "restore order to the body politic." The double entendre would have appealed to Foucault. Wearing black hats and bright red coats, the Masters of Wrath led royal processions and displayed to the public the brute power of their sovereign. In appointing provincial governors, the Shah bestowed on them both a Mir Ghazab and a jeweled dagger to symbolize his royal prerogatives over life and death.

Sir John Malcolm, an early-nineteenth-century British envoy at the Qajar court, noted that the Shahs preserved the enormity of public executions by minimizing their use but maximizing their "inventive cruelty."[5] Jafar Shahri, the author of a social history of Tehran, reminisces that in the late nineteenth century the Masters of Wrath performed their duties in public squares—flogging feet and backs; gouging out eyes; and chopping off fingers, feet, ears, and tongues. They also executed the condemned by hanging them in public squares, hurling them from city walls, or blowing them away with cannon shots.[6] The last was probably a recent innovation inspired by the British in India.

The condemned were paraded through the bazaar before ascending the public scaffold. In nineteenth-century Tehran, the scaffold was an octagonal brick platform with a mastlike pole in the Maydan-e Qayeq (Boat Square) adjacent to the Ark-e Shahi (Royal Citadel). At the turn of the twentieth century, executions were moved to the expansive Maydan-e Tupkhaneh (Cannon Square) inside the Royal Citadel between the ministries, the telegraph office, and the Anbar-e Shahi (Royal Storehouse), a warehouse used also as an imperial dungeon. This *anbar* became synonymous first with *habs* (dungeon) and later with *zendan* (prison). It was also known colloquially as the Falakeh both because its courtyard had a circular view of the sky (*falak*) and because the bastinado (*falak*) was administered there. Victims could enjoy a heavenly view while receiving their lashes.

Shahri claims that the Masters of Wrath and their footmen routinely tortured suspected criminals in the royal dungeon. His list of tortures includes starvation, sleep deprivation, chaining in dark, damp cells, heavy rocks on chests, submersion in water, sitting on hot bricks, walking on red coals, limestone and feces in the mouth, weights on the testicles, hot fat on the skin, the strappado (hanging from pullies), and, of course, the most common of all, the bastinado. He adds that the Masters of Wrath were under constant pressure to obtain appropriate "confessions" from the "guilty."

The ultimate in the spectacle of cruelty came in the Babi executions of 1852. Accused of attempted regicide and heresy— they had proclaimed their leader to be the Bab (Gate) to the Hidden Messiah—thirty Babis were found guilty of "sowing corruption on earth" and "taking up arms against God and His Representatives." They were paraded in chains through Tehran, given a final opportunity to recant, and then portioned out for execution to various groups—to the royal family, the Qajar tribe, the clergy, the ministries, the military, the merchants, and the bazaar guilds. Some were blinded before being shot; others were stabbed repeatedly, then decapitated; yet others were beaten mercilessly before being strangled. The leaders were hacked in two after being "turned into torches"—having candles inserted throughout their bodies. For the sake of royal decorum, Nasser al-Din Shah handed his designated victim over to the state chamberlain.

The British envoy tried to persuade the chief minister to forgo these "revolting tortures," arguing that they would "disgust" Europe and tarnish the country's reputation of "advancing towards civilization."[7] But the chief minister retorted that this was "not the time for trifling" and that the "responsibility" for the executions had to be "spread out." Lady Sheil, the British envoy's wife, writes that once the guilty had received their just "deserts," the Master of Wrath distributed sweets among the participants as a token of royal gratitude and "admission into the brotherhood." The whole community—not just the monarch and the state—was to be seen as the grand executioner. Lady Sheil adds: "It was said that the general impression produced on the people by all this bloodshed was not favorable. Indignation at the attempt on the Shah's life was lost in sympathy for the fate of the sufferers."[8]

Although such extravaganzas were not repeated, public punishments continued well into the early twentieth century. A diary for 1893–1904 describing public events in Shiraz lists in that city alone 118 amputations—41 of fingers, 39 of feet, and 38 of ears—110 floggings, 48 decapitations, 17 hangings, 11 drawing-and-quarterings, 4 live-wallings, and 2 disembowelings.[9] These punishments were carried out in public view and the bodies left on display as an *'ebrat* (example) to others. Most of the executed were tribesmen accused of rural banditry and highway robbery.

Thus the traditional legal systems of Iran and Europe had much in common. Both rejected circumstantial evidence, relying heavily on judicial torture and public confessions. Both treated punishment as a grand spectacle to deter and impress the public with the awesome power of the monarch. Both located punishment mainly on the body and rarely incarcerated prisoners for prolonged periods. They had dungeons and jails but no prisons or penitentiaries. If physical punishment happened to be more prevalent in Iran, it was simply because Europe could banish criminals to its colonies and galley navies. Iran did not enjoy such overseas luxuries.

The two, however, differed in one significant aspect. Whereas Europe sporadically launched witch-hunts against "Satan and his agents," Iran, like the rest of the Middle East and the Eastern Orthodox world, did not—even though its elite as well as its masses believed in the existence of Satan (*shaytan*) and little devils (*jinn*s) capable of wreaking havoc on the community. Witch-hunts did not take place probably because the public, including the lower clergy, readily countered "bad magic" with folk remedies: visits to fortune-tellers, invariably "wise old women"; animal sacrifices; alms; prayers to saints; pilgrimages to holy shrines, including Qom, Najaf, Karbala, Mecca, Medina, and Mashed (literally, "the place of martyrdom"); and, most prevalent of all, amulets containing special charms, herbs, stones, seashells, and Koranic quotations. Good spells—tacitly tolerated by Islam—could heal the ill, revive sick animals, overcome barrenness, locate lost property, prevent butter from curdling, and even ward off natural disasters. What is more, the family structure (early female marriages and grandmothers integrated into extended households) produced few impoverished old women—the main targets of European witch-hunts. In short, Iranian society believed in the existence of witches but did not produce European-style witch-hunts with their inquisitional methods, live burnings, and public recantations.

Judicial Reforms

Judicial reform came to Iran gradually. It came first as a trickle in the last quarter of the nineteenth century; then as a stream during the first quarter of the twentieth century; and finally as a full torrent once Reza Shah established his Pahlavi dynasty in 1926. Inklings of change appeared in the last years of Nasser al-Din Shah (1848–96) when a small group of reformers, known as the *munavar al-fekr* and *rushan fekran* (both literally mean "enlightened thinkers"), raised fundamental questions about the traditional judicial system. They questioned the lack of uniformity between urf and sharia courts; the ambiguous line between the two; the rejection of circumstantial evidence; the inordinate power of the clergy; the subordinate position of women and non-Muslims; the notion of vengeance and blood money; the corporal punishments that produced limbless and thus unproductive citizens; the premise that law mediated not between state and citizen but between feuding families, clans, and tribes; and the harsh sentences mandated for such victimless crimes as drunkenness, apostasy (*kafer*), homosexuality (*lavat*), and fornication (*zanan*; sex between unmarried couples).

What is more, they began to perceive judicial torture and corporal punishments as signs of barbarism, medievalism, and, to borrow Foucault's terminology, the "surplus power of Oriental Despotism." In the same way that nineteenth-century Russian reformers denounced serfdom as the shameful badge of "Asiatic backwardness," their Iranian counterparts saw judicial torture and corporal punishments as the embarrassing hallmarks of "Oriental Despotism."

Nasser al-Din Shah tried to address the new "discourse" by modifying the horrors of public executions and, on a number of different occasions, outlawing judicial torture—at least in political cases. Torture, however, continued to be used extensively on common criminals both to extract confessions and to locate stolen goods. Significantly, when Nasser al-Din Shah was assassinated, the new monarch refused his Master of Wrath permission to torture the assassin even though the latter was convinced that such methods would uncover a wide network of hidden accomplices. The assassin was hanged in public with a military band drowning out his final speech. This was a sharp contrast to the 1852 Babi executions.

The pressure for judicial reform intensified during the

1905–9 Constitutional Revolution. In fact, the revolution was sparked by the public flogging of prominent merchants scapegoated for rising sugar prices. In the eyes of the constitutionalists, public floggings were demeaning; royal footmen were the "lowest of the low"; and the Nasaqchis and Mir Ghazabs were no better than "common torturers and sadists."[10] One newspaper ran a long series of cartoons in color entitled "Punishments under the Despotic Monarchs" graphically depicting the Masters of Wrath carrying out the most horrendous of the traditional executions—public beheadings, live burials, quarterings, eye gougings, and disembowelings.[11] The cartoons claimed to "illustrate" the incorrigible backwardness of the ancien régime—even though many of these punishments had already fallen into disuse. The very same cartoons were reprinted in 1980 to illustrate the iniquities of all monarchies.[12]

After 1909, the constitutionalists implemented some mild reforms despite conservative resistance. They renamed the urf the Adliyeh (Justice Ministry) and set up a central office to decide which cases went to the sharia courts. They repeated the ban against judicial torture and promised to respect the independence of the judiciary. Moreover, they restricted executions to hangings and firing squads. When Fazlallah Nuri, the leading conservative cleric, was sentenced to death, he was swiftly hanged. A Revolutionary Tribunal found him guilty of "sowing corruption and sedition on earth" because his *fatwas* (religious decrees) had urged the faithful to "spill the blood" of the parliamentary leaders on the grounds that they were "apostates," "atheists," and "secret Babis." For some, the sharia gave senior clerics the authority to issue such fatwas against the *kuffar* (unbelievers)—although such fatwas trespassed on royal prerogatives. The same tribunal condemned to death two other prominent royalists. Fazlallah was hanged before a large jeering crowd in Cannon Square. The other two were shot by a firing squad in a walled garden hidden from public view.

Furthermore, the reformers employed Swedish officers to establish a rural gendarmerie, an urban *shahrbani* (police force), and city jails that were soon dubbed "shahrbani." Teh-

ran obtained a Central Jail (Zendan-e Markazi)—known officially as the Zendan-e Movaqqat (Temporary Detention House)
and colloquially as the Falakeh as it was located on the site of
the old royal dungeon. A two-story, square building around a
large courtyard, the Central Jail had one huge entryway and
three smaller gates separating the inner part (*darouni*) of the
building from the outer (*berouni*). The outer part contained
offices and guard rooms. The inner part contained eight cell
blocks, four on each floor. The first floor had small solitary
cells, two meters by one. These had metal beds and shared with
the other solitary cells on the same corridor a common toilet
and washroom. The second floor contained large wards, each
capable of housing as many as thirty to fifty inmates. According
to one inmate, the first floor was dreaded not only because of
its solitary cells but also because it was damp and dark.[13] Another writes that burglars were often placed there to persuade
them to reveal their hidden loot.[14] The provincial jails were
even worse; they lacked such amenities as beds, showers, and
proper toilets.

Real judicial reform did not come until the late 1920s—after
Reza Shah had consolidated the Pahlavi regime. He assigned
the task of judicial reform to Ali-Akbar Davar, the justice minister, Firuz Mirza Farmanfarma, the finance minister, and
Abdul-Hossein Timurtash, the court minister. This triumvirate
had degrees from European universities—two of them in law,
the field favored by sons of the landed aristocracy. Later generations disparaged them as *kravatis* (tie-wearers) and *gharbzadeh* (mesmerized by the West). But they—unlike their
successors—realized that such traditional practices as
religious discrimination and corporal punishments could not
be eliminated without a root-and-branch revamping of the
whole judicial system.

Their outlook is reflected in an essay by Firuz Mirza entitled
"Penal Codes."[15] It sketched the evolution of European law beginning with *lex talion* (law of vengeance) in primitive tribes
and ending with the establishment of uniform state codes in
the nineteenth century. Firuz Mirza focused on the contribu-

tions of Beccaria, Rousseau, Kant, Montesquieu, and Bentham. Interestingly, he overlooked their concern about protecting the individual against the state. His own concern was not to protect the individual from the state but rather to safeguard the state from what he perceived to be the shackles of tradition—tribal chiefs, local magnates, and, most serious of all, retrogressive clerics.

The triumvirate used handpicked parliaments to revamp the judiciary. They created a Justice Ministry named the Dadgustari. They established courts on the county, regional, and provincial levels—as well as a Supreme Court on the national level. They abolished the sharia, tribal, and guild courts. They required all lawyers and judges to obtain some modern legal training—either from the West or from the new law school at Tehran University. They drew up penal and criminal codes modeled on those of Italy and Switzerland. Applicable to all— Muslim as well as non-Muslim—the new codes accepted the modern rules of evidence, especially circumstantial evidence; rejected the concept of family vendetta and blood money; diminished corporal punishments in favor of prison sentences; stressed the importance of incarceration and rehabilitation; and reserved capital punishment chiefly for murder, high treason, and armed rebellion. These codes gave to the sharia only one significant concession: they incorporated their rulings on marriage, divorce, and child custody.

The reformers also moved most executions out of public view. In fact, few executions were carried out in these years for the simple reason that violent crime rapidly diminished once the state established control over the highways and stamped out rural banditry.[16] It should also be noted that the Pahlavi regime—unlike previous dynasties in Iran—did not need to impress the public with gruesome spectacles. For the first time in history, the state was armed with the full machinery of modern government—a central bureaucracy, a standing army, and a national police force. In short, it had the Maxim gun and thus could dispense with the public gallows.

The replacement of corporal punishments with prolonged

incarceration placed a heavy burden on prison facilities. The Tehran Central Jail, designed for 400 inmates, contained more than 1,000 by the late 1920s.[17] The Mashed jail, intended for 200, housed more than 900.[18] To meet the new demand, the regime drew up plans to build five large prisons (each housing more than 100 inmates); fifty medium-sized ones (more than 50 each); and thirty small ones (housing less than 30). In fact, most of these were not built until the 1960s.

The most famous of those built in the 1920s was Qasr. Its full name was Qasr-e Qajar (the Qajar Palace) because of its location near the ruins of a royal summer retreat on the cool northern hills of Tehran. A large, tall building perched prominently on the hilltops next to an army barracks, Qasr became a symbol of both the new Pahlavi state and the modern judicial system. Its thick walls not only absorbed the inmates but also concealed the wardens and the occasional executions from public view. A former prisoner writes that those driving past were easily intimidated—as they were supposed to be—by the thick, high walls covered with barbed wire, armed guards, searchlights, and gun turrets.[19] Some dubbed it the Iranian Bastille. Others called it the *faramushkhaneh* (house of forgetfulness): the outside world was supposed to forget its inmates; its inmates were supposed to forget the outside world.

Despite Qasr's later reputation, the first transfers from the Central Jail were impressed by its cleanliness, sunlit windows, wide corridors, spacious courtyards, flowered gardens, and, most of all, running water and shower rooms.[20] Although inspired by Bentham's Panopticon and the Philadelphia Penitentiary, Qasr discarded their most inhumane features—the treadwheel, the absolute silence, the ever-present eye, the obligatory hoods, the totally solitary cells, and the constant religious indoctrination. The modern prison had come to Iran via the modified and more humanitarian systems of early-twentieth-century Western Europe. Like much else in Pahlavi architecture, ancient Iranian motives were grafted onto the building to give it an "authentic" look. The Western penitentiary had been Iranianized.

The building contained a major communal block, three large blocks housing 10 to 20 inmates each, and five smaller ones with multiple double and single cells. Block 1 housed short-term inmates—petty thieves and, paradoxically, murderers awaiting execution. Blocks 5 and 6 held common criminals, with the more "dangerous" in chains. Block 8—with its small cells—was soon to be used for privileged prisoners such as former ministers, tribal chiefs, and prominent bankrupts. Some had private rooms with easy access to nearby cells. Political prisoners were placed in the neigboring block 7. The corridors of blocks 7 and 8 led to the prison courtyard and garden. Other wings contained solitary cells, baths, guard rooms, prison offices, the workshop, and the infirmary. A separate women's section was planned for the future.

In its first year of operation, 1929–30, Qasr housed 300—18 of them political prisoners. By 1940, it housed more than 2,000—200 of them political prisoners.[21] More than 50 of them were crammed into block 7, which was built for 20. Others were in blocks 2 and 4. Not surprisingly, Qasr soon obtained the reputation of being the regime's main political prison. It retained this reputation until the 1970s.

Communist Prisoners

The first political prisoners in Qasr were from the Communist party. They were to set the pattern for prison life for forthcoming generations of political inmates. Some two hundred communists were arrested in 1929–30 soon after organizing a series of strikes—in an Isfahan textile mill, in the Mazandaran railways, in the Mashed carpet workshops, and, most sensational of all, in the British-owned oil industry. Some were soon released. Others were sent into "internal exile"—northerners to the intolerable heat of Bushire, southerners to Turkish-speaking Azerbaijan. But thirty-eight were incarcerated in Qasr. Seven died there—all from natural causes. The other thirty-one remained there until 1941 when the Anglo-Soviet invasion forced the government to grant a general amnesty to all political prisoners.

The thirty-one remaining communist prisoners spent much of these eleven years in block 7. There they set up their own *komun* (commune) with a three-man steering committee to co-ordinate their activities, pool their meager resources, organize their daily routines, and help those in need of financial and medical assistance.[22] In fact, after the 1930 arrests in Iran and the Stalinist purges in Russia—which took a heavy toll from Iranian exiles—the Communist party of Iran ceased to exist for all practical purposes outside the walls of Qasr.[23]

The regime intentionally created the impression that these communists had been convicted for espionage. In fact, they were not brought to court until 1938–39, and then they were tried retroactively under a 1931 law banning all forms of *maram-e ishteraki* (collectivist ideology).[24] This 1931 law threatened anyone advocating "collectivism" or joining an organization—defined as more than two persons—that advocated "collectivism" with three to ten years in "solitary confinement." It also threatened those opposing the "constitutional monarchy" with prolonged incarceration and those taking up arms against the same monarchy with the death penalty. Reza Shah decreed this law without parliamentary discussion, knowing well that its sweeping language would be highly controversial, even for his handpicked deputies. Although these communists were not tried for espionage, some historians remain under the false impression that they had been convicted of spying for the Soviet Union.

The one major espionage trial of the reign did not implicate these thirty-eight. In 1930, Georges Agabekov, the head of the Soviet secret service in the Middle East, defected to France and presumably revealed what he knew of his agency. Soon the Iranian police rounded up thirty-two Soviet agents—many of them functionaries in the Ministry of Post and Telegraph. Two were executed, three were sentenced to life, and the others were given terms varying from five months to fifteen years.[25] Only

one was to participate in the subsequent communist movement. In his memoirs, Agabekov mentions in passing that his
superiors were so fearful of double agents that they strictly forbade the recruitment of local communists.[26] Agabekov himself
seems to have been remarkably ignorant of the Iranian Communist party—of both its internal workings and its recent
history.[27] The Soviets probably compartmentalized their espionage and revolutionary activities.

In Qasr, the communists distanced themselves from these
spies. They looked down on them as weaklings who had ratted
on each other, as simpletons who had been fooled into making
self-incriminating confessions, and as "moral degenerates" in-
dulging in opium and card gambling.[28] What is more, they felt
that anyone who had spied for money would again do the same
for the prison authorities. According to one communist, such
"highly dubious" characters were to be "avoided" at all costs.[29]
Another revealed in his interrogation that the party expelled
anyone suspected of being a Soviet spy on the grounds that they
were too untrustworthy.[30] The lone spy who participated in the
later communist movement—Sayyed Baqer Emami, the son of
Tehran's Imam Jom'eh (Friday Prayer Leader)—continued to
be handicapped by the reputation of being a dangerous ultra-
leftist—perhaps even an "agent provocateur."[31]

Prison memoirs—most of them published after the 1979 revolution—reveal much about the social composition of the
thirty-eight communist prisoners and thus of the early
communist movement in Iran. (See table 1.) The thirty-eight
were predominantly ethnic minorities. Two were Jews, another
two were Armenians, and twenty-four were Azeris (Turkish-
speakers originally from Iranian Azerbaijan). Persians num-
bered no more than four, and two of them had Turkic-speaking
mothers. Ethnicity, however, does not appear to have been of
great importance to them and hardly figures in their writings.
At one time, the steering committee of their komun was composed of one Azeri and two Armenians.[32]

The group was relatively young. At the time of arrest, most
were in their late twenties or early thirties. This meant that they

had been in their impressionable teens at the time of the Russian Revolution. Few had higher degrees. Only two had completed college—both at the Medical College in Baku. Two had no formal education whatsoever. Eleven had been to primary school. Twenty had finished secondary school. Many had briefly attended the Communist University of the Toilers of the East located in Moscow. This was known in Iran by its Russian acronym, KUTIV. The Iranian regime considered KUTIV a school for espionage. In fact, it was an ideological institute designed to give party organizers a smattering of Marxism-Leninism. One alumnus estimates that some one hundred Iranians attended KUTIV at one time or another during the 1920s and 1930s.[33]

Among the thirty-eight were thirteen teachers, three office employees, two doctors, one pharmacist, and one bookseller. There were also thirteen workers—many of them printers, carpenters, and skilled artisans. The early labor movement in Iran, as in many other countries, was located not so much in modern factories—which were few—as in the skilled crafts and trades.[34] Only one among the thirty-eight had been born into the wealthy upper class.

Three of the thirty-eight—Jafar Pishevari, Yousef Eftekhari, and Ardashir Ovanessian—played particularly important roles both inside prison and, later, in national politics. They—as well as some of the others—were to publish prison memoirs in later years. Pishevari, the eldest of the three, was a founding member of the Communist party. Born in Iranian Azerbaijan as Jafar Javadzadeh, he and his family had emigrated to Baku when raiding tribesmen destroyed their home and livelihood. His father—an educated *sayyed* (presumed descendant of the Prophet)—earned a living running a small grocery store. After completing his schooling in Baku, Pishevari taught Turkish language and Persian literature at the local municipal high school. In his words, "The drama of the Russian Revolution had swept me into radical politics."[35] He joined the Adalat (Justice) party formed by pro-Bolshevik Iranians in Baku. He participated in the famous Jangali Revolt in Gilan and served as

Table 1
Imprisoned Communists, 1930–41

Name	Dates	Province of Birth	Province of Activities	Ethnicity
1. Alizadeh, Ibrahim	?–1993	Gilan	Tehran & Khuzestan	Azeri
2. Amir-Khizi, Ali	1894–1979	Azerbaijan	Tehran	Azeri
3. Asadi, Abulqassem	1895–1944	Azerbaijan	Tehran	Azeri
4. Cheshmazer, Qassem	1914–	Azerbaijan	Azerbaijan & Kurdestan	Azeri
5. Dehqani, Mohammad	1905–85	Azerbaijan	Azerbaijan	Azeri
6. Eftekhari, Yousef	1902–	Azerbajian	Tehran & Khuzestan	Azeri
7. Enzebi, Mohammad	1914–34	Azerbaijan	Tehran	Azeri
8. Eskandrani, Abulqassem	1880–1945	Azerbaijan	Azerbaijan	Azeri
9. Farhakhti, Hossein		Azerbaijan	Gilan	Azeri
10. Farhi, Abulfasel	1895–1955	Khurasan	Khurasan	
11. Faruhid, Ismael	1903–	Gilan	Gilan	Azeri
12. Gurgian, David	1895–1991	Azerbaijan	Azerbaijan	Armenian
13. Hamdad, Rahim		Azerbaijan	Tehran & Khuzestan	Azeri
14. Hejazi, Morteza	1902–30	Tehran	Tehran	Persian
15. Hesabi, Abbas			Tehran	
16. Javid, Salamallah	1898–1988	Azerbaijan	Tehran	Azeri
17. Kaviyan, Jafar	1902–	Azerbaijan	Azerbaijan	Azeri
18. Keshavarz, Karim	1900–86	Gilan	Gilan	Persian
19. Mosavi, Abulqassem	1888–1943	Azerbaijan	Azerbaijan	Azeri

Profession	Class Origins	Education	Previous Politics	Subsequent Politics
Office employee	Merchant	German high school	Oil strike	Tudeh & DP
Office employee	Shopkeeper	High school & KUTIV	Rail strike	Tudeh & DP
Teacher	Shopkeeper	High school	1905 Revolution & Gilan	Tudeh
Teacher		High school	DP & Justice party	Tudeh & DP
	Lower middle class	High school	None	Tudeh & DP
Teacher	Merchant	High school & KUTIV	Oil strike	Anti-Tudeh politician
Printer	Lower middle class	Primary school	Oil strike	Died in prison
Printer			1905 Revolution & Justice party	DP
Teacher		High school & KUTIV	Justice party	Tudeh
Teacher	Lower middle class	High school	DP & unions	Tudeh
Teacher	Lower middle class	High school	Cultural Society	None
Artisan	Urban poor	Primary school	DP	Tudeh
Office employee		High school & KUTIV	Oil strike	None
Printer	Urban poor	Primary school & KUTIV	Printers' strike	Died in prison
Teacher		High school & KUTIV	Justice party	None
Doctor	Middle class	Baku Medical College	Justice party	DP
Baker	Urban poor	Primary school	Justice party	DP
Translator	Merchant	French School in Tehran	Cultural Soceity	Tudeh supporter
Shopkeeper	Lower middle class	High school	1905 Revolution & Justice party	DP

Table 1 *(continued)*

Name	Dates	Province of Birth	Province of Activities	Ethnicity
20. Najjar, Ghulam	?–1931	Gilan	Gilan	
21. Nikravan, Hossein	1898–	Gilan	Gilan	
22. Nungarani, Momi	1907–	Azerbaijan	Azerbaijan	Azeri
23. Omid, Ali	1900–74	Kerman	Khuzestan	Persian
24. Ovanessian, Ardashir	1905–90	Gilan	Tehran	Armenian
25. Pishevari, Jafar	1893–1947	Azerbaijan	Tehran	Azeri
26. Rusta, Reza	1903–67	Gilan	Gilan	Azeri
27. Sadeqpour, Mohammad	?–1931	Azerbaijan	Azerbaijan	Azeri
28. Shafii, Ismael	1903–	Gilan	Gilan	Azeri
29. Shakiba, Ayub	1898–1946	Azerbaijan	Tehran & Khuzestan	Azeri
30. Sharifi, Mohammad	1898–1970	Gilan	Gilan	Azeri
31. Sharqi, Ali	1888–1936	Azerbaijan	Tehran	Azeri
32. Simonian, Qazar	1901–	Isfahan	Tehran	Armenian
33. Tahmasbi, Mehdi	1905–31	Tehran	Khurasan	Persian
34. Tanha, Mohammad (Ismaeli)	?–1933	Isfahan	Khuzestan	Persian
35. Taqizadeh, Dadash	1901–46	Azerbaijan	Mazandaran	Azeri
36. Yaqubzadegan, Yaqub	1911–90	Gilan	Gilan	Jewish
37. Yasari, Mohammad	1910–80	Azerbaijan	Mazandaran	Azeri
38. Zavlun (Hossein Nuri)	1907–46	Georgia	(Turkey)	Jewish

Profession	Class Origins	Education	Previous Politics	Subsequent Politics
Carpenter	Urban poor	Primary school & KUTIV	Unions	Died in prison
Teacher-journalist	Lower middle class	High school	Cultural Society	Tudeh
Shop assistant	Peasant	Primary school	Justice party	Tudeh & DP
Oil worker	Peasant	None	Oil strike	Tudeh
Pharmacist	Middle class	American School & KUTIV	Unions	Tudeh
Teacher	Lower middle class	High school & KUTIV	Justice party	DP
Teacher	Peasant	High school & KUTIV	Cultural Society	Tudeh
Worker	Peasant		Unions	Died in prison
Doctor	Middle class	Baku Medical College	Cultural Society	Tudeh
Teacher	Lower middle class	High school	Justice party Oil strike	DP Executed
Teacher	Middle class	High school	Cultural Society	Tudeh
Factory worker	Urban poor	Primary school & KUTIV	Unions	Died in prison
Translator-teacher	Middle class	High school	Tudeh	
Printer	Urban poor	Primary school & KUTIV	Unions	Died in prison
Printer	Urban poor	Primary school	Unions	Died in prison
Railway worker	Urban poor	None	Unions	Tudeh, Executed
Shopkeeper-bookseller	Urban poor	Primary school	Unions	Tudeh
Railway worker	Peasant	Primary school	Rail strike	Tudeh
Intellectual			CP in Palestine	Tudeh & DP, Killed in 1946

interior commissar of the short-lived Soviet Socialist Republic of Iran. When the Adalat party reconstituted itself as the Communist party, he was elected to its central committee. After the demise of the Jangali Revolt, he went first to KUTIV and then to Tehran where he opened a bookstore and helped edit the trade union paper *Haqiqat* (Truth). He was arrested in 1930 when funds destined for striking oil workers in Abadan were traced back to him in Tehran. The police, however, failed to link him to the Jangali Revolt, probably because he had changed his name to Pishevari (Artisan).

Eftekhari had a similar background. His father, also a shopkeeper in Azerbaijan, had died young, forcing the family of four brothers to emigrate to Baku. There the eldest brother started a small business while the younger ones taught at local schools and joined the Iranian Communist party. Eftekhari and one other brother also studied at KUTIV, where they attended lectures given by Trotsky, Bukharin, Kamenev, and Zinoviev. After returning to Iran in the mid-1920s, Eftekhari first set up a teachers' union in Tehran. He then moved to Abadan with three fellow Azeris determined, as he boasts, to organize the oil workers against the British.[36]

By May Day 1929, Eftekhari had organized Iran's first oil strike, bringing the whole industry, including the refinery—which at that time was the largest in the world—to a total standstill. He mobilized the workers through literacy classes and public theaters; through protests against racial discrimination (the oil company discriminated in favor of British and Indian employees); and through demands over such bread-and-butter issues as the minimum wage, paid Fridays, job security, and the eight-hour day. The strike was not broken until the military arrested more than forty-five labor organizers. The British "thanked" and "congratulated" Reza Shah for his decisive intervention.[37] Eftekhari, however, won fame as the man who had shaken the British Empire as well as the Pahlavi state.

Ovanessian had been born into an Armenian family living in Rasht. His father—originally from Tabriz—was a salesman-turned-pharmacist who apprenticed his sons to Alexander Atabegyan, a local Armenian pharmacist who later succeeded Prince Kropotkin as one of Russia's foremost intellectual anarchists. On completing his apprenticeship, Ovanessian forsook pharmacy for revolutionary politics. In his memoirs, he writes that one of his first recollections was that of the Jangalis holding enthusiastic rallies in Rasht.[38]

Ovanessian soon joined the Cultural Society—the hotbed of radicalism in Rasht. There Armenian and Muslim intellectuals, including women, organized literacy classes, book readings, chamber concerts, soccer games, and theatrical shows, including Molière's anticlerical play, *Tartuffe*.[39] Conservatives denounced the society as a den of iniquity—even of Babis. The British Consul kept close tabs on the society, suspecting it of being a den of Soviet spies.[40] After all, did it not proudly display Lenin's portrait every May Day?[41] Similar cultural societies existed in nearby Qazvin and Enzeli (Pahlavi).[42]

Ovanessian joined the Communist party in 1923 and was sent to KUTIV in 1925. On his return in 1926, he organized a pharmacists' union in Tehran and served as the party's troubleshooter in the provinces, traveling frequently to Rasht, Qazvin, Mashed, and Tabriz. On one such visit to Tabriz, he was arrested and transferred to Tehran. He spent the next eleven years in Qasr. The British Embassy later described Ovanessian as one of the premier "brains" and "dominating personalities" of the Iranian communist movement.[43]

The prison memoirs of these three—and others—document many hardships but few actual incidents of physical brutality. They were kept in limbo for years without being formally charged.[44] The long wait drove one to attempt suicide. Some were never brought to trial.[45] Others were sentenced to ten years—the maximum permitted by the 1931 law. Of course, the time spent awaiting trial was not taken into account. Those completing their sentences were invariably banished to the provinces. The police chief later testified that the Shah had instructed him to send these prisoners into "indefinite exile"— preferably to the deep south.[46]

Moreover, prisoners were occasionally forced to watch

executions. When a group of bandits tried to break out of Qasr, their leader was hanged in the main courtyard in full view of all inmates.[47] In addition, prisoners were often deprived of books, newspapers, visitors, food packages, and proper medical care. Of the seven communists who did not survive prison, most died from lack of medicine: one succumbed to appendicitis, two to heart attacks, and at least two to typhus epidemics. What is more, any blatant infringement of prison regulations was punished with solitary confinement. Pishevari described this as the very worst punishment in Qasr.[48] He added that this was real "torture" because humans are by nature social beings in dire need of companionship, conversation, and the sharing of such everyday pleasures as tea, cigarettes, and laughter.

The absence of physical violence turned interrogations into battles of wit. Eftekhari writes that when he was arrested his interrogator threatened him with torture, but he mockingly dismissed this as a bad joke, knowing well that physical violence was not permitted.[49] It took the interrogator months to discover even his name and identity.

Ovanessian reminisces that his initial interrogation in Tabriz lasted two days, beginning early in the morning and ending late at night. He describes his two interrogators as persistent and experienced but correct and cordial. They shared meals with him and flattered him and other educated prisoners by praising their learning and insisting that they respected their social ideals. They tried to trick them into thinking their accomplices had already implicated them. The prisoners, in turn, tried to put the interrogators on false trails. Ovanessian's Tabriz contact pretended he did not know Ovanessian's identity but claimed that his forehead bore the calluses of someone who diligently performed his daily Muslim prayers. Ovanessian writes that his interrogator had pointed out to the Shah in 1930 that advocating socialism was not in itself a crime. After his 1941 release, Ovanessian remained on cordial terms with some of his interrogators. One even phoned in 1944 to congratulate him on his election to parliament.[50]

The interrogators used similar tactics with Pishevari. They

claimed that his accomplices had already testified that he had been sent by the Comintern with a false identity to participate in the Jangali Revolt, launch a communist newspaper, and foment unrest among oil workers. Demanding a "face-to-face" confrontation with these "liars," Pishevari offered a number of plausible explanations for his past life. He had been a mere observer of the Jangali Revolt. His Persian had not been good enough to enable him to write newspaper articles. He had come to Tehran because his in-laws resided there. His knew some of the oil strikers by sight because they occasionally visited his bookstore. He had adopted a new name only because the government had recently ordered all citizens to obtain identity cards. He added that it was true he had been an ardent revolutionary in his youth but age had mellowed him. When asked to name fellow students at KUTIV, he listed those who had either died or remained outside Iran. He repeated these explanations ten years later when brought to trial. He added caustically that the passage of time had faded his memory and that the 1931 law could not possibly apply to him because he had been in prison since 1930.[51] He commented that the main strategy of the police was to to break down prisoners by offering them bribes and threatening them with solitary confinement.[52]

This conspicuous absence of torture can be explained in a number of ways. First, the law explicitly banned the use of physical force to extract information. In 1941, at his own trial, the police chief successfully pleaded that he had respected the law banning such "abhorrent" investigatory methods.[53] Ovanessian writes that the prison authorities—with the notable exception of the notorious "doctor" in the Central Jail—were on the whole "decent," "reasonable," "sympathetic," and even "European-trained products of the Constitutional Revolution."[54] The police chief was himself an accomplished classical violinist.

Second, the Comintern kept close tabs. Eftekhari and his two colleagues were convinced that they were not tortured because the regime shunned bad foreign publicity, especially from the Comintern.[55] Leo Karakhan, the Soviet deputy foreign minister, visited Qasr on his 1933 tour of Iran—just before falling victim to the Stalinist purges.

Third, the communist prisoners were willing to organize hunger strikes to protest outrageous behavior. Such strikes erupted in Tabriz, in the Central Jail, and in Qasr. In 1929–30, prisoners in Tabriz and the Central Jail protested the mass detentions without formal charges. Likewise, prisoners in Qasr went on a hunger strike to demand the right to earn pocket money in the prison workshop. Ovanessian writes that destitute prisoners needed this income to ward off bribes offered by the prison authorities. These three strikes were partially successful. Less important detainees were released. Political prisoners gained access to the workshop on condition they did not use it during the same hours as the Lurs and Kurds—these tribesmen were segregated in their own cell blocks. The wardens feared fraternization between communists and such "dangerous" inmates. After the Qasr strike, the warden exclaimed that Ovanessian could no longer deny being a communist because "only communists organize hunger strikes." Ovanessian retorted that Gladstone—the Conservative prime minister of Britain—had himself once organized such a strike. He later commented that this was pure fabrication, but he figured the warden had not read enough European history to know better.[56]

Fourth, the regime did not have a pressing need to use torture. It was not seeking vital security information as the Communist party had rejected the notion of armed struggle. And it was not in the business of extracting ideological recantations and winning over hearts and minds. A few minor figures were released once they pledged in writing to stay out of politics. These pledges were never published. Ovanessian explains that the government was reluctant to acknowledge even the existence of politically committed citizens.[57] He adds that those who signed such pledges terminated their political careers because they were stigmatized as "sellouts" and "corrupt collaborators."[58] For its part, the regime rarely sought such pledges. In a revealing passage, Pishevari writes that one worn-out prisoner offered to write His Imperial Highness a letter pledging full support and recanting his ideological past. The warden laughed, retorting that the "regime wanted not active citizens but obedient and apolitical subjects."[59] The regime was more interested in keeping subjects passive and outwardly obedient than in mobilizing them and boring holes into their minds. Reza Shah had created a military monarchy—not an ideologically charged autocracy.

Physical force, however, continued to be used on common criminals, on suspected spies, and on those accused of plotting regicide. Criminals, especially burglars, were subjected to the bastinado and the strappado to reveal their hidden loot. Suspected spies and assassins were beaten, deprived of sleep, and subjected to the dreaded *qapani*—the binding of arms tightly behind the back. Sometimes this caused the joints to crack. It was rumored that this excruciating torture had been imported from Western Europe. Ovanessian writes that the qapani prompted some spies to seal their own fates.[60] Although political prisoners were often threatened with the qapani, they were rarely subjected to it.

On the whole, political prisoners were treated reasonably well. Block 7 was clean and well ventilated—unlike block 5, reserved for common criminals. They were allowed to bring in their own clothes, blankets, bedding, and sometimes books. They received home meals and pocket money—friends and relatives entrusted money to the warden, and the warden, in turn, issued prisoners weekly *jetons* (coupons). They were permitted visitors; by the mid-1930s, Tuesdays, Fridays, and national holidays were designated visiting days. Forty years later, Ovanessian reminisced that on their release in 1941 he and his fellow prisoners had been hailed as heroes for having survived the "Iranian Bastille." But, he adds, Qasr did not really deserve this sinister reputation.[61] Of course, Ovanessian, like many, had an exaggerated notion of the original Bastille.

The main concern of the political prisoners was not torture but boredom and lack of privacy. One inmate writes that everyone, including the jailers, was deadened by the monotony of

waking up every morning at the same hour, eating the same
tasteless breakfast, walking in the same courtyard, listening to
the same complaints, and hearing the same trampling of boots,
the locking and unlocking of the same iron gates.[62] Prison, he
adds, was like a small village where everyone poked their noses
into other people's business:

> The one thing you must keep in mind is that the occupants
> of these villages inhabit a tiny world. They tend to squab-
> ble over small things and obsess over their neighbors' sex
> lives. They gossip when an older inmate goes around with
> a younger one. What is more, the overcrowding leads to
> petty squabbling over such issues as whose bedding
> should make room for walking space, who should go to
> the courtyard when, and how much should the window
> be left open. What a relief it is to get away from one's own
> cell even if for a short spell.[63]

To break the monotony, the prisoners organized a wide variety of activities. They spent as much time as possible in the
courtyard walking, exercising, and playing soccer and volleyball. Some grew plants and vegetables in the prison garden.
Others—especially from the Cultural Society in Rasht—put on
skits and shows. They played chess and recited poetry—especially Hafez, Saʿdi, and Lahuti (their contemporary revolutionary poet who had fled to the Soviet Union). Ferdowsi was
shunned as a royalist. They read both smuggled-in newspapers
and permitted books—the favorite titles were Dumas's *Mount
Cristo* and Remarque's *All Quiet on the Western Front*. Some
translated Chekhov's plays, Tolstoy's *Anna Karenina*, and Pe-
trushevky's *Islam in Iran*. They organized literacy and language
classes. Ovanessian added French to his working knowledge of
Turkish, Persian, Armenian, Russian, and English. Pishevari
mastered colloquial Persian—which he had not been able to
speak fluently in the 1920s.[64]

They also socialized with inmates from other blocks during
their periodic visits to the prison clinic. They invited guests to
their komun dinner parties to celebrate May Day and the Oc-

tober Revolution. They told each other stories. Eftekhari comments that a story, however interesting, becomes boring when heard for the umpteenth time. For example, the Bakhtiyari tribesmen drove him up the wall by telling and retelling how one of their heroines had saved the Constitutional Revolution.[65] The poorer communists earned pocket money making toys in the prison workshop. Those with craft skills trained others to make goods that were then sold to the outside market through the prison guards, who, of course, took their commissions. The money thus earned bought the inmates cigarettes and citrus fruits considered essential to survive disease, especially the typhus epidemics that periodically hit the prisons.[66]

The communist prisoners also spent considerable time discussing the hot issues of the day—especially the debate over "World Revolution" versus "Socialism in One Country." Ovanessian, Eftekhari, and Pishevari took different positions. Ovanessian, who later used the pen name Ahan (Iron), supported the official party line, arguing that industrialization and collectivization would inevitably lay the groundwork for democracy and socialism in the Soviet Union. Eftekhari, who lost a brother in the purges, denounced Stalin for "betraying" Lenin, failing to export the revolution, and using brutal methods to crush the opposition. Meanwhile, Pishevari, while still loyal to the Comintern, argued that ultra-revolutionary slogans about class struggles were counterproductive in such backward semicolonial countries as Iran.[67] He insisted that radicals in these countries should think more in terms of creating a cross-class progressive organization—such as the Democratic party that had played a crucial role in Iran from 1906 to 1921.[68] One communist prisoner repeated the old Persian saying: "If you put two Iranians in one place you will get at least three different political views."[69]

Other Political Prisoners

Monotony was broken—especially in the mid-1930s—by the sudden appearance of fallen dignitaries. Ovanessian writes that Qasr inmates were the first to feel the shifts in national politics:

dignitaries would arrive at all hours of the night, sometimes after having spent the same evening playing cards with the royal family.[70]

Seven prominent figures passed through Qasr before meeting their deaths in the Central Jail: Timurtash and Firuz Mirza, two of the triumvirate who had reformed the judicial system; Abdul-Hossein Diba, Timurtash's confidant and the uncle of the future empress Farah Diba; Sardar As'ad, a Bakhtiyari leader and war minister; Khan Baba As'adi, his brother; Sowlat al-Dowleh, the Qashqayi chief; and last, but not least, Mohammad Forrokhi-Yazdi, a well-known poet and the editor of *Tofan* (Storm) who was arrested after visiting Moscow and publishing in the émigré communist paper *Peykar* (Struggle). Forrokhi-Yazdi was murdered probably because he satirized the marriage of the crown prince to Princess Fawzieh of Egypt. Expecting a similar fate, Davar, the other member of the triumvirate, committed suicide.

These murders were committed in the Central Jail rather than in Qasr to avoid prison unrest. They were carried out by Lieutenant "Doctor" Ahmadi, a self-taught pharmacist promoted through the ranks and given a crash course on nursing. It was said—probably apocryphally—that he had received his promotion as compensation for having inadvertently eaten poisoned stew intended for one of the prisoners.

Two other national figures—Sayyed Hassan Modarres, the chief cleric in parliament, and Shaykh Khaz'al, the main Arab leader in Khuzestan—were both strangled after spending years in internal exile. To discredit all these dignitaries, the regime accused them of bribery and embezzlement. Such smears easily stuck as the public tended to view the elite as inherently venal and financially corrupt. The regime did not try to extract public confessions from them. Financial accusations were deemed more than adequate.

While in prison, Timurtash and Firuz Mirza were constantly ridiculed for having collaborated with Reza Shah and having built Qasr. Firuz Mirza wrote in his *Prison Memoirs*—not published until 1986—that he was proud of his model prison and was tempted to remind his fellow inmates of the old dungeons and their "horrendous filth."[71] Nevertheless, he was so "ashamed" of being incarcerated in the same prison as "pickpockets and petty crooks" that he forbade his children to visit him. After watching Moharram flagellations in the courtyard, he commented that it was a pity the regime had not diverted such "deep and genuine energies" into creating a strong modern nation-state. He found Shi'ism to be closer to Christianity than to Sunni Islam with its "passive fatalism." Firuz Mirza filled his cell—which enjoyed a skyline view of Tehran—with carpets and his private library. There he composed his memoirs, wrote the history of legal reform, and translated Oscar Wilde's *De Profundis*—this probably suited his self-pity and the pain of misplaced affection.

Timurtash was needled even more. Pishevari writes that Timurtash was disliked because of his role in the execution of the Jangali leaders, his drafting of the 1931 law, and his constant self-pity, weeping, and childlike behavior.[72] He pleaded with the guards to shoot some harmless owls nesting in the prison courtyard on the grounds that they were bringing him bad luck. The guards could not oblige; they were not permitted to bring guns into the prison compound. According to legend, the master builder of the Tower of London had been one of its first inmates. With Qasr this was no legend.

Three lesser figures were executed for plotting a coup: Colonel Fouladin, the governor of Azerbaijan; Samuel Haim, the Jewish Majles deputy; and Alimardan Khan, a Bakhtiyari rebel leader. Fouladin insisted on giving the order to fire at his own execution. Haim, who spent seven years in prison refusing to answer questions about Fouladin, devoted his last hour to giving Eftekhari his daily French lesson. Alimardan Khan went cheerfully to the firing squad, refusing a blindfold and distributing his possessions to his fellow prisoners. Ovanessian writes that he published his prison memoirs in part to "keep alive the memory of such courageous figures as Alimardan Khan"—even

though he came from the upper class.[73] Pishevari contrasts
their fortitude with the panic that broke out among the convicted spies as they approached the gallows.[74]

Many other dignitaries spent time in Qasr: Amir Mojahed
and Manoucher As'ad, two other Bakhtiyari leaders; Nasser
Khan, a Qashqayi chief; Dabir Azam Bahrami, a court minister;
Qavam Shirazi, the Shah's future son-in-law; Moshir Homa-
yun, the former mayor of Tehran; Abu-Nasr Azod, a wealthy
Qajar landlord who had sent a letter critical of the Shah to a
French newspaper; Generals Jahanbani and Shahybani; Amir
Khosrow Khan, the chief of the Kalhor tribe from western Iran;
Salar Zafar Sanjabi and Sardar Rashid Ardalan, two Kurdish
chiefs (the latter spent eleven years in Qasr); Mirza Taher Tu-
nekaboni, a cleric on the Supreme Court; Movarrekh al-
Saltaneh Sephar, a senior bureaucrat who fell victim to typhus
while in prison; Zaka al-Dawleh Ghaffari, a law professor who
had questioned the financial wisdom of building the Trans-
Iranian Railway; Abdul-Qadir Moshkinfam, a maverick journalist who changed his name to Azad (Free) while in prison;
and Ali Dashti, a journalist who had started his political career
by singing loud praises for Reza Shah.

Dashti was in Qasr for only a few months. Suffering from
acute insomnia, he was transferred to a mental asylum where
he translated Le Bon's *Sociology* and composed his *Prison Days*,
which was not published until 1948. *Prison Days* contains little
on prison life but much on fate, love, death, suicide, divine
providence, Christ, and Thomas Jefferson. It belongs less to the
genre of modern prison literature than to that of medieval
courtiers bemoaning their unfair fate. Dashti describes prison
as a "cemetery," chastises Europe for inventing such horrors,
and depicts incarceration as "torture worse than death."[75] Ovanessian comments that prisoners of Dashti's ilk enjoyed many
privileges in Qasr, including private rooms, opium pipes, and
personal servants—common criminals who cleaned out their
cells and did their daily chores.[76]

In addition to these dignitaries, a colorful array of personalities passed through Qasr. They included Mr. Lapidus, a wealthy Polish businessman who often bribed his way out to fancy restaurants; "Alexander," a White Russian officer who entertained cellmates with artful portraits; and Sayyed Farhad, a bandit who made a rare escape from Qasr—when gendarmes took his eighty-year-old father hostage, the old man told them he could produce for the Shah another Sayyed Farhad if given nine months of freedom.[77] At one time, the cells housed a group of "simple peasants" from Azerbaijan who had dreamed of an unnamed figure heralding the dawn of freedom. The communists jested that these villagers had invented a new form of high treason—subversive dreams.[78]

Some remained in Qasr until 1941. These included Yousef "The Armenian" (in fact, he was Assyrian), a bandit who bribed the guards to smuggle in his wife for overnight visits; Matous Melikian, the octogenarian principal of the Armenian high school who had protested the closing of his teaching establishment; Ahmad Ispahani, a young literary friend of the famous Nazem Hekmat of Turkey (Ispahani had been caught crossing the border into Iran); Ruhollah Kazemzadeh, an air force pilot who had tried to escape abroad in his airplane; and eight young officers accused of forming a fascist organization. Their leader, Lieutenant Mohsen Jahansouz, was a Beirut-educated aristocrat who had translated Hitler's *Mein Kampf.* Suspected of plotting to assassinate the Shah, Jahansouz was deprived of sleep, subjected to the qapani, and then executed.[79] His seven associates remained in Qasr; two of them soon converted to Marxism.

For the veteran communists, however, by far the most interesting of all the newcomers were a group of young Marxists known as the Fifty-three. They were to form the nucleus of the future Tudeh party. Ovanessian reports that their arrest struck Qasr like a lightning bolt. "We were all eager," he writes, "to see, talk to, and get to know these famous newcomers."[80] Pishevari recounts that by the mid-1930s the communist komun had grown gloomy: few radicals were coming in, and the state appeared to have the whole country in its tight grip. "We had concluded Iran was either dead or in deep sleep. The arrival of the Fifty-three shook us out of our gloom."[81]

The Fifty-three

In November 1938—soon after the famous Moscow show trials—Iran staged the most sensational of its political trials. Using the ambiguous 1931 law, it indicted a group of fifty-three—many of them young intellectuals from prominent families—with the clear intention of intimidating the country's intelligentsia. In the past, dissidents had been put away quietly. Now they were placed in the limelight to illustrate to all and sundry the dangers of dallying with radical "alien ideas."

Imitating the Russian practice of labeling political trials with the total number in the dock, the Iranian government billed the group as "the Fifty-three." In fact, one of the famous trials preceding the Moscow purges had been known as the Case of the Fifty-three. It was jested that Reza Shah wanted to keep up with his northern neighbor. Not surprisingly, the Iranian Fifty-three soon became a household term in Tehran. In later years, ten of them—in addition to Bozorg Alavi, the author of the best-seller *The Fifty-three*—published memoirs describing their arrests, trials, and prison experiences.

The case began inadvertently in March 1937 when border guards came across three men smuggling themselves into the country from the Soviet Union. The three escaped, but their abandoned luggage led the police to a theater troupe in Khuzestan. This, in turn, led the police to associates in Tehran, Qazvin, and Isfahan. By early May, the police had compiled a list of more than sixty suspects and had begun to round them up. Most were taken—often by public transport—to Tehran's Central Jail for "routine questioning." This turned into lengthy interrogations lasting eighteen months. Some were released. One escaped. But fifty-three were brought to trial in November 1938.

The regime claimed these fifty-three constituted a tight-knit party under direct Comintern control. In fact, they were formed of two loosely linked groups: intellectuals too young to have had a political past and veteran labor activists from the near-defunct Communist party. The intellectuals, numbering thirty-three, averaged twenty-seven years of age. The labor activists, totaling fourteen, averaged thirty-four. The two groups were joined by a handful of university-educated professionals—some of whom had belonged to the youth section of the Communist party in their teens. (See table 2.)

In terms of profession, they included one judge; five professors, including two at the Medical College; two physicians; one factory manager; one museum director; four lawyers; two headmasters; three teachers; nine office employees, almost all civil servants; and twelve university students. Eighteen came from titled families. Among them were also two mechanics, two tailors, two printers, one locomotive driver, one cobbler, and one factory worker. No women were brought to trial, although among those initially rounded up was the wife of one of the veteran communists.

In terms of ethnicity, Persians dominated—in sharp contrast to the early communist movement. Forty came from Persian-speaking homes; the other thirteen, from Turkic (Azeri, Qajar, Afshar, and Turkoman) families. Almost all the intellectuals were from Persian and Persianized households. Of the total, thirteen had been born in Tehran; twenty-two, in the central regions, including Qazvin; and nine, in the Caspian provinces. Two of the six born in Azerbaijan had been raised in Persian-speaking districts outside Azerbaijan. At the time of arrest, forty-one resided in Tehran; the others, in Abadan, Isfahan, Qazvin, Gilan, and Mazandaran. None resided in Azerbaijan. All but one came from Shi'i backgrounds. The lone exception came from a Bahai family.

The main figure in the dock was Dr. Taqi Arani—regarded by some to be his generation's most promising intellectual. Born in Tabriz, he had been raised in Tehran by his mother and her family. He disliked his absent father—a civil servant—for being an incorrigible Casanova.[82] Graduating from the Dar

Table 2
*The Fifty-three**

Name	Birthdate	Place of Birth	Residence	Ethnicity
1. Arani, Taqi	1902	Tabriz	Tehran	Azeri
2. Kambakhsh, Abdul-Samad	1902	Qazvin	Tehran	Qajar
3. Bahrami, Mohammad	1898	Tafresh	Tehran	Persian
4. Shureshyan, Mohammad	1885	Gilan	Tehran & Abadan	Persian
5. Sadeqpour, Ali	1904	Qazvin	Tehran	Persian
6. Boqrati, Mohammad	1904	Gilan	Tehran	Persian
7. Alamutti, Ziya	1913	Qazvin	Tehran	Persian
8. Pazhuh, Mohammad	1906	Qazvin	Tehran	Persian
9. Farjami, Mohammad	1905	Gilan	Tehran	Persian (Bahai)
10. Azeri, Abbas	1900	Isfahan	Tehran	Azeri
11. Ezazi, Nasratallah	1901	Tehran	Tehran	Persian
12. Khamehei, Anvar	1917	Tehran	Tehran	Persian
13. Jahanshahlu, Nasratallah	1914	Tehran	Tehran	Turkic (Afshar)
14. Alamutti, Emad	1911	Qazvin	Qazvin	Persian
15. Afshar, Akbar (Fatouli)	1909	Tehran	Tehran	Turkic (Afshar)
16. Makinezhad, Taqi	1915	Arak	Tehran	Persian
17. Sajjadi, Mojtaba	1913	Arak	Tehran	Persian
18. Alavi, Bozorg	1904	Tehran	Tehran	Persian

*The Fifty-three are listed in the order of those receiving the longest sentences as announced in *Ettel'at,* 17 November 1938. Forty-seven were sentenced on that day; the other six were tried separately, and the press never announced their sentences. Biographical information has been obtained from interviews, memoirs—especially those printed since 1979—and the coverage of the trials published in *Ettel'at,* 2–17 November 1938.

Profession	Class Origins	Higher Education	Previous Politics	Subsequent Politics (1941–47)
Professor	Civil servant	Berlin University	Nationalist	Died in prison
Factory manager	Aristocrat	Moscow University	CP	Tudeh
Physician-professor	Physician	Berlin	CP	Tudeh
Mechanic & actor	Poor	None	CP	Tudeh
Mechanic	Poor	KUTIV	CP	None
Headmaster	Physican	Dar al-Fanon & KUTIV	CP	Tudeh
Civil servant	Teacher	High school	Cultural Society	Tudeh
Teacher	Bookseller	KUTIV	Cultural Society	Tudeh
Civil servant	Merchant	KUTIV	Cultural Society	Tudeh
Cobbler & railway worker	Poor	None	None	Tudeh
Civil servant		None	CP	Tudeh
University student	Clerical	Tehran University	None	Tudeh
University student	Tribal chief	Tehran University	None	Tudeh
Civil servant	Teacher	High school	Cultural Society	Tudeh
Typesetter	Poor	None	None	Tudeh
University student	Senior clerical	Tehran University	None	Tudeh
University student	Clerical-landed	Tehran University	None	None
Writer-teacher	Merchant	High school in Germany	None	Tudeh

Table 2 *(continued)*

Name	Birthdate	Place of Birth	Residence	Ethnicity
19. Rasai, Mehdi	1898	Qazvin	Tehran	Persian
20. Iskandari, Iraj	1908	Tehran	Tehran	Qajar
21. Yazdi, Morteza	1907	Yazd	Tehran	Persian
22. Radmanesh, Reza	1906	Gilan	Tehran	Persian-Gilaki
23. Maleki, Khalel	1900	Tabriz	Tehran	Azeri
24. Sajjadi, Morteza	1912	Arak	Tehran	Persian
25. Sajjadi, Hossein	1910	Arak	Isfahan	Persian
26. Shandramini, Ali	1917	Gilan	Abadan	Azeri-Persian
27. Qodreh, Mohammad	1912	Arak	Tehran	Persian
28. Shahin, Taqi	1916	Tabriz	Tehran	Azeri
29. Razavi, Morteza	1915	Qazvin	Gurgan	Persian
30. Sayyah, Seyfollah	1901	Isfahan	Isfahan	Persian
31. Hokmi, Alinqali	1915	Tehran	Tehran	Persian
32. Etiqechi, Ezatollah	1917	Tehran	Tehran	Persian
33. Khajavi, Vali	1893	Qazvin	Qazvin	Persian
34. Alamutti, Rahim	1899	Qazvin	Tehran	Persian
35. Zamani, Shayban	1916	Babul	Gurgan	Persian
36. Ashtari, Abul-Qassem	1915	Tehran	Tehran & Shiraz	Persian
37. Tarbiyat, Hossein	1908	Khuzestan	Abadan	Persian
38. Garkani, Fazollah	1918	Tehran	Tehran	Persian
39. Soqfi, Yousef	1913	Qazvin	Tehran	Persian
40. Naini, Jalal	1915	Tehran	Qazvin	Persian
41. Nasimi, Rajbali	1917	Tabriz	Tehran	Azeri
42. Shomali, Bahman	1913	Khalkhal	Qazvin	Azeri
43. Laleh, Mehdi	1900	Tehran	Tehran	Persian

Profession	Class Origins	Higher Education	Previous Politics	Subsequent Politics (1941–47)
Office employee		None	Cultural Society	Tudeh
Lawyer	Aristocrat	Grenoble University	None	Tudeh
Surgeon-professor	Senior clerical	Berlin University	CP	Tudeh
Professor	Landed	University of Paris	Cultural Society	Tudeh
Teacher	Merchant-landed	Berlin University	None	Tudeh
Physican	Clerical-landed	Berlin University	None	None
Physician	Clerical-landed	Berlin University	None	None
Tailor	Poor	None	Cultural Society	Tudeh
University student	Senior clerical	Tehran University	None	Tudeh
Civil servant		None	None	Tudeh
Civil servant		None	Cultural Society	Tudeh
Textile worker	Poor	None	None	Tudeh
University student		Tehran University	None	Tudeh
University student	Merchant	Tehran University	None	Tudeh
Villager	Villager	None	None	None
Tailor	Poor	None	None	Tudeh
Cobbler	Poor	None-illiterate	None	Tudeh
Museum director		Dar al-Fanon	None	None
Headmaster	Merchant	Dar al-Fanon	CP	Tudeh
University student	Senior clerical	Tehran University	None	None
Teacher			None	None
Civil servant	Middle clerical	None	None	None
Civil servant		None	None	None
Mechanic		None	None	None
Professor-banker	Merchant	None	None	None

Table 2 *(continued)*

Name	Birthdate	Place of Birth	Residence	Ethnicity
	Sentenced Separately			
44. Tabari, Ehsan	1917	Sari	Tehran	Persian
45. Naraqi, Abbas	1914	Kashan	Tehran	Persian
46. Daneshvar, Mehdi	1915	Khamseh	Tehran	Persian
47. Habibi, Hassan	1916	Kermanshah	Tehran	Persian
48. Alamutti, Nuraldin	1903	Qazvin	Tehran	Persian
49. Ibrahimzadeh, Reza	1902	Mazandaran	Mazandaran	Azeri
50. Enqelab, Khalel	1913	Tabriz	Tehran	Azeri
51. Manou, Fereydun			Tehran	Persian
52. Turkoman, Ana (Babayi)	1898	Gurgan	Gurgan	Turkoman
53. Hakim-Allahi, Razi	1917	Tehran	Tehran	Persian

al-Fanon—the elite high school—at the top of his class in 1920, Arani took a two-year crash course in medicine in Tehran and then went to Germany to study chemistry in the Berlin Technical University. His stay there lasted from 1922 to 1930. While working toward his doctorate, he took courses in philosophy, taught Persian to supplement his meager family stipend, and published pamphlets and articles on Omar Khayyam, Sa'di, Nasser Khosrow, Aristotle, Azerbaijan, and Iranian history. These articles appeared in two nationalistic journals published in Germany, *Iranshahr* (Land of Iran) and *Farangestan* (Europe).

During these Berlin years, Arani moved to the left. He had arrived a staunch nationalist, full of praise for ancient Iran and the Persian language. His articles on the Persian language urged the purging of Arabic words. His articles on history listed Zoroaster, Farabi, Ibn Sina, Omar Khayyam, Ferdowsi, Cyrus

Profession	Class Origins	Higher Education	Previous Politics	Subsequent Politics (1941–47)
		Sentenced Separately		
University student	Clerical	Tehran University	None	Tudeh
Lawyer-student	Landed	Tehran University	None	Comrades party
University student		Tehran University	None	None
University student	Middle clerical	Tehran University	None	None
Judge	Senior clerical	Seminary	DP & Cultural Society	Tudeh Justice minister
Railway worker	Oil worker	None	CP	Tudeh
University student		None	None	Tudeh
Lawyer		Tehran University	None	None
Lawyer			None	None
Printer		None	None	None

the Great, Darius the Great, and Anusheravan the Just as the true heroes of Iran. Conspicuously absent was Mazdak, the hero of the left, who had been executed by the Zoroastrian establishment for advocating economic egalitarianism. What is more, Arani's articles on Azerbaijan urged the government to replace Turkish with Persian on the grounds that the Mongol invaders had imposed their "foreign tongue" on northwestern Iran. Praising Azerbaijan as "the cradle of Iranian civilization," he described its people as pure Aryans coerced by the Mongols to give up their indigenous Iranian language.[83]

By the time he returned to Iran, Arani had joined the Revolutionary Republican party—a short-lived leftist organization—and had befriended a number of Iranian Marxists, including Morteza Alavi, the editor of the Communist party paper *Peykar*.[84] Arani later told the police that Morteza Alavi had introduced him to Marxism in 1927 and that he had returned home in 1930 a convinced communist.[85] It is not clear what this meant as Arani never admitted to having formally joined the Communist party.

Back in Tehran, Arani lived with his mother and devoted his time to intellectual pursuits, allowing himself only two diversions—long walks and Western music. He taught science at the Dar al-Fanon and Tehran University; chaired the teaching department in the Ministry of Industries; and published booklets on physics, chemistry, biology, psychology, and dialectical materialism. The first two works were adopted as high school textbooks. The booklet on psychology linked the workings of the mind to the physical structure of the brain.

He also convened at home a number of separate informal discussion groups—for colleagues from Europe, for students from Tehran University, and for pupils from the Dar al-Fanon and the Ministry of Industries. Meeting on different days, most participants were unaware of the existence of the other groups. They discussed philosophy and modern political theory. They read Victor Hugo's *Les miserables* and Henri Bergson's *Les deux sources de la vie.* Some translated—from French and German— Engels's *Ludwig Feuerback and the End of Classical German Philosophy* as well as Marx's *Capital, Communist Manifesto,* and *Wage Labor and Capital.* Others translated Bukharin's *ABC of Communism* and *Historical Materialism.*

These discussions inspired some to spend hours in the Majles library devouring all they could find on political philosophy.[86] They had an insatiable thirst for modern political ideas. Autobiographies published in later years—particularly in the 1980s—gloss over the importance of these political ideas and instead dwell on individual foibles and personal animosities. The authors are probably embarrassed by their "youthful follies," and feel readers would find Freud and Kafka, not to mention Marx and Bukharin, off-putting and passé. The removal of political ideals from individuals who were motivated primarily by political ideals makes them appear one-dimensional, lifeless, and even meaningless. This self-selected memory not only distorts the past but also does their authors a gross disservice.

In addition to organizing discussion groups, Arani obtained a government license to publish a journal named *Donya* (The World). He borrowed the title from *Le Monde*—the paper edited by Henri Barbusse, the famous French communist.[87] In all, twelve issues of *Donya* appeared between February 1934 and June 1935. Its aim was to bring academic Marxism to the Iranian intelligentsia. As its masthead declared: "This journal will examine scientific, technical, social, and cultural issues from the materialistic point of view."

To pass the censors, *Donya* avoided inflammatory language, used a dry academic style, and published abundant nonpolitical articles on Persian literature and the modern sciences—on radium, cancer, television, nuclear physics, mathematics, car construction, sleep and dreams, aeronautical engineering, and electrical power plants. It also translated works from European languages—an article on blindness by Helen Keller; *White Flowers*, a short story about a teenage girl in Germany; and *I Am Black*, an indictment of racism in the American Deep South. *Donya* was definitely avant-garde.

Its forte, however, was articles on social sciences. Their titles are self-explanatory: "Dialectical Materialism," "The Materialist Concept of Humanity," "Art and Materialism," "Mysticism and Materialism," "Law and Materialism," "Women and Materialism," "Determinism and Free Will in History," "The Material Foundations of Life and the Brain," "Value, Price, and Labor," and "The Evolution of the Species." The last summarized Lamarck and Darwin. Older readers were often troubled that this new framework left little room for God, the metaphysical, and the supernatural.[88] One youngster remembers Shariat Sangalaji, the chief reforming cleric, throwing him out of his mosque for raising questions about the existence of God.[89] Academic Marxism came to Iran coupled with Darwin and the modern sciences. *Donya* was unique for its time. It remains so.

Donya also challenged the notion of Aryan superiority—a notion gaining currency as officials traveled to Nazi Germany and dabbled in the ideas of Count Gobineau, the nineteenth-century European racial theorist. Some suspected the censors tolerated *Donya* because they deemed it too dry and academic. Others joked that the censors had confused *diyalektik* (dialectic) with *alakdolak* (hair sieve).[90] One university student spoke for his age cohorts when he said *Donya* captured his attention from the very moment he saw the first issue.[91] Another wrote that *Donya* had whetted his generation's appetite, for it had discussed for the very first time in Persian such subjects as historical materialism.[92]

In publishing *Donya*, Arani was helped mostly by his two closest colleagues: Iraj Iskandari and Bozorg Alavi. The three used pseudonyms—Arani, the pen name Qazi (Judge); Iskandari, Jamshid (an ancient Iranian name); and Bozorg Alavi, Nakhoda, which means shipmaster as well as atheist and freethinker. Arani signed his own name only when writing purely scientific articles.

Iskandari was a French-educated lawyer from a highly respected family. His father—a Qajar prince—was revered as a martyr of the Constitutional Revolution. His uncle was the founder of the Socialist party and the leader of the nonclerical parliamentary opposition to Reza Shah. His own French education had been cut short when he forfeited his state scholarship by participating in student political activities. On his return home, he had met Arani and found employment as a Supreme Court attorney.

Bozorg Alavi—the founder of prison literature—was the younger brother of Morteza Alavi in Berlin. He had already established a literary reputation by publishing a collection of essays entitled *Suitcase*. His grandfather, a wealthy businessman, had supported the Constitutional Revolution and sat in the first Majles. His father, a businessman, had emigrated to Germany in the late 1910s and had committed suicide there after going bankrupt. His uncle was a well-known professor of Persian literature at Tehran University. Growing up in the Weimar Republic, Bozorg Alavi had been influenced by Freud and Kafka as well as Schiller, Marx, Engels, and Darwin. Returning home in 1928, he befriended other young intellectuals, pub-

lished short stories, and translated Schiller and Hermann
Hesse. He earned his living teaching German at the Ministry of
Industries. At the time of his arrest, he was married to a Jewish
refugee from Nazi Germany. In later years, he married the
granddaughter of Ayatollah Tabatabai—one of the leading clerics of the Constitutional Revolution.

Many of the other intellectuals among the Fifty-three came
from similar backgrounds—from prominent, even titled, but
not necessarily wealthy, families. Dr. Mohammad Bahrami, a
Berlin-educated professor of medicine, was the son of a titled
court physician. Dr. Morteza Yazdi, a Berlin-trained surgeon,
was the son of a senior cleric who had participated in the Constitutional Revolution. After his father's death, Yazdi had been
raised by Hakim al-Mamalek, a court doctor and frequent cabinet minister as well as member of parliament. Similarly, Dr.
Reza Radmanesh, a Sorbonne-educated physicist, and Nuraldin Alamutti, a senior judge, came from prominent families in
Gilan and Qazvin, respectively. In their teens, these five had
belonged to the youth section of the Communist party.

Khalel Maleki, a science teacher, came from a family highly
respected both in Tabriz and in Sultanabad (Arak). Although
in central Iran, Sultanabad contained a large Azeri-speaking
community. Like Iskandari, Maleki had not been able to complete his European degree because of his student activities.
Nasratallah Jahanshahlu, a leader of a recent strike in the Medical College, was the scion of an Afshar tribal leader from Zan-
jan. Mohammad-Reza Qodreh, another student who had
organized a strike at the Teachers' College, came from a clerical
family well known in central Iran. His family was related to the
future Ayatollah Khomeini. Taqi Makinezhad, yet another
strike leader at the Engineering College, came from a similar
family in Arak. Both his father and his maternal grandfather
had been senior clerics. Drs. Hossein and Morteza Sajjadi,
brothers, had close relatives in the Majles and in the higher
ranks of the state bureaucacy. Ehsan Tabari, one of the youn-
gest of the group, was a second-year law student and the grandson of a prominent cleric in Mazandaran. A facile writer and

learner of foreign languages, Tabari in later years became the chief popularizer of Marxism in Iran.

The police dragnet missed three other intellectuals who at the time happened to be out of the country: Sadeq Hedayat, Eprim Eshaq, and Abdul-Hossein Noshin. Hedayat, the towering figure in modern Persian prose, had, together with his friend Bozorg Alavi, introduced Kafka and Freud into Iran. From 1941 until his suicide in 1951, Hedayat worked so closely with the Tudeh that the police were to jump to the wrong conclusion that he was a secret member.[93] Eshaq, a young Assyrian, was in England studying with Keynes. Considered to be one of Keynes's best students, Eshaq later became a don at Oxford. Noshin, a prominent stage director, was in France trying to join those going to fight in the Spanish Civil War. After 1941, Noshin, together with some innovative actors, including his famous wife, Loreta, organized the county's first professional theater. Not surprisingly, many felt that Arani had attracted the best and the brightest of the new generation.

The labor organizers were led by Kamran Qazvini (Nasrollah Aslani). A KUTIV graduate, Qazvini had been sent to revive the Communist party. He formed a communal household in Tehran composed of veteran labor organizers. He worked in an Isfahan textile mill where he had organized a successful May Day strike. He collected strike money from such sympathizers as Arani, Bozorg Alavi, and Iskandari. He also asked Arani to print a May Day manifesto praising the Comintern and demanding the release of all political prisoners.[94] Qazvini, however, was not in the dock with the Fifty-three; he escaped from the Central Jail before the trial began.

The chief liaison between the labor organizers and the intellectuals was a Russian-trained pilot named Abdul-Samad Kambakhsh. The son of a Qajar prince living in modest circumstances in Qazvin, Kambakhsh had grown up partly in Qazvin, where he participated in the Cultural Society, and partly in Russia—both before and after the revolution—where he attended high school and obtained an Iranian government scholarship to study aeronautical engineering. On his return to

Iran, he taught at the Military Academy and wrote technical pamphlets for the War Ministry. He was married to the grand-daughter of the famous Shaykh Fazlallah Nuri, who was hanged in 1909. His wife—one of the first women to study modern medicine in Iran—had also been active in the Qazvin Cultural Society. Kambakhsh knew eleven of the Fifty-three from his hometown. They became known in prison as the "Qazvin group." He also had contacts in the armed forces, which he kept to himself for the next twenty years.

Much of the pretrial imprisonment was spent in the Tehran Central Jail where many met for the very first time most of their supposed fellow conspirators. They were confined initially in solitary cells, then in three separate but interlocking wards. Those from prominent families—notably Iskandari, Kambakhsh, and Yazdi—were assigned to the "bourgeois ward." Those from less prominent families—including Arani, Bahrami, and Jahanshahlu—were sent to the "petty bourgeois ward." Those from humble homes, including the labor organizers, were sent to the "proletarian ward." The last enjoyed less pocket money, less home-cooked food, and fewer family visits. Anvar Khamehei—one of the few intellectuals in the last ward—claims in his book *The Fifty and the Three* that this separation was designed to undermine resistance and inflame "class differences." He adds that "his first exposure to working-class life" gave him two surprises: uneducated males were heavily dependent on cigarettes, and they found it quite natural to wash and mend their own clothes.[95]

The interrogators tried to trick the prisoners into giving self-incriminating information, pretending that others had admitted that the discussion groups were sinister covers for the Comintern and the Communist party. The police intimidated the prisoners with the full force of the 1931 law—five years in solitary confinement for promoting Marxism plus ten years in solitary confinement for joining a communist organization. They held out the specter of death sentences on the grounds that the accused had spied and plotted an armed uprising on behalf of a foreign enemy. What is more, they tried to get the prisoners to rat on each other by claiming that others—especially Arani and Kambakhsh—had already implicated them. Some bore lifelong grudges against Kambakhsh.[96] Even now—sixty years later—some insist he betrayed them; others insist he protected them.[97] Unknown to them, many had been betrayed by a young returnee from Europe who had named names in exchange for his own release.[98]

The police occasionally used more brutal methods with the suspected ringleaders. Arani was briefly subjected to the qapani and then placed in a cold solitary cell without shoes, blankets, or mattress. Bahrami was punched on the face and deprived of proper food for three days. Kambakhsh was warned that his wife could be arrested and that he—as a War Ministry official—could face the firing squad. Radmanesh was slapped. Bozorg Alavi was subjected to the qapani for half an hour. One labor organizer was force-fed when he began a hunger strike. Some were denied home-cooked meals and family visits. Others were "insulted" by being called "shameless," "unpatriotic," "atheistic," and "foreign spies." They considered this "torture." Although Khamehei claims to have been "tortured," he admits that no one was actually flogged, burned with cigarettes, or put on the rack. He claims that "Westerners had not yet introduced such modern techniques into Iran."[99]

Students from privileged homes were treated with kid gloves. Jahanshahlu writes in his *Recollections* that he was well treated simply because his interrogator had studied under his uncle at the Military Academy.[100] He adds that his mother—as well as Iskandari's mother—monitored the investigations for the president of the Majles, a family friend. The president, in turn, monitored them for his two friends, the justice minister and the court minister. In later years, Iskandari reminisced that "family" mattered in those days, and that his uncle, a gendarmerie colonel, had been his own interrogator's classmate.[101] Maleki, as well as Iskandari, stresses that "the very worst tortures in those days" were mild compared to what was to come in later decades.[102]

Intimidation had limited success. Some gave names, but

mostly of those already in custody or out of the country. Although Kambakhsh was rumored to have "spilled the beans," he defended himself by arguing that he could not have identified people unknown to him and that his arrest had followed—not preceded—many of theirs. The older intellectuals pleaded that they had severed their ties with the Communist party long ago. The younger intellectuals pleaded that their discussion groups had dealt only with academic issues. Dr. Morteza Sajjadi insisted he had visited Arani's home only once. A handful, however, were pressured or tricked into describing their discussion group as a *tashkilat* (organization) and a *ferqeh* (party).

Arani admitted being a Marxist but denied forming an organization or joining the Communist party.[103] He insisted that some of the accused had not even attended the disussion groups and that he had rebuffed Qazvini's offer to finance *Donya* because he did not want to turn the journal into a Communist party organ. He further insisted that the only people he knew to be party members were Morteza Alavi and Qazvini.[104] The former was in exile, and the latter had escaped custody.

Iskandari and Bozorg Alavi both argued that their interests had been cultural and that *Donya* had been purely an intellectual journal. It was true that they had read Bukharin and Marx; but they had also read Freud, Pushkin, Victor Hugo, Le Bon, Darwin, Bergson, and Hitler. Iskandari insisted that they had never once talked of creating a party or any such organization. Bozorg Alavi argued that he had lost contact with his brother; his recent honeymoon had distracted him from even intellectual pursuits; he had found *Capital* to be too boring to read; and his contributions to *Donya* had dealt with literature and psychology, not with politics. He added cryptically that the very first time he heard of the existence of a ferqeh or tashkilat was from his police interrogator.

Although the lengthy investigations failed to unearth an underground organization linked to the Comintern, the regime was determined to stage a show trial. It gave the trial a great deal of publicity and permitted the press to summarize some of the defense speeches. This was the first time in Iran that a political trial had been given extensive coverage. The British Legation reported that the secret police watched the public galleries for signs of sympathy and that the government publicized the trial to "broadcast a plain warning to all that it will tolerate nothing remotely savoring of communism."[105] The regime also permitted the defendants to have three well-known defense attorneys: Dr. Alexander Aghayan, a European-educated jurist; Amidi-Nuri, a flamboyant journalist who later became a prominent senator; and Ahmad Kasravi, a former judge and leading historian of the Constitutional Revolution.

The prosecutor demanded the maximum penalty under the 1931 law.[106] He argued that the accused had propagated "atheism" as well as "materialism," formed a subversive party at the behest of international communism, and thereby undermined the "security and independence of the royal kingdom." As evidence, he produced *Donya*, the May Day Manifesto, and the unfinished translations of Bukharin's *ABC of Communism* and *Historical Materialism*. The emphasis on Bukharin was probably for Stalin's ears. As further evidence, the prosecutor cited the border crossings, the strike fund, the university strikes, and the "secret discussion cells." "These ungrateful creatures," he declared, "have taken advantage of the unprecedented generosity of the Shah and the hardworking people of Iran."

The defense lawyers retorted that their clients had done no more than take part in innocent discussion groups. They categorically denied Comintern links. One lawyer argued that such scions of "respectable families," of "well-known clerics," and of "the privileged class" could not possibly harbor "communistic and atheistic notions." Another declared that the law could not ban books and that in Western Europe such works as *Capital* were essential reading: "One is not considered educated in Europe unless one has read Karl Marx." Yet another declared that these defendants should be congratulated because so many of their contemporaries did their best to avoid reading serious books. The lawyers for the labor organizers depicted their clients as simple folk uninterested in esoteric and high-flown theories.

Arani, in a four-hour speech, denounced the trial as a blatant violation of the constitutional laws—especially the clauses on freedom of thought.[107] Needless to say, the press did not reprint this speech. Referring to other famous trials in history—those of Socrates, Galileo, the Inquisition, the Reichstag Fire, and the recent "Fifty-three" in Russia—Arani reprimanded the judges for knuckling under to political pressure, abdicating moral responsibility, and betraying the Constitutional Revolution for which "thousands of Iranians had sacrificed their lives." He argued that the Fundamental Laws had been designed not only to make the judiciary independent of the executive but also to protect freedom of speech—especially the right to read books. Freedom of thought, he argued, was valued by Voltaire, Rousseau, and Montesquieu, as well as by the most advanced countries of the world—namely, America, Britain, France, and Switzerland. "Free speech," he continued, "is stifled mostly in colonized countries, such as Palestine and India." This was hardly the voice of a Stalinist.

Arani accused the regime of violating due process of law. He dismissed the 1931 law as invalid, both because it violated freedom of thought and because it had not been discussed by parliament. He argued that the police had coerced naive youngsters into false statements about the existence of a nonexistent political party. He categorically denied creating a political organization or writing the May Day Manifesto. He stressed that his interests had been academic—reading books, discussing ideas, and editing *Donya*, which, he reminded the judges, had been licensed by the government itself. "You," Arani declared, "may dislike my democratic and socialistic ideas, but you cannot ban them any more than you can ban other things Western. Like it or not, you are obliged to borrow much from the West—Western clothes, Western food, Western architecture, Western laws, Western civilization, and Western political concepts." Arani—unlike recent intellectuals—was a self-avowed modernizer and Westernizer. Some would consider him a gharbzadeh—one bewitched and bedazzled by the West.

The court meted out stiff sentences. Arani was given ten years of "solitary" imprisonment for belonging to a communist organization, three years of "correctional" imprisonment for propagating communism, and another three years for writing the May Day Manifesto. To maximize the impact, the court did not mention whether these sentences ran consecutively or concurrently. It also mentioned solitary confinement, even though Iranian prisons rarely placed anyone in total isolation for prolonged periods. In short, the impression was created that Arani had been sentenced to sixteen years—ten of them in solitary.

Eleven others, including Kambakhsh and Bahrami, were each sentenced to ten years in solitary; four, to eight years in solitary; two, to seven years in solitary; one, to six years in solitary; twenty-one, including most of the young intellectuals, to five years in solitary; nine, to four years; and one, to two years. Three with lesser terms were soon released. The British Legation commented that the sentences were unduly harsh considering the defendants had merely belonged to a "student debating society with leftish tendencies."[108] Bozorg Alavi writes, "Many concluded we were given such stiff sentences to warn youth away from dangerous ideas."[109] He adds that this succeeded: the public, especially the middle class, soon took shelter behind silence and bland conformity.[110]

The Fifty-three were moved from the Central Jail to Qasr in July 1938—some five months before the trial. Many remained there until 1941. "Our lives," Khamehei writes, "improved in Qasr."[111] Some—including Iskandari, Yazdi, Radmanesh, and Bozorg Alavi—were placed in block 7 together with the veteran communists. Others—notably Arani, Kambakhsh, and the labor organizers—were placed in block 2, which had been emptied of its nonpolitical prisoners to "protect" them from "dangerous ideas."[112] Block 7 became known as the "dignitaries' ward" (*band-e a'yan*); block 2, as the "proletarian ward" (*band-e proletariya*). Despite the fact that the hardened communists were in block 7, Khamehei boasts that the more "dangerous" prisoners, like himself, were in block 2.[113]

Each block set up its own *sandoq* (common fund) to buy

food, especially fruit. Because block 7 inmates were better off financially, its common fund had more money to dispense. Block 7 inmates were also assigned common criminals to clean out their cells, make their beds, and warm up their food. Khamehei comments caustically that class privileges were recognized even inside Qasr.[114] Although these "household servants" were supposed to spy on their "masters," their sympathies often lay more with them than with the wardens.

The Fifty-three were treated better than the veteran communists—in part because of family connections and in part because they could afford to bribe. Jahanshahlu writes that the jailers were helpful because they were "decent folk" in dire need of extra cash.[115] Bozorg Alavi remembers that on the whole they and the guards left each other alone. He also remembers telling a noisy guard to lower his voice outside the baths because there was a *shahzadeh* (prince) inside—the prince being Iskandari. The guard deferentially obliged.[116]

The prisoners had visiting hours for friends as well as family members. They could send and receive letters. They could also receive from home clothes, meals, medicines, and bedding. They could spend as much as five hours a day in the courtyard walking, exercising—both individually and collectively—and playing soccer and volleyball. Some grew flower and vegetables in the prison garden. They socialized with inmates from other blocks in the courtyard, in the baths, and in the infirmary. To reach the infirmary, they passed through block 4, which housed other political prisoners. To reach the baths, they passed through block 8, reserved for special dignitaries. They arranged dinner parties to celebrate May Day, the October Revolution, and Nowruz (Persian New Year). They put on skits and played chess but avoided opium and cards—pastimes favored by the old elite. They interpreted dreams using a smuggled-in handbook on pop psychology. They practiced traditional fortune-telling, which consists of opening up at random the works of Hafez and Sa'di. They told each other stories and jokes. Arani—who had a great sense of humor—was an endless source of Mulla Nasraldin jokes. Yazdi—famous for his voice—often filled the ward with his loud laughter. Some studied art with one of the veteran communists who happened to be an accomplished sculptor.

Bribes got them special perks. They brewed vodka. They smuggled in books, newspapers, and even magazines with pictures of scantily dressed women. Some kept pets: Maleki, a stray cat; Bahrami, an owl from the courtyard. During typhus epidemics, they stayed up all night nursing the sick and thus saving lives. The four physicians among them were allowed to practice medicine. When Bozorg Alavi needed his appendix removed, he was operated on by his family doctor in a private hospital in downtown Tehran. When Jahanshahlu came out of an interrogation session at the Central Jail, he was allowed to wander the streets while his guards paid a leisurely visit to a nearby teahouse.[117]

The prisoners also pursued their intellectual interests—especially after 1938 when the Shah ruled they could have "nonpolitical books." This ruling, Bozorg Alavi notes, was greeted with joy even though it produced some absurd results. The warden allowed German but not French books on economics simply because the latter used the term "political economy" instead of "national economy."[118]

"These intellectuals," writes Ovanessian, "turned Qasr into a lively university."[119] Some read textbooks hoping to complete their degrees some day. Others exchanged language classes. Tabari studied English, German, Russian, and Istanbul Turkish—the latter with Ispahani and a Jewish communist who had spent years in Istanbul. Bozorg Alavi learned some Russian, English, and Armenian. He also translated Bernard Shaw's *Mrs. Warren* and tried out on his cellmates segments of his *Prison Scrap Papers*. He later reminisced that his decision to become a professional writer had been made in Qasr.[120] Arani exchanged German for Russian lessons with Ovanessian. Maleki taught French and German and learned some English. Others composed poetry and read literature, especially Hafez and Sa'di. Tabari and Pishevari spent hours discussing classical Persian poetry. Some lectured on their areas of professional expertise—Maleki on chemistry, Radmanesh on physics, Yazdi and Bahrami on medicine. Iskandari formed a small group to translate *Capital*—a task he had started before his arrest.[121] Jahanshahlu writes, "Free to do as we wished from 8 A.M. to 6 P.M., we were probably the most fortunate prisoners in the whole world."[122] Khamehei quotes one cellmate as saying his four years in Qasr were easier than his four months in military service.[123]

They also spent long hours with the veteran communists listening to their accounts of the early radical movement, the Jangali Revolt, and the 1929 oil strike—all forbidden subjects in Reza Shah's Iran. But the relationship between the veteran communists and the Fifty-three was not always smooth—both because of age and social differences and because of the long-standing animosities between Ovanessian, Pishevari, and Eftekhari. Jahanshahlu portrays the older prisoners as "blind worshipers of Russia" and as "illiterate northern commonfolk with no more than a smattering of KUTIV-style Marxism."[124] Khamehei describes them as unread, unsophisticated, and uncultured activists burning with the simple desire to throw the British out of Iran.[125] Similarly, Maleki depicts them as *khoshk* (dry; austere) admirers of the Soviet Union, who, because they had never seen Western Europe, were easily impressed by Moscow's wide streets and large hospitals.[126]

For their part, the veteran communists considered the new arrivals to be mostly "pampered feudalists" and "inexperienced intellectuals."[127] Years later Pishevari gave Bozorg Alavi's *Fifty-three* a mixed and patronizing review. While praising Arani as "a sincere Marxist intellectual who may or may not have been a member of the Communist Party," he dismissed his disciples as immature youngsters, who, like the rest of their generation, had done nothing more than read a few books. "Readers of *The Fifty-three*," he cautioned, "may get the wrong impression that when political prisoners are arrested the only thing on their mind is their next cigarette."[128]

Their relationship was further complicated by the ongoing crisis in the Comintern, especially the Moscow show trials.

Eftekhari often denounced Stalin as a new tsar, and relished reading off the list of prominent Bolsheviks executed as "saboteurs," "foreign agents," and "imperialist spies."[129] Ovanessian retorted by denouncing Eftekhari as a "treacherous Trotskyist." Meanwhile, both Ovanessian and Eftekhari shunned Pishevari, claiming that he had lost faith in communism and that his policy of forming a broad movement was designed to dilute Marxism and curry favor with the reactionary classes.

In the competition to sway the Fifty-three, Ovanessian won hands down. This revealed much about that generation's political outlook. Pishevari carried little weight among radicals fired with the concepts of class warfare and working-class revolution. Eftekhari, while listened to, convinced no more than four—and even they soon deserted him. In a revealing passage written half a century later, Khamehei admits he still does not understand the Moscow trials even though they spent hours in prison discussing them.[130] Maleki—who later became Iran's main Marxist critic of Stalinism—comments that in those days criticism of the Soviet Union was synonymous with opposition to the Great October Revolution, and that opposition to the October Revolution was synonymous with rejection of Socialism, Democracy, and Historical Progress itself.[131] When in 1944 the Tudeh convened its first party congress, the delegates— some of them from the Fifty-three—denounced Eftekhari as a reactionary, barred Pishevari from the proceedings, and overwhelmingly elected Ovanessian to their central committee. The latter had put to good use his long years in Qasr.

Although the Fifty-three were treated reasonably well in Qasr, they experienced one noteworthy incident of police brutality. One afternoon in September 1939, Maleki got into a fist-fight with one of the prison guards. Some say the guard had interrupted his siesta; others, that the guard had made a pass at a younger prisoner; yet others, that Maleki had caught the guard stealing his toothpaste. Whatever the reason, Maleki was given fifteen lashes and thrown into block 5, which was reserved for common criminals. Protesting these "insults," some one hundred political prisoners in blocks 2 and 7 launched a hunger strike. "Political prisoners," declared Iskandari, "should not be treated and flogged like common criminals."[132] The strikers included all the veteran communists and most of the Fifty-three. Some with short sentences abstained, hoping to receive amnesty at the upcoming royal wedding. This decision was to blemish their future revolutionary credentials.

The hunger strike lasted five days. It ended only when Maleki was returned to his cell, and ten strike leaders—including Arani, Kambakhsh, Ovanessian, Eftekhari, and Bahrami—had their feet flogged in the prison courtyard. Iskandari comments, "A country in which doctors and professors are whipped cannot be deemed civilized."[133] Khamehei claims the warden exempted Iskandari from the whipping simply because he was an old family friend.[134] The warden later argued that the flogging did not constitute "torture" as its intention was to enforce prison regulations, not to extract "information" or "confessions."[135]

This crisis reinforced earlier ordeals to create a strong sense of solidarity. Khamehei writes that the group—despite internal differences—cooperated against adversity and thought in terms of "We" rather than "Me."[136] Maleki remembers that his colleagues developed a strong esprit de corps even though many had not known each other before their arrests.[137] Bozorg Alavi uses the hunger strike as the climax of his *Fifty-three*, describing it as their greatest single feat and stressing that it had been instrumental in forging very disparate individuals into a single group. "Qasr created the Fifty-three."[138]

Immediately after the hunger strike, eight of the ten strike leaders were sent to the malaria-infested port of Bandar Abbas. Although Ovanessian and Eftekhari were not on speaking terms, they were transported literally chained together. They remained there until the 1941 amnesty—even leading a prison strike. The other two, Arani and Kambakhsh, were transferred to the Central Jail and thrown into damp solitary cells without proper food, bedding, shoes, or clothing. Arani died five months later during a typhus epidemic. Some claimed the prison "doctor" had given him a lethal injection. Others claimed typhus-infested clothes had been placed in his cell. He probably succumbed to typhus because he had no cellmate to nurse him through the high fever.

Soon after Reza Shah's fall, four of his henchmen—including the Qasr warden and the Central Jail "doctor"—were charged with violating privacy laws, taking bribes, unlawful detention, and murdering political prisoners, including Arani, Diba, Firuz Mirza, Farrokhi-Yazdi, Modarres, Shaykh Khaz'al, and Sardar As'ad Bakhtiyari. It is significant that torture did not figure in the indictments. After a well-publicized trial in which members of the Fifty-three gave evidence, the four henchmen were found guilty of murdering a number of prisoners—but not Arani. The court ruled that Arani's death had been caused by the cumulative effects of typhus and medical neglect. The new Shah promptly pardoned three of the four but, in a rare return to public executions, permitted the "doctor" to be hanged in Cannon Square. The British ambassador commented that the execution was "greeted with great satisfaction."[139] The hanged "doctor" was an apt symbol for the fallen regime—phony, brutal, and even deadly, but not one that tortured.

2

Mohammad Reza Shah

> In our elaborate precautions, we
> (in 1953) failed to take into
> account the possibility of torture.
> We never imagined we would be
> dealing with fascism.
> *Tudeh officer cited in G. Baqeyi,*
> The Reasons

Interregnum (1941–53)

Royal autocracy collapsed with Reza Shah's abdication in August 1941 and did not reemerge until August 1953 when Mohammad Reza Shah, together with Britain and America, carried out a military coup. Iranians consider this thirteen-year interregnum to be their second constitutional era—the first being the period between 1905 and 1921.

Between 1941 and 1953, Mohammad Reza Shah retained full control over the military—but little else. Like his father, he made all the important appointments as well as decisions in the armed forces—from war minister and chiefs of staff all the way down to field commanders, especially of the armored divisions and tank brigades. Instructions went directly from the Military Office in the Royal Palace to the chiefs of staff and the field officers, bypassing civilian institutions. To keep the military isolated from the government, the Shah handpicked the war ministers and used them as mere grand quartermasters for the armed forces.

To cement his military ties, the Shah lobbied aggressively for the armed forces. He called for higher officer salaries, larger battalions, and, most persistently, more modern weapons. As early as 1948, an exasperated American ambassador advised President Harry Truman to give the Shah "harpoon therapy" to deflate his "extravagant" aspirations and "astronomical figures" for modern weapons—especially tanks and jets.[1] The Shah was demanding jet fighters almost as soon as they came off the assembly lines in America. Moreover, the Shah invariably wore military uniforms for public ceremonies; participated in army maneuvers, academy graduations, and field inspections; protected his father's cronies and promoted his own classmates from the Military Academy; showered trusted officers with privileges and sinecures; and, most important, personally scrutinized all promotions above the rank of major.

The Shah also created within the military the Rokn-e Dovom (Second Bureau) modeled after the famous French Deuxième Bureau. This organization carried out the surveillance work previously done by the urban police (sharbani), which was now under the civilian interior minister. Reporting directly to the Shah, the Second Bureau monitored civilians as well as military personnel. In the words of the British Legation, the Shah, being "doubtful of popular enthusiasm for his dynasty," jealously "guarded his control over the military" and thereby "assumed the title as well as the real authority of the Commander-in-Chief of the Armed Forces."[2] Unaware of these court-military ties, the public formed the notion that the Shah began his reign as a genuine constitutional monarch and was later dragged into politics by circumstances outside his control. Many still harbor this misconception.

While retaining the armed forces, the Shah lost control over the civilian population—especially over the press, the Majles, the cabinet, and the judiciary. The press—after being muzzled for fifteen years—overnight produced some two dozen national newspapers run by muckraking editors eager to take on the royal dynasty as well as the old aristocratic families. The Majles divided into aristocratic parties, with the royalists constituting only one of the many rival groupings. The cabinet—with the exception of the war minister—was now beholden not to the monarch but to parliament. The interior minister—not the war minister—administered the rural gendarmerie as well as the urban police and the whole prison system. What is more, the judiciary regained its independence. The justice minister— elected by the Majles—made appointments to the Supreme Court, appeals court, provincial courts, and district courts. Similarly, defendants regained the rights to have legal counsel, habeas corpus, access to the media, and open civilian trials. Inevitably, political prisoners, not to mention police torture, became rare. It should also be noted that in these years corporal punishments continued to recede from the public arena.

During the interregnum, the country was stirred by one major charismatic politician, Dr. Mohammad Mossadeq, and one major political movement, the Tudeh party. Mossadeq, a veteran statesman banished to his village by Reza Shah, soon stirred the nation by denouncing the Majles as a "den of thieves," criticizing the royal family for its unconstitutional activities, and advocating strict neutrality in foreign affairs. He insisted that the monarch should neither reign nor rule and that the nation should preserve independence by pursuing a policy of "negative equilibrium"—withholding concessions to all the Great Powers. Although an aristocrat, Mossadeq drew his supporters from the urban middle classes: first from university students; later from other sectors of the middle class once his National Front launched the campaign to nationalize the Anglo-Iranian Oil Company. In this, Mossadeq was helped by Ayatollah Abdol Qassem Kashani—one of the few clerics active in national politics. Most others, including the future Ayatollah Khomeini, advised the faithful to keep out of politics—which, in practice, meant staying aloof both from the oil campaign and from the struggle to limit royal power. Apologists for the clergy tend to overlook this.

The Tudeh party was founded at a closed meeting in September 1941—a few days after the release of the first batch of political prisoners. The founders—numbering less than thirty—

knew each other mostly from their days in Qasr. The meeting was convened primarily by Iraj Iskandari, Arani's close disciple. Ovanessian later wrote that Iskandari's intention was to bring Marxists together with the *melli* (nationalists) and the *melliyun* (patriots) to create a broadly based progressive movement—not necessarily a pure communist party.[3]

Iskandari convened the meeting at the home of his uncle Solayman Iskandari, the grand old man of the Iranian left. A radical prince expelled from the Dar al-Fanon by Nasser al-Din Shah, Solayman Iskandari had barely escaped execution in the Constitutional Revolution—he had been praying when court footmen had come to hang him as a "Babi heretic." His brother, Iraj's father, had not been so lucky. In the 1910s, Solayman Iskandari had been prominent in the Democratic party. In World War I, he had served on the Committee of National Resistance formed to oppose the Anglo-Russian occupation. And in the 1920s, he had chaired the Socialist party and had been forced out of politics because of his opposition to the establishment of the Pahlavi dynasty. Although an aristocrat, he lived in a modest apartment in Tehran. Some think he would have rivaled Mossadeq in popularity had he not died in 1944.

Also attending the founding meeting was Imanallah Ardalan (Hajj Az al-Mamalek), Solayman Iskandari's friend since the days of the Committee of National Resistance. A former minister and Kurdish aristocrat, Ardalan himself had not been imprisoned, but some of his close relatives had spent much of the 1930s in Qasr. The others at the meeting included Bozorg Alavi, Bahrami, Yazdi, Radmanesh, Boqrati, and Tabari, all from the Fifty-three; Noshin, the theater director who had escaped the 1937 roundup; Hossein Khairkhah and Hassan Khas'e, two of his theater colleagues; and Pishevari, Reza Rusta, Cheshmazar, Nikravan, Amir-Khizi, Asadi, Sharifi, and Farhi, all veteran communist prisoners.

The others were Abbas Iskandari, Iraj Iskandari's cousin and the editor of *Siyasat* (Politics); Shaykh Mohammad Yazdi, the brother of Dr. Yazdi from the Fifty-three; Amir-Khizi's elder brother, who had fought in the Constitutional Revolution; Ali

Kobari, a civil servant who had been active in the early Communist party in Gilan; Hossein Jahani, a carpenter and labor organizer from the early Communist and Socialist parties; and Ahmad Razavi, an engineer from a prominent Kermani family who later served in Mossadeq's cabinet. Two other former inmates from Qasr also attended the meeting: Azad, the maverick politician who had just launched a newspaper under his name; and Azod, the landed aristocrat who had been imprisoned for his article in a French newspaper. Both had served time in the same block as the wealthier members of the Fifty-three. Some believe that the Iskandaris had also invited Mossadeq to participate in this founding meeting of the Tudeh party.

At Iraj Iskandari's suggestion, the group adopted the label Hezb-e Tudeh-e Iran (the Party of the Iranian Masses), elected Solayman Iskandari the organization's chairman, and named Abbas Iskandari's *Siyasat* its official organ. It pledged to get the other political prisoners released; hold a memorial service at Arani's grave in Abdul Azim Cemetery to mark the second anniversary of his "martyrdom"; and campaign actively in the forthcoming parliamentary elections—in fact, it won nine seats. It also drafted a party platform stressing the importance of constitutional and "individual rights." The platform spoke of protecting "democracy" and "judicial integrity" from fascism, imperialism, militarism, and the vestiges of the fallen despotism. It stressed "the importance of safeguarding democracy as well as all social and individual freedoms—the freedom of language, speech, press, thought, and social activity"; "the necessity to make the judiciary fully independent of the executive branch"; and "the creation of a special high court to punish those who had violated social and individual rights during the twenty-year dictatorship."[4]

At Solayman Iskandari's urging, the party initially barred women from membership, organized Moharram processions, and designated a special prayer room in its main clubhouse. It also celebrated Constitution Day. Years later, Iraj Iskandari admitted that they had intentionally not created a conventional communist organization in part because of the 1931 law, in part because of the traditional environment, in part because of the need to create a broad front, but mostly because the preeminent issues of the day were democracy, freedom, political rights, and constitutional government.[5] In short, the Tudeh began as a liberal rather than a radical party.

The Tudeh, however, moved rapidly to the left in the next few months—especially after the release of Ovanessian and Kambakhsh. These two, helped by Reza Rusta, systematically eased out those deemed to be either too unpredictable, such as Pishevari, Asadi, and Azad, or too "corrupted" by wealth, such as Azod, Ardalan, Razavi, Abbas Iskandari, and Mohammad Yazdi. Ovanessian, who lived in a one-room apartment and often had to forgo meals, tolerated aristocrats with radical commitments but not those with grand lifestyles. He managed to supplant them with members of the Fifty-three whom he had befriended in Qasr—Marxist intellectuals such as Maleki, Khamehei, Jahanshahlu, Makinezhad, Omid, Qodreh, Shahin, Etiqechi, Tarbiyat, Ibrahimzadeh, and the Alamuttis.

By the time the Tudeh convened its first party congress in August 1944, the militant Marxists dominated. Of the 168 delegates at the congress, 24 were from the Fifty-three, 10 were their close friends, and 2 were former officers imprisoned with them. Fourteen others were older communists from Qasr. Another fifteen were labor organizers who had been in and out of prison during the previous two decades.

The congress—presided over by Ovanessian—elected a central committee and an inspection commission. The central committee included seven from the Fifty-three (Nuraldin Alamutti, Bahrami, Iskandari, Radmanesh, Kambakhsh, Boqrati, and Tabari); two from the old Communist party (Ovanessian and Amir-Khizi); and two newcomers, Dr. Fereydoun Keshavarz and Parvin Gonabadi. The former was the brother of the elder Keshavarz imprisoned for communist activities in the 1930s. A French-educated professor at the Medical College in Tehran, Keshavarz had a considerable following in his hometown, Enzeli, where his father had been a famous merchant-philanthropist active in the Constitutional Revolution. He himself was a novice to politics. Gonabadi was a well-known literary figure in Mashed where he edited a newspaper, published poetry, and ran the main girls' high school. In the 1920s, he had been active in the local trade unions and the Socialist party. His father had been a prominent cleric in central Khorasan. In later years, Gonabadi helped the famous writer Dehkhoda produce his famous *Loghatnameh* (Lexicon).

The inspection commission was also packed with Qasr alumni. It included Yazdi, Maleki, and Ziya Alamutti, all from the Fifty-three; Noshin, the theater director; and Reza Rusta, the veteran communist. The others were young well-educated militant Marxists—Dr. Nuraldin Kianuri, Dr. Hossein Jowdat, Ahmad Qassemi, and Ali Olavi. Kianuri—who was to lead the Tudeh during the Islamic Revolution—was a German-trained architect teaching at Tehran University. His grandfather was the conservative Shaykh Fazlallah Nuri who was executed in 1909. His father, however, had fought on behalf of the constitutional revolutionaries. Kianuri's wife, Maryam Firuz, was also active in the Tudeh and was the sister of Prince Firuz Mirza, who was murdered by Reza Shah. Kianuri's sister was married to Kambakhsh and had been active in leftist circles since the late 1920s.

Jowdat was a Sorbonne-educated physics professor at Tehran University. Four decades later he was to be executed by the Islamic Republic. Qassemi, a prolific pamphleteer and Marxist theorist, was a former school principal who had given up a promising career for full-time party activities. He knew some of the Fifty-three from his days at the Law College. Olavi came from a Turkish-speaking family that had emigrated from the Caucasus to Iran in the 1930s via Germany, where he had obtained a civil engineering degree. Olavi was executed after the 1953 coup.

Immediately after the congress, the central committee named Iraj Iskandari, Nuraldin Alamutti, and Bahrami as its co-chairmen to replace Solayman Iskandari, who had died recently. It also named a politbureau composed of Nuraldin

Alamutti, Iraj Iskandari, Bahrami, Ovanessian, and Amir-Khizi. Thus of the twenty top leaders, ten were from the Fifty-three, two were their close associates, and three were veteran communists. Only five were newcomers. Fifteen of the twenty knew each other from Qasr. Not surprisingly, some felt left out by this inner core from Qasr.

In terms of professional background, the leadership included six professors, three in medicine; one judge; one lawyer; three high school principals; two high school teachers; two civil servants; one pharmacist; one theater director; one factory manager; one engineer; and one full-time writer. In terms of ethnicity, the group was composed of twelve Persians; five Azeris; two Qajars; and one Armenian. Their average age was thirty-seven. Like the Fifty-three, they represented the young generation of the Persian-speaking intelligentsia from fairly privileged but not necessarily wealthy families.

The congress resolutions reflected the ongoing shift to the left. While continuing to mention constitutional and individual liberties, it increasingly stressed the rights of women, ethnic and linguistic minorities, and, most important of all, the "laboring classes"—"workers, peasants, craftsmen, and progressive intellectuals." It called for social justice, economic development, land reform, eradication of feudalism, wealth redistribution, health care, and labor legislation—especially the eight-hour day. The party handbook explained:

> In August 1941 many thought that Reza Shah's abdication had overnight ended the dictatorship. We now know better; for we can see with our own eyes that the class structure created by him remains intact. What is more, this class structure continues to create petty Reza Shahs—oligarchy in the form of feudal landlords and exploiting capitalists, who control the state through their ownership of the means of production.[6]

Thus the party was initially a hybrid of socialism and communism, parliamentary liberalism and revolutionary radicalism, Marxism from Western Europe and Leninism from the

Bolshevik Revolution. Years later Iraj Iskandari wrote that some labeled him a "rightist" because he recognized the importance of individual rights, parliamentary politics, and constitutional laws.[7] But even Iraj Iskandari was willing to contemplate the use of arms to protect party buildings and personnel from physical attacks launched by tribal chiefs, local landlords, and hostile government officials. The central committee asked Kambakhsh—who had contacts in the military from his own days in the air force in the 1930s—to set up an informal network within the armed forces as a precautionary measure to keep an eye on right-wing groups there.

The central figure in this network soon became Captain Khosrow Rouzbeh—probably the most controversial as well as the best-known martyr of the communist movement in Iran. A popular teacher at the Military Academy, Rouzbeh was the author of a number of pamphlets on chess, artillery warfare, and, together with Ovanessian, the country's first political lexicon, *Vocabulary of Political and Social Terms.* Rouzbeh deemed some of the Tudeh leaders "mere reformers," "bourgeois liberals," and "parliamentary lobbyists." In his memoirs, Ovanessian praises Rouzbeh as a sincere but impatient radical in need of a firm hand.[8] The removal of this firm hand in 1946 was to have dire consequences.

The Tudeh program had instant appeal—especially among the young intelligentsia and the urban working class. By early 1945, the party had managed to create the first mass organization in Iran's history. According to secret police records, it had more than 2,200 hard-core members—700 of them in Tehran.[9] It also had tens of thousands of sympathizers in its youth and women's organizations and hundreds of thousands of sympathizers in its labor and craft unions. The Central Council of the Federated Trade Unions claimed 33 affiliates and a membership of more than 275,000.[10] When Reza Rusta, the chairman of the Central Council, was arrested for leading unauthorized strikes and demonstrations, more than 230 well-known writers, professors, and newspaper editors volunteered to join him in the dock. They included luminaries such as

Sadeq Hekmat, the unofficial poet laureate Malek al-Sha'ar Bahar, and the historian Sa'ed Nafisi. The courts soon released Reza Rusta—as they did most labor and party organizers arrested in this period.

The Tudeh appeal was somewhat tarnished in 1944–46 by two concurrent events: the Soviet demand for an oil concession in northern Iran and the Soviet sponsorship of ethnic revolts in Kurdestan and Azerbaijan. Despite strong reservations, the Tudeh leaders supported the Soviets on grounds of "socialist solidarity," "internationalism," and "anti-imperialism." The oil issue was especially embarrassing because the Tudeh Majles deputies had been vociferous in demanding the nationalization of the whole petroleum industry. Ovanessian was so outraged that he had a shouting match with the Soviet ambassador at an embassy reception. Khamehei writes that he was locked up in the embassy and not released until the Tudeh central committee intervened.[11] Although the trade unions organized a street demonstration in support of the Soviet oil demand, most of the party leaders were conspicuously absent from the event. One party organizer writes that this crisis made the Tudeh vulnerable for the first time to being smeared as a *beganeh-parast* (worshiper of foreigners).[12]

The Azerbaijan and Kurdish revolts were also damaging. In September 1945, Pishevari, who until then had been oblivious to the whole ethnic issue, suddenly, on a visit to Tabriz, discovered the Azeri card. Helped by some veteran communists who had remained aloof from the Tudeh, Pishevari formed the Ferqeh-e Demokrat-e Azerbaijan (Democratic Party of Azerbaijan) and championed the inalienable right of Azerbaijan to have its own schools, newspapers, and provincial autonomy. He also took the Tudeh to task for "failing to represent the people of Azerbaijan." In prison he had called for the revival of the old Democratic Party of Iran; he now created the Democratic Party of Azerbaijan. The immediate reaction of the Tudeh leaders in Tehran was to denounce him as an "irresponsible adventurist." But the Soviet authorities intervened to muffle their denunciation and persuade them to support the "legitimate rights of the downtrodden nationalities." Parallel events occurred in Kurdestan.

Although the revolts were initially successful in establishing autonomous governments, both collapsed a year later as soon as the Soviets evacuated the region and the Iranian army reoccupied the two provinces. Post-1979 memoirs reveal that the subsequent reprisals were far bloodier than previously thought. Overruling the premier, who recommended leniency, the Shah placed the region under tight martial law, set up military tribunals, and signed 178 execution warrants—including those of 58 military deserters and 3 veteran communists from Qasr (Taqizadeh, Shakiba, and Zavlun).[13] Another 95 died in skirmishes and summary executions. It is estimated that more than 7,000 fled to the Soviet Union.[14] Ovanessian and Iraj Iskandari—both of whom had opposed the uprisings—were now officially blamed for them and charged with high treason and armed insurrection. They fled the country and were sentenced to death in absentia.

In the aftermath of these setbacks, three members of the Fifty-three—Maleki, Khamehei, and Makinezhad—led a group of intellectuals out of the party. This weakened Tudeh influence over the intelligentsia and provided the future National Front with a circle of anti-Soviet Marxist intellectuals. Despite these setbacks, the Tudeh survived to convene a second congress, woo back some lost members, recruit new ones, and gradually rebuild the labor movement. The British Embassy was soon reporting that the Tudeh had regained "the sympathy of the general public," recovered from the 1946 debacles, and survived the Shah's attempt to destroy it. It concluded that there had been a "marked swing in opinion" and that many members of the "middle class" were openly asking why they should not support the Tudeh.[15] In February 1949, the Tudeh held its first public meeting in three years when it revived the annual memorial service at Arani's grave.

On the same day, a lone gunman tried to shoot the Shah while the latter was visiting Tehran University. The Shah promptly declared martial law, pointed his finger at the Tudeh, closed down many opposition newspapers, and banished from the capital numerous politicians, including Mossadeq and Ayatollah Kashani. Even before the assassination attempt, the U.S. and British embassies had suspected that the Shah was seeking an opportunity to strengthen his position vis-à-vis the opposition, including the parliamentary opposition.[16]

The Tudeh bore the brunt of the crackdown. Citing the 1931 law and accusing it of attempted regicide, the government banned the Tudeh, confiscated its assets, dissolved affiliated organizations, especially the Central Council, and rounded up some two hundred leaders and cadres. They were taken to a new block built in Qasr. One prisoner writes that first impressions were deceptive because the clean cells with their toilet facilities were designed to place the inmate in maximum security and total isolation: "Once inside one realized one had been buried alive in a vault."[17] This period of isolation did not last long. They were soon moved to a large communal ward and permitted to socialize in the courtyard. Years later, one of the imprisoned cadres remarked that conditions in Qasr were relatively tolerable in those days since "SAVAK [Persian acronym for State Organization for Security and Intelligence] had not yet been created and the forms of torture practiced in the Reza Shah era had ceased."[18] Like others, he had an exaggerated notion of Reza Shah's prisons.

Most of the two hundred were released within a few months, but fifty were formally charged with undermining the constitutional monarchy, advocating collectivism, supporting secessionists in Azerbaijan and Kurdestan, organizing illegal strikes and demonstrations, and publishing articles in praise of Mirza Kermani and Haydar Khan (the former had assassinated Nasser al-Din Shah in 1896, and the latter had tried to blow up Mohammad Ali Shah in 1907). Finding no credible links between the Tudeh and the lone gunman at Tehran University, the government quietly dropped the original charge of attempted regicide.[19]

The fifty were tried in early 1949. For the sake of symbolism, the Tudeh put their number at fifty-three and billed them as the second "Fifty-three."[20] They were tried in small batches in military courts, but in the presence of independent journalists and proper defense attorneys. The military magistrates often reached split decisions. These sentences, in turn, were often reversed or reduced by higher courts. The defense attorneys included Amidi-Nuri, the flamboyant lawyer who had defended some of the original Fifty-three; Manou, a member of the Fifty-three who had given up politics for the bar; and Dr. Ali Shayegan, Mahmud Nariman, Dr. Mehdi Azar, and Abdul-Ali Lofti—four Mossadeq associates. Azar, who later became Mossadeq's minister of education, was the brother of a leading Tudeh army officer who had defected to the Azerbaijan rebels. Lofti, Mossadeq's justice minister, was a sharia-trained lawyer who had been imprisoned briefly by Reza Shah for speaking up on behalf of constitutional liberties. He too had close relatives in the Tudeh.

Fifteen leaders and thirty-five party organizers comprised the fifty. Top leaders, such as Boqrati, Kianuri, and Qassemi, each received ten years. Less important ones, as well as the party organizers, received lighter sentences; a few were even acquitted. (See table 3.) But leaders who had escaped abroad, such as Ovanessian, Kambakhsh, Iraj Iskandari, Amir-Khizi, Tabari, and Reza Rusta, or gone underground, such as Radmanesh, Bahrami, Keshavarz, Forutan, and Mrs. Kianuri, were sentenced to death in absentia.[21] These verdicts clearly lacked consistency. Bozorg Alavi, a member of the central committee, was even released without trial; his new father-in-law was the Shah's personal adviser. Obviously, the Shah did not take seriously the regicide charges.

The defendants reflect the social composition of the Tudeh party. The professions of the fifteen leaders were as follows: three professors, three school principals and teachers, one theater director, one engineer, one civil servant, one oil worker, one railway worker, one carpenter, one tailor, one mechanic, and one stonecutter. All were males from Muslim homes. Eleven were Persians; the other four were Azeris. Their average age was forty-five.

Table 3
Tudeh Leaders on Trial, 1949

Name	Profession	Age	Ethnicity	Previous Activities	Sentence
Boqrati, Mohammad	School principal	45	Persian	Fifty-three	10 years
Omid, Ali	Oil worker	49	Persian	Communist prisoner	10 years
Kianuri, Nuraldin	Professor	35	Persian	Joined 1942	10 years
Qassemi, Ahmad	School principal	33	Persian	Joined 1942	10 years
Shandramini, Ali	Tailor	32	Azeri-Persian	Fifty-three	7 years
Shureshyan, Mohammad	Mechanic	64	Persian	Fifty-three	7 years
Yazdi, Morteza	Professor	42	Persian	Fifty-three	5 years
Jowdat, Hossein	Professor	40	Azeri	Joined 1942	5 years
Alamutti, Ziya	Civil servant	36	Persian	Fifty-three	3 years
Olavi, Ali	Engineer	45	Azeri	Joined 1941	3 years
Mohazeri, Ibrahim	Stonecutter	38	Persian	Prisoner 1931–34	2 years
Sharifi, Mohammad	Teacher	51	Azeri	Communist prisoner	1 year
Noshin, Abdul	Theater director	44	Persian	Joined 1941	1 year
Jahani, Hossein	Carpenter	59	Persian	Trade unions 1921–29	6 months
Hakimi, Samad	Railway worker	60	Azeri	Prisoner 1937–41	Acquitted

Among the thirty-five cadres and second-ranking leaders were four office employees, four workers, four street vendors, three journalists, three housewives, three students, two lawyers, two coffeehouse owners, two booksellers, two engineers, one teacher, and one doctor. Most resided in Tehran; a few were from the Caspian provinces. Ony two came from Armenian homes. The average age was twenty-seven. Four were women—the first in a political trial. They were incarcerated in a special cell at the Central Jail.

Few of the fifty remained in prison for long. In fact, ten of the top leaders made a sensational escape from Qasr in December 1950: Yazdi, Boqrati, Jowdat, Kianuri, Noshin, Qassemi, Olavi, Hakimi, Shandramini, and Rouzbeh, who had been court-martialed separately. The escape was facilitated by Kianuri, who, before his arrest, had won an architectural prize to design a royal hospital and, on his frequent trips from Qasr to the construction site, had ample opportunity to communicate with the other party leaders. On a designated day, a Tudeh captain, together with a military truck and ten party members wearing army uniforms and carrying rifles—but no ammunition so as to avoid bloodshed—presented the Qasr warden with forged instructions to transfer the ten to the Central Jail in downtown Tehran. Noshin was reluctant to join the escape as he had almost completed his sentence and was busy reinterpreting Ferdowsi's *Shahnameh* to show that, despite conventional belief, it was not a royalist epic. Once out of Qasr, the ten hid in safe houses dispersed throughout the city.

This dramatic escape—one of the few in Qasr's history—fueled the rumor that General Razmara, the premier, had lent a helping hand so as to undermine the Shah. Forutan—the Tudeh leader in charge of the whole venture—ridicules this rumor, pointing out that the escape embarrassed the whole military establishment—the general as much as the Shah.[22] The Shah got his revenge two decades later when he executed the captain who oversaw the escape after giving him a free pass to return from his Soviet exile.

The inmates left behind in Qasr soon organized a hunger

strike to demand more books, longer visiting hours, and the transfer of all political prisoners to Tehran. Meanwhile, the party set up a defense committee to collect contributions and wage an international campaign on their behalf. This campaign achieved success once Mossadeq was elected prime minister and his Supreme Court—much to the chagrin of Britain, the United States, and, of course, the Shah—overruled the 1949 sentences on the grounds that the defendants should have been tried in civilian courts. The courts soon became revolving doors, with lenient judges releasing demonstrators and strikers as fast as the military authorities arrested them. What is more, the justice minister and some members of the Supreme Court questioned the legal standing of the 1931 decree as well as the 1949 ban on the Tudeh. They paid a high price for this after the 1953 coup. Lofti, the seventy-year-old justice minister, died in a military hospital after being beaten up by a royalist goon squad. The judges themselves were put on trial.

Tudeh Dismantled (1953–71)

After the 1953 coup, the secret police—first the Second Bureau and then the newly created SAVAK—selectively used torture on Tudeh activists suspected of withholding information on safe houses, arms caches, printing presses, and contacts in the armed forces. Years later, Kianuri reminisced that after the 1953 coup "torture had been used mostly in the initial interrogation and then only to obtain organizational information. . . . After that prisoners were left alone."[23] Another Tudeh leader writes that the "barbaric practices" introduced in 1953 were rarely used by the end of the 1950s.[24] Likewise, a Khomeini supporter admits that he and his friends, arrested in 1956 for plotting to assassinate the prime minister, were not subjected to physical torture. "Such methods," he remarked in passing, "came in later years."[25]

The forms of torture practiced in this period were crude. They involved indiscriminate beatings, whippings of backs and limbs (but rarely of the feet), smashing of chairs on heads,

breaking of fingers, and slapping of eardrums. A few were subjected to the dreaded qapani or suspended from hooks—but
for no more than fifteen minutes.[26] In a revealing passage, a
senior member of the Tudeh military network writes that his
organization had over the years taken elaborate security pre-
cautions, even developing a complicated cryptographic code,
but had failed to take into account the effectiveness of primitive
brute force. "Torture did not figure in our calculations simply
because we had never expected to be dealing with fascism."[27]
For those who had grown up in the 1930s and 1940s, torture
was a distant abstraction found in fascist Europe or in the bad
old Qajar days. They were to receive a rude awakening.

A Tudeh book of martyrs documents eleven torture deaths
in the period between 1953 and 1958.[28] The victims—most of
whom succumbed from brain hemorrhages—included Farhi,
the central committee member who had been in Qasr during
the 1930s; Lieutenant Mohammad Monzavi, the son of the religious scholar Ayatollah Bozorg Tehrani (his killers were executed after the Islamic Revolution); Galoust Zakharian, an
Armenian intellectual described by Kianuri as the party's
"ablest theoretician";[29] and Vartan Salakhanian, another Armenian intellectual, whom Ahmad Shamlu, the country's preeminent poet, eulogized as a heroic martyr who preferred to
die rather than betray his comrades. Leftists, including Tudeh
opponents, were reciting Shamlu's ode to Vartan even as late
as the 1980s.[30]

Despite the likes of Vartan, brute force, together with the
breaking of the cryptographic code—probably with CIA know-
how—unearthed the whole Tudeh underground. Between 1953
and 1957, the security forces tracked down 4,121 party members—477 of them in the armed forces. This constituted more
than half the party membership and almost the entire military
network—only 37 officers escaped abroad. General Zibayi, the
chief interrogator, named the 4,121 arrested members in his
book, *Communism in Iran*. This book was commissioned by
SAVAK in the late 1950s but was not readily available until the
1980s.[31] The occupations of 2,419 are known. Of these, 1,276

(53%) were from the intelligentsia, including 386 civil servants, 201 college students, and 165 teachers; and 860 (36%) were from the working class, including 125 skilled workers, 80 textile workers, and 60 cobblers. Most of the remaining 11 percent were shopkeepers, with a sprinkling of peasants and house-wives—mostly from middle-class homes.[32]

British and American authorities felt the crackdown had not gone far enough. The British Foreign Office complained that "family influence and graft were playing a large part in securing the release of people arrested."[33] The American Embassy insisted that only massive "suppression" could destroy the Tudeh as the prospects of economic development would have no effect on a membership that was entirely "employed," "literate," and relatively well off: "The notion that communism feeds on suppression is a communist-inspired notion."[34] Not surprisingly, many felt that the main drive for the brutal crackdown came from the West—especially the CIA.

The magnitude of the dragnet forced the regime to over-crowd Qasr and the Central Jail as well as the main provincial prisons; the jail in Rasht became so overcrowded that it erupted into a bloody uprising in which three prisoners were killed. The regime also improvised. It converted Qezel Qal'eh (Red Fort)— a Qajar armory in western Tehran—into a prison for some two hundred inmates. It used the nearby Zarhi barracks as a temporary detention center; most of the casualties from torture occurred in its bathrooms. It packed Maleki supporters as well as Tudeh militants into the old Falak al-Falak fortress in Khor-ramabad. Clearly, the disparate groups were put together for malevolent reasons. What is more, it dispatched some one hundred twenty prisoners to the godforsaken island of Khark in the Persian Gulf. In the past, Khark had been reserved for highly dangerous common criminals.

Karim Keshavarz has detailed this place in his *Fourteen Months on Khark.*[35] A survivor of Qasr from the 1930s, Kesha-varz depicts Khark less as a regular prison than as place of unhealthy and inhospitable banishment. The guards, living in a separate compound, provided the prisoners with bare necessities and periodically counted heads but otherwise let them have free range of the island. The prisoners formed a komun that had its own joint banks and elected officials. They cooked and baked bread, cleaned house, herded goats, washed clothes, collected rainwater for drinking, swam in the salty water (always on the lookout for sharks), brewed vodka, and visited the ancient ruins. They sang, performed folk dances, and put on plays—one was staged for the local population. They celebrated Nowruz, January 1, May Day, Constitution Day, and the Autumn Equinox—an old Persian festival revived by the Tudeh. They listened to a homemade radio as well as to classical music on an old gramophone. They played volleyball and incessant games of chess—the best players competed in tournaments. They gave illiteracy and language classes—mostly Persian, Azeri, English, French, and Russian. They read the few books available and the periodicals that sporadically arrived from Tehran—the older prisoners tried to shield the younger ones from temptation by removing from these magazines all pictures of scantily clothed women. When finances permitted, they bought fresh fruits and vegetables from local smugglers and the small Arab-speaking community. They had cordial relations both with the Arab *kadkhuda* (headman) and with the prison warden—who happened to be a childhood friend of one of the prisoners.

In addition to their large komun, the Khark prisoners had a number of smaller social *dowreh*s (circles). One was composed of intellectuals who favored an alliance with Mossadeq; one, of intellectuals who opposed such an alliance; one, of workers and "simple folk" who insisted on addressing the intellectuals as "engineers" and "doctors"; one, of veterans from the Azerbaijan revolt; and one, of Armenians, almost all from the same slum in Tehran. Khark also contained a few individuals from the National Front and the Fedayan-e Islam. The komun exempted the oldest inmates from physical chores. This gave Keshavarz the opportunity to study the local dialects and archaeological sites. According to him, their worst ordeals were summer heat and humidity; disease and tooth infections; and lack of vitamins, medicines, and sanitary facilities—the sea was their toilet. The group contained four doctors and four medical students, but they lacked penicillin and basic medicines.

The 1953–58 dragnet caught most of the remaining top leaders, including Bahrami, Yazdi, and Olavi. It also caught 22 colonels, 69 majors, 100 captains, 193 lieutenants, 19 noncommissioned officers, and 63 military cadets. This military network was so extensive that some National Front supporters complained that the Tudeh could have saved Mossadeq. But in actual fact, few Tudeh officers held field commands—especially in the crucial tank divisions around Tehran. The officers came mostly from the military academies, the gendarmerie, the police, and the medical corps. Coups are carried out—as well as forestalled—by tanks and motorized brigades, not by cadets and academy lecturers. The Shah's screening of the tank division had paid off. Ironically, a Tudeh colonel had been in charge of the Shah's personal security—as well as that of Vice President Richard Nixon when he visited Iran. The Tudeh had the opportunity to assassinate the Shah and the U.S. vice president but not to launch a coup. Incidentally, many of these officers came from the lower middle class—even from religious bazaar families. Lacking political clout, their families rushed to Qom in search of clerics willing to lobby on their behalf.

Military tribunals meted out varied sentences in camera. Those in the military organization—whether uniformed or civilians assigned to them—were treated harshly. But others— even party leaders—were treated fairly leniently so long as they did not withhold information on safe houses and hidden printing presses. The 31 executed in 1953–58 were all either military personnel or their close civilian associates. They included 7 colonels, 6 majors, 8 captains, 5 lieutenants, 2 sailors, and 3 civilians—one of them being Olavi, the central committee's main liaison with the military organization. Tabari—one of the Fifty-three—later claimed that Olavi, in contrast to Yazdi and Bahrami, had been executed because he lacked their "social connections."[36] Although to some extent true, this overlooks the military factor. Of the other military officers, 144 got life, 119 got fifteen years, and 79 got ten years.

The condemned were executed in four batches. A Reuter's correspondent who observed the first batch filed a confidential report to the U.S. government describing how the condemned had gone to their death singing patriotic songs, hailing the Tudeh, denouncing the Shah, and refusing Muslim rites.[37] He warned that leaked reports of this "bravado" were "impressing large segments of the public." He added that they had to be dispatched with pistol shots because the firing squads had missed either "through nervousness or deliberate avoidance." The regime dispatched the others in total secrecy and circulated the false rumor that the condemned had to be drugged to fortify their failing courage. It also encouraged the rumor that the Americans had overruled the Shah's desire to grant clemency.[38] A Foreign Office expert commented that these "necessary executions" aroused strong protests inside and outside the country, with prominent figures such as Jean-Paul Sartre and Albert Camus signing letters urging clemency.[39] He added that the executed officers had "a reputation for honesty and efficiency" and that the Shah had promised to educate their children at his personal expense.[40] It is not clear if the promise was kept. The British ambassador noted that many were "impressed" by the officers' refusal to seek clemency and their willingness to "face torture and execution."[41]

The regime portrayed the trial of the officers as one of treason and espionage. Denouncing the Tudeh as a "fifth column," General Timour Bakhtiyar, the military governor of Tehran, issued two works—*The Black Book* and the *Evolution of Communism in Iran*—claiming that the officers had confessed to passing on secret information to the communist bloc. But, in fact, the Zibayi book—the documentary basis for Bakhtiyar's books—has next to nothing on gathering information and absolutely nothing on the passing of such information to the Soviet Union. One of the condemned confessed that every morning he had to pass information to a foreign official—his American superior. Likewise, memoirs published by SAVAK officials after 1979 provide much information on Tudeh "subversion"—but not on foreign espionage.

Instead of proving espionage, the Zibayi book provides reams of documentation on how the organization read and distributed Marxist books, wrote in secret codes, kept tabs on right-wing officers, made hand grenades, stored arms, smuggled people out of the country, embezzled money from state banks, provided firearms to party members and the Fedayan-e Islam, and, most serious of all, helped a pro-Mossadeq revolt among the Qashqayis by disabling some planes and sending arms and ammunition to the tribesmen. The published trial transcripts show that the real charges were not "espionage" but "sedition" and "communism." In fact, it turned out that the Soviets did have an agent in the Iranian armed forces, but he was neither in the Tudeh nor in its military organization. He escaped detection until 1977, by which time he was a full field marshal in charge of intelligence agencies in all three branches of the armed forces. A SAVAK officer writes that this field marshal had been giving information to the Soviets since his days in the Military Academy in the 1940s.[42] It seems the Soviets continued to keep their espionage and their communist contacts strictly separate.

Rouzbeh—the military organization's de facto head—was one of the last to be apprehended. Wounded after a shootout in July 1957, he was interrogated—we do not know under what conditions—tried in camera, and executed secretly in Qezel Qal'eh in May 1958. Zibayi reveals that Rouzbeh confessed to having assassinated Mohammad Massoud, a maverick newspaper editor, in 1948 as well as four party members suspected of selling information to the police after the 1953 coup. One of the four was Hesham Lankrani, a member of a prominent clerical family from Azerbaijan. Rouzbeh, however, emphasized that he had carried out the Massoud assassination without the party's knowledge.[43] In fact, the party had dissolved its military network in 1946 and had not re-created it until 1950–51. Contemptuous of the party for being too "moderate," Rouzbeh had resigned in 1946 and not rejoined until the early 1950s. He confessed he had thought the assassination of such a popular anticourt journalist as Massoud would polarize Iran and thus radicalize the Tudeh. Rouzbeh was a radical in the tradition of Bakhunin—not of Marx and Engels.

SAVAK never published Rouzbeh's damaging confessions, probably because his defiant death made him an instant revolutionary icon. Further coverage would have given him more publicity. Besides, the Shah preferred to make his adversaries—whether dead or alive—into nonpersons. In begrudging praise, the British Embassy described Rouzbeh as the "Red Pimpernel, who, in a series of disguises walked into and out of innumerable baited police traps with the swashbuckling courage that made him a figure of legendary proportions, both to the Party, the security authorities, and the general public."[44]

On the eve of his execution, Rouzbeh composed a seventy-page testament denouncing capitalism, praising socialism, and explaining why he was willing to die for the "great revolutionary cause" of the Tudeh party.[45] The party posthumously elevated him to the central committee and made him into an icon on a par with Arani. It published laudatory articles every year commemorating his martyrdom. It erected a statue in his honor in Italy. Shamlu composed a couplet eulogizing him. And many leftists—including non-Tudeh members—named their newborn sons after him. In short, he became the symbol of uncompromising opposition, heroic resistance, and ultimate self-sacrifice.[46]

Few of the others remained in jail for long—even Yazdi and Bahrami, whose death sentences were commuted to life imprisonment. Most were granted amnesty after signing short announcements known as *nadamat nameh* (letter of regret), *tanaffar nameh* (letter of disgust), or *enzejar nameh* (letter of revulsion), expressing loyalty to the Shah, promising to abstain from politics, or declaring their disgust with the "treacherous" Tudeh party. Such letters were signed by 2,844 of the 4,121 arrested between September 1953 and May 1957. In most cases, the main inducement was reduced sentences rather than torture. Some avoided signing by giving bribes or convincing the police they had never belonged to the Tudeh.[47] Mahmud Behazin, a prominent intellectual, writes that he got released within two months because relatives pulled strings and he signed a promissory note that he would abstain from politics. He claims that the authorities knew perfectly well he had no intention of keeping his promise.[48]

The longest letters came from Yazdi and Bahrami. Yazdi sent a full paragraph to the Supreme Court and the Shah seeking repeal of his death sentence "in consideration of the medical contribution he could make to the country and of his past opposition to the dangerous elements in the Tudeh leadership."[49] At his trial, he refused to work with his court-assigned attorneys but pleaded that while on the central committee he had argued against armed actions and the re-creation of the military network.[50] He stressed that the party had tried to work within the constitutional laws but that hotheaded individuals had initiated illegal actions without the central committee's approval. Those he named as hotheaded, such as Kianuri, were safely out of the country. A fellow prisoner reports that Yazdi's arm had been broken during his initial interrogation.[51]

According to the British ambassador, Yazdi's life was saved by the unexpected intercession of Sayyed Ziya Tabatabai, the most pro-British and anticommunist of the old-time politicians. Sayyed Ziya, who happened to be a childhood friend of Yazdi's older brother, advised the Shah that more executions would be counterproductive because the whole concept of "martyrdom" had a "great deal of emotional appeal" for the average Iranian.[52] According to a cellmate, further clemency pleas came from Yazdi's brother-in-law, a general in the army, and Ibrahim Hakimi, his foster father, who had served the monarch both as a court tutor and as prime minister.[53] Yazdi was released after serving five years of his life sentence. He spent these five years writing a book on medicine and keeping himself separate from the Tudeh komun. After his release, he opened a clinic that welcomed the indigent and former Tudeh members. He remained friendly with members of the Fifty-three who continued to lead the Tudeh in exile until as late as 1979.

Bahrami's letter was longer. He began with his "fall into communism" in prewar Germany, his friendship with Arani, his membership in the Fifty-three, and his role in the creation and leadership of the Tudeh. He continued with a litany of reasons for being "disgusted" with the Tudeh—the Soviet oil demand, the Azerbaijan revolt, the refusal of hotheaded adventurers to listen to the leadership, and the "conspiracies" to subvert the armed forces and the "constitutional monarchy." He exhorted party members still at large to turn themselves in and concluded with, "Long Life to the Promising Young Shah. Death to the Foreign-worshipping Tudeh."[54] A fellow prisoner writes that Bahrami signed the letter only after his wrists had been placed inside red-hot handcuffs. Forty years later, the fellow prisoner noted that he had screamed exactly the same phrase as Galileo: "What do you want from me?"[55] Bahrami was released in 1957—just before succumbing to diabetes from which he had suffered even when incarcerated with the Fifty-three in the 1930s. Rouzbeh became the symbol of bravery, heroism, and resistance; Bahrami, the epitome of the exact opposite. Neither deserved their reputations.

Most of the 2,844 letters, however, were not taken seriously—by either the public or the signers or even the authorities themselves. They were one-shot deals appearing in the daily *Ettela'at*. They were short—often less than a paragraph and sometimes less than two sentences. They were perfunctory, giving only name, identification number, profession, and vague reason for resignation. The wardens often pleaded with them to sign and get on with their lives; some even reminded them that "promises made to governments were not morally binding."[56] The letters were clearly pro forma: the authorities composed them, and the petitioners merely added their signatures. They sounded ironic in the wake of the CIA coup as they hailed the Shah as a "constitutional monarch" and denounced the Tudeh as "foreign-worshiping." They even became the butt of public humor when some Armenians signed letters stating that they were "disgusted" with the Tudeh because it had "failed to show proper respect for Islam." Karim Keshavarz narrates how "shocked" Armenians in Khark beseeched their Muslim comrades to be considerate of their Christian sensibilities and take more care performing their daily Muslim prayers.[57]

It was rumored that the authorities took bribes and turned a blind eye when concerned relatives forged signatures. It was also rumored that the leadership permitted and even encouraged some to sign. Mehdi Kaymaram, a party organizer, writes that leaders ordered—through smuggled notes and Morse code messages—specific members to get out of prison by signing these letters.[58] Mehdi Khanbaba-Tehrani, a militant student who left the Tudeh with the complaint that the party was not revolutionary enough, writes that these letters were not really "testimonials of disgust but merely expressions of desire to return to private life." Besides, he adds, the Tudeh leaders had been bound more by "legalism" than radicalism.[59] He could have added that some leaders were physically exhausted, having been in hiding since 1949. It is significant that the Tudeh did not ostracize the signers but, on the contrary, invited most of them back into the fold as soon as conditions permitted in 1979.[60]

The Tudeh reserved its venom for those who actively collaborated with the regime either by becoming paid informants or by contributing to the short-lived SAVAK journal *'Ebrat* (Example). This journal specialized in critiquing Marxism, translating works from the CIA-financed Congress for Cultural Freedom, and denouncing the past record of the Tudeh party— especially its support for the Soviet oil concession and the Azerbaijan rebellion. The Tudeh drew a sharp line between signing "letters of regret" and collaborating actively with the regime. Years later Kianuri confided that contributors to *'Ebrat* remained barred from the Tudeh—even after the 1979 revolution.[61]

It is surprising that the regime did not demand more of its prisoners—especially since the 1953 coup coincided with the height of McCarthyism in United States and the Slansky trials in Eastern Europe. The regime in Iran preferred that the public forget the immediate past as soon as possible. It also preferred that opponents withdraw from politics rather than remain on the scene—even if active on behalf of the regime. Public shows in the style of the House Un-American Activities Committee would have drawn more attention to the opposition and would have kept alive the memory of the days when the Tudeh had been a mass movement. Besides television had not yet come to Iran.

National Front leaders were treated more leniently. Mossadeq and most of his ministers were tried and sentenced but released within four years. Mossadeq was banished to his village, where he died in 1967. Others, such as Shayegan, were encouraged to leave the country. Only two suffered serious repercussions. Lofti, the justice minister, died in a military hospital after being beaten up. Hossein Fatemi, the foreign minister, was executed after being found guilty of plotting to overthrow the "constitutional monarchy." He had advised Mossadeq to declare a republic. He had taken shelter in the Tudeh underground after the coup. Even more serious, before the coup he had openly denounced the Shah as a "venomous serpent."

Once the bulk of the Tudeh prisoners were released, the makeshift jails closed down. Khark returned to its original use. Falak al-Falak shut its doors; it was later turned into a tourist attraction. Provincial jails ceased to house political prisoners. And the military barracks—with the exception of Qezel Qal'eh—lost their inmates once Tudeh officers were pardoned in large batches. Among the early releases was Captain Abbasi, Rouzbeh's right-hand man, who had saved his own neck by cooperating with the authorities. In his *Memoirs of a Tudeh Officer*, Abbasi describes how the taxi driver taking him home from prison kissed him, refused payment, and praised the communist officers when he discovered Abassi had been one of them. Abbasi preferred to be treated as a Tudeh officer rather than as an informer.[62]

Two of the officers produced literary masterpieces. Ex-Lieutenant Ali Mohammad Afghani, while serving a life sentence, wrote *The Husband of Ahu Khanum*—a one-thousand-page novel that avoided overt politics but explored the sensitive issue of polygamy in traditional families. Published in 1961, it received immediate acclaim—even winning a royal prize. Ahmad Mahmud, a fellow prisoner, wrote a trilogy entitled *Neighbors, Tale of a City*, and *Burnt Land*. A fictionalized biography, the trilogy describes the life of a Tudeh officer beginning with his youthful commitments, continuing with his prison experiences, and ending with his social alienation and political disillusionment. Needless to say, Mahmud received literary recognition only after 1979. These four books detail the culture of the traditional middle class. Meanwhile, a third young officer, Abdul-Rahman Qassemlou, after being pardoned, went to Czechoslovakia, where he studied history, wrote *Kurdestan and the Kurds*, and revived the Kurdish Democratic Party of Iran. He remained at its head until his assassination in 1989.

By the late 1960s, the number of Tudeh prisoners had dwindled to less than two dozen. Their nucleus was seven military officers who refused to sign the conventional letters of regret. Remaining incarcerated until the revolution, they became—with Nelson Mandela—the world's longest-serving political prisoners. When in 1970, Behazin, the well-known author, spent three months in Qasr for trying to revive the Writers' Association, he found few long-term political prisoners besides these seven holdouts and a group of religious extremists accused of plotting to assassinate the prime minister.[63] The others were short-term prisoners—like Behazin himself. Mohammad Ali Amoui, one of the seven holdouts, writes in his unpublished memoirs that the bulk of the Tudeh officers had been released after being persuaded by the party leadership to sign the perfunctory letters of regret.[64]

The prisoners organized themselves into two komuns divided along generational lines. Significantly, religious extremists were willing to be in the same komun as the Tudeh prisoners. Their daily routine did not differ much from that of their predecessors—except they now had a radio, television set, reading room, Ping-Pong table, and indoor gym equipped with exercise machines. They spent time playing chess, exchanging language lessons, and reminiscing about their own political experiences. They were even allowed to decorate their cells with pictures of world-famous communists.[65] Amou writes that they could read Marxist texts such as "The Manifesto," "The Holy Family," "Eighteenth of Brumaire," as well as biographies of Beethoven, Gandhi, Garibaldi, Napoleon, and Peter the Great. He adds that his favorite book was a study of the Decembrists who had tried to "liberate the serfs and bring freedom to Russia."[66] Behazin spent his short time in prison reading Dostoevsky's *House of the Dead* and translating Sholokhov's *And Quiet Flows the Don*. Readers of Behazin's prison memoirs could well conclude that the generation that had eagerly burst into politics in 1941 had by the late 1960s withdrawn from the national scene—either because of defeat, middle age, repression, or disillusionment, or sheer physical and psychological exhaustion.

SAVAK versus Guerrillas (1971–77)

The mood changed drastically in 1971. In February of that year, a small band of armed Marxists assaulted the gendarmerie post in the Caspian village of Siahkal. This Siahkal incident became a historical landmark. It sparked an intense guerrilla struggle and inspired an increasing number of young Muslims as well as Marxists to take up arms against the regime. It also marked the entry onto the national scene of a young generation of the intelligentsia equipped with new energy, new aspirations, new tactics, a new ethos, and even new political terminology.

The older generation had given priority to political struggles—political parties, trade unions, and parliamentary as well as extraparliamentary strategies. The new generation felt these strategies had reached a dead end and the only way forward was through armed struggle—guerrilla warfare, heroic martyrdom, and inspiration to self-sacrifice. In their words, "the question was no longer whether but when and how one should take up arms."[67]

For older radicals, the exemplars were Marx and Engels; the

preferred symbols, the red rose, the north star, and the hammer and sickle. For the younger ones, they were Che Guevara, Mao, Ho Chi Minh, the rifle, and the machine gun. In fact, the term "armed struggle" became a litmus test for dividing the two. The old were acceptable to the new only if they had been "martyred"—such as Vartan and Rouzbeh—or if they incorporated into their discourse the language of "armed struggle." Others were dismissed as "liberals," "reformists," "revisionists," "petty bourgeois," and even "effeminate." For their part, the old felt the new to be contaminated with "anarchism," "adventurism," "infantile ultra-leftism," and *chapzadeh* (awestruck by the left). In fact, "chapzadeh" was coined at the same time as the better-known term "gharbzadeh" (awestruck by the West).

In the six years following Siahkal, 368 guerrillas lost their lives.[68] Of these, 197 died in gun battles; 93 were executed by firing squads after being condemned by military tribunals; and the remaining 78 were summarily executed, died under torture, or committed suicide just before capture (see table 4). According to their organizations, 45 died under torture, but this probably includes some who blew themselves up with hand grenades or took cyanide pills to prevent capture. They carried cyanide pills for such contingencies. These guerrillas posed a major threat to the regime not so much for their military actions as for the wide appeal they enjoyed among their contemporaries. Every year on December 7—the unofficial student day—the campuses throughout the country closed down as radicals staged demonstrations denouncing the regime and praising the guerrillas. The guerrillas had become the new generation's folk heroes.

In terms of political affiliation, the vast majority of the martyred guerrillas came from three main organizations: the Marxist Fedayi (Self-Sacrificers) that had launched the Siahkal assault; the Muslim Mojahedin (Holy Warriors), a new group inspired by both Islam and Marxism; and the Marxist offshoot of the Mojahedin, which after the revolution took on the name Peykar (Struggle). A few came from smaller Muslim or Marxist

Table 4
Dead Guerrillas, 1971–77

	Fedayi	Mojahed	Marxist Mojahed	Other Marxist	Other Islamic	Total
Killed fighting	106	41	31	11	8	197
Executed	38	17	10	12	16	93
Tortured to death	10	16	6	9	4	45
Missing	6	6	3	2		15
Suicide	7	1	1			9
Murdered in prison	7	2				9
Total	172	83	51	34	28	368*

*The political affiliations of a few remain unknown.

groups such as Tofan (Storm) and the Sazman-e Enqelab-e Hezb-e Tudeh (the Revolutionary Organization of the Tudeh Party)—both Maoist offshoots of the Tudeh. The Fedayi founders had mostly begun their political careers in the Tudeh and the National Front. Some were children of Tudeh organizers. The Mojahedin founders had all been active in the Liberation Front—an organization created by Mehdi Bazargan and other religious-minded liberal supporters of Mossadeq.

In terms of social background, almost all were from the young generation of the intelligentsia. Only ten were older than thirty-five. As a whole, they differed in two subtle ways from previous radicals—both of the Tudeh and of the Communist parties. First, the Armenian element had shrunk to one. Much of the Armenian population that had produced radicals in the past had migrated in the 1950s to the Soviet Union. Second, women made their first significant appearance. Constituting 11 percent of the dead, they scored a number of firsts in Iranian history—the first woman to face a firing squad, die under torture, take cyanide to evade capture, lose her life in a street shootout, and write her prison memoirs.[69] (See table 5 for the occupations of these guerrillas.)

The regime took measures to counter the guerrilla challenge. It expanded SAVAK to over five thousand full-time employees and an unknown number of part-time informants. It trained SAVAK personnel in the United States and Israel. It coordinated SAVAK, military intelligence, the gendarmerie, and the urban police by setting up the Komiteh (Committee) against Terrorism. This Komiteh was located on the site of the old Central Jail in Tehran, and soon attained a macabre reputation as initial interrogations were invariably carried out there. The

Table 5
Occupations of Dead Guerrillas

	Fedayi	Mojahed	Marxist Mojahed	Other Marxist	Other Islamic	Total
College students	73	44	25	14	7	163
High school students	1				7	8
Teachers	17	5	6	1	1	30
Engineers	19	14	3	1		37
Office employees	7	4		1	8	20
Doctors	3	1		1		5
Intellectuals	4			1		5
Other professionals	11	6	2	1		20
Housewives	8	1	4			13
Conscripts	5					5
Shopkeepers		2			1	3
Workers	12	1	1	7		21
Not known	12	5	10	7	4	38
Total	172	83	51	34	28	368
(Women	22	3	15	2		42)

term "Komiteh" became synonymous with prison brutality. The guerrillas suspected that this committee—like many other innovations—was an import from Latin America via the United States.

The regime also modernized the prisons. In addition to the Komiteh, it added two new blocks to Qasr—one for women, another for political prisoners. It built maximum security prisons in Shiraz, Tabriz, Isfahan, Mashed, and Khorramabad. In the Tehran region, it converted the Qezel Qal'eh into a public park but built three maximum security penitentiaries: at Qezel Hesar (Red Fort) on the road to Karaj (this housed more than 2,000); at Gohar Dasht (Jeweled Field) also on the road to Karaj (its foundations were laid in 1978); and, most important of all, at Evin, a private scenic garden at the foot of the Alburz mountains on the northwestern outskirts of Tehran. These maximum security prisons were modeled on those of United States.

Evin soon supplanted Qasr as the country's Bastille. This time the reputation was well deserved. It was designed in 1971 to house 320—20 in solitary cells and 300 in two large communal blocks. By 1977, it had expanded a number of times to house more than 1,500—with 100 solitary cells in block 209 reserved for the most important political prisoners. A three-floor building, block 209 contained six interrogation chambers in its basement. Evin also contained an execution yard, a courtroom, and separate blocks for women and common criminals. No prisoner ever succeeded in breaking out of Evin. Most cells had only one tiny window out of eye reach. Ironically, Evin was built by business associates of Bazargan and his liberal Liberation Movement. Leftist prisoners found this to be more than ironic.

What is more, SAVAK was given a loose leash to torture suspected guerrillas—few of whom enjoyed any family ties to the ruling elite. Social connections that had protected previous dissidents had evaporated. Not surprisingly, torture increased dramatically—in scope, intensity, variety, and sophistication. One SAVAK interrogator links this directly to Siahkal and argues that the day after the attack the regime permitted his organization to use as much physical pressure as necessary to uncover accomplices and arms caches.[70] He adds that this pressure worked wonders.

A senior SAVAK officer later wrote that after Siahkal interrogators were sent abroad for "scientific" training to prevent unwanted deaths from "brute force."[71] Brute force was supplemented with the bastinado; sleep deprivation; extensive solitary confinement; glaring searchlights; standing in one place for hours on end; nail extractions; snakes (favored for use with women); electrical shocks with cattle prods, often into the rectum; cigarette burns; sitting on hot grills; acid dripped into nostrils; near-drownings; mock executions; and an electric chair with a large metal mask to muffle screams while amplifying them for the victim. This latter contraption was dubbed the Apollo—an allusion to the American space capsules. Prisoners were also humiliated by being raped, urinated on, and forced to stand naked. Some embellished these tortures with horror stories of prisoners being thrown to bears, starved to death, and having their limbs amputated. Some claimed religious leaders were forced to sit naked before stripteasing prostitutes.

Despite the new "scientific" methods, the torture of choice remained the traditional bastinado. It was excruciatingly painful but rarely led to death. It was quick, whereas most modern methods needed time; for SAVAK, time was of the essence as its primary goal was to locate arms caches, safe houses, and accomplices. Guerrilla handbooks warned that the bastinado was by far the most painful of the tortures—especially when the victim was tied to a metal bed and lashed with a thick knotted electrical cable known as the *kable*.[72] Victims agree this was by far the most painful of SAVAK tortures.[73] The pain bolts like lightning from the highly sensitive nerve endings at the soles of the feet into the rest of the body through the whole nervous system, including the brain. Victims would have difficulty placing any weight on their feet for days on end. Some needed compresses and antibiotics to avoid infections. SAVAK compounded the agony by forcing victims to walk around the cell between the rounds of lashings. For SAVAK, the bastinado had one drawback: its overuse could permanently damage the kidneys and the central nervous system. Such damage could be embarrassing.

The guerrillas issued handbooks on how to manage torture. They advised forgoing food so as to lose consciousness in the first twenty lashes. They set the strict rule that no vital information should be given in the first twenty-four hours so that colleagues could have the opportunity to relocate themselves. They had learned from hard experience that prolonged whipping could break even the most committed. They recommended focusing their minds on martyred comrades and heroic poems while the interrogators were demanding the *adres* (address) of safe houses and future meetings. They also recommended wasting time by giving false addresses and useless information—especially about the dead. They warned that the police would try devious tricks. They would move the hands of the clocks in the torture chambers forward. They would claim the bastinado was merely a prelude to worse torments to come. They would threaten to strip them naked, and rape their wives, sisters, and even mothers.

These handbooks introduced readers to SAVAK euphemisms. Interrogators addressed each other as "doctors" or "engineers." They referred to the bastinado as the *tamshiyat*—a double entendre meaning both "raising awareness" and "making one walk farther" (on swollen feet). Torture chambers became known as Tamshiyat Rooms. The handbooks also stressed that torture should be considered an integral part of the ongoing war against the regime—as important as the actual armed struggle. Death under torture was itself a major victory. It proved the caliber of true revolutionaries and their ideological superiority over the regime as well as over ideological competitors. Even more important, it would inspire others to similar deeds of heroism, self-sacrifice, and revolutionary martyrdom.

SAVAK killed in cold blood on one notorious occasion. A SAVAK interrogator later admitted that in 1975 he and his colleagues had lined up against a wall and machine-gunned seven Fedayis and two Mojaheds, all serving life sentences— one of them was Bezhan Jazani, a founding leader of the Fedayi.[74] These killings were carried out to revenge a series of assassinations, including those of a police informer and a prominent military judge. "The guerrillas," the interrogator declared, "had killed our people so we killed theirs." The next day, the government announced that the nine had been shot trying to escape from Evin. The same interrogator later pleaded that the orders for the killings had come down from the highest level—from the Shah himself.[75]

By the mid-1970s, the total number of political prisoners reached a new peak, 7,500. Most were in Evin; others were in Qasr, Qezel Hesar, Mashed, Shiraz, and Tabriz. Conditions in Evin were much harsher compared both to the other prisons and to the previous decades. In fact, Qasr was now considered a place of rest compared to Evin. Evin was under SAVAK supervision. Its guards—all military personnel—were changed every month to prevent fraternization. Inmates were confined to their immediate wards. They could spend no more than two hours per day in the courtyard. They could not receive home-cooked food. They had to wear blindfolds outside their cells— even when going to the interrogation rooms. Visits were restricted to immediate family members—and then only as a special privilege. Visiting rooms had glass barriers, mesh wire, and telephones to prevent all direct contact.

Evin—unlike Qasr—had no reading room. Its cells were frequently searched for books and other contraband. Newspapers—already government controlled—were further censored. Radios were banned as they could tune in to foreign stations. Television was screened to prevent the viewing of inappropriate programs—documentaries on communism as well as Hollywood shows such as "Mission Impossible" were forbidden in case they conveyed "dangerous messages." Inmates felt— whether true or false—that they were being constantly monitored by hidden cameras. The Evin wardens tried to ban communal gym and communal eating but backed down when confronted by a hunger strike. What is more, Evin inmates often remained incarcerated even after completing their sentences. These prisoners were known as the *mellikesh*—a sardonic reference to the national lottery, implying they were being kept gratis at national expense. Financed by SAVAK, Evin had three advantages over most other prisons. It could afford better food, unlimited hot showers, and more floor space for sleeping. Modernity had some advantages. Amoui, who knew the prisons inside out, comments that the modern maximum security ones like Evin were infinitely worse because they deprived inmates of privacy as well as of all aspects of nature—trees, gardens, flowers, and sky views. "Here there was nothing but iron and steel."[76]

Prisoners outside Evin followed a daily routine similar to those of previous generations. They woke up at 6:00 A.M.; exercised in the courtyard; ate breakfast at 8:00; read in silence for two hours until snack time; had group discussions until lunch; after lunch walked for half an hour in the courtyard and then had a siesta until 3:00 P.M.; held classes from 3:00 until dinner at 6:00; and spent the period from dinner until bedtime walking, watching television, reading, or even writing—although writing implements were strictly forbidden. Jazani managed to write his *Thirty-Year History of Iran* in the prison bathroom after lengthy discussions with veterans from the Tudeh and Fedayan-e Islam. Although lights remained on all night for security reasons, prisoners went to sleep at 11:00 P.M. At all times, there was a strict taboo against sex, so much so that during television hours two prisoners—usually one from the Mojahedin and one from the Fedayi—sat on each side of the television set with a large drape to block the view if any scantily clothed women unexpectedly appeared on the screen.

As special punishment, political prisoners were transferred to criminal wards. Thus they were cut off from colleagues. They had to tolerate chaotic conditions: there was no komun to clean the place, arrange a daily routine, or mediate personal disputes. Other inmates—especially the psychiatric cases—could be a source of irritation and even danger. What is more, youngsters were exposed to sexual threats. Despite these dangers, some did not mind this punishment because it gave them the opportunity to proselytize among the "common people" and obtain political news from the outside world.

Prison life differed from that in the Reza Shah period in one significant way: class privileges had become less apparent as modern egalitarianism had crept in. Prisoners, irrespective of income and social background, were put in the same cells and had access to the same privileges—or at least, lack of them. In addition, Mohammad Reza Shah—unlike his father—rarely placed disgraced members of the elite in prison. He preferred to banish them either to embassies abroad or to the private business sector. Prisons, thus, ceased to contain "aristocratic wards."

The prisoners, however, continued to organize themselves into komuns. During the early 1970s, each major block had one large komun and many small and flexible eating *sofrehs* (literally, "tablecloths")—for Fedayis, Mojaheds, older advocates of the "political struggle," prisoners with long sentences, and those from particular regions such as Kurdestan, Lurestan, Azerbaijan, Khorasan, and the Caspian. The number of religious sofrehs increased in 1974 when groups of ayatollahs, including Khomeini, issued fatwas against the formation of the Resurgence party, arguing that the Shah was trying to turn Iran into a one-party totalitarian state. For the first time, Evin and Qasr contained numerous clerics and their followers.

Komuns elected their leader (*shahrdar;* literally, "mayor") and administrators (*masoul-ha*), who, in turn, rotated daily chores among the members. Komuns also had a communal bank that collected money from relatives outside, purchased goods, especially fruits and vegetables from the prison store, and then shared them equally between its members. Gifts sent from outside were also shared equally. The main ethos of the komuns was equality—in terms of both participation and distribution. The komuns used Morse code to communicate with other komuns in the same prison. In fact, most solitary cells had the code inscribed on their walls for the benefit of newcomers. Living in close-knit komuns, the prisoners developed their own jargon. In addition to *mellikesh*, they coined such terms as *boycot* (boycott), placing someone in silence; *borideh* (broken), meaning one who had given up the struggle; *mozugar*, someone "taking issue" with the authorities; and *falange*, a fanatical Muslim. Ironically, the last term came from the Phalange, the Christian Maronites in Lebanon.

Communal solidarity was shattered in 1975 when the falange raised for the very first time the archaic issue of *najes* (religious impurity). According to the strict interpretation of Shi'ism, holy prayer is invalidated if the one who is praying touches such impurities as blood, urine, semen, feces, pigs, dogs, and *kafer*s (infidels). Convention had defined infidels as Christians, Jews, Hindus, and, in some circumstances, Sunnis. But in the midst of the Marxist-Muslim split within the Mojahedin, an ultra-conservative cleric circulated an unpublished fatwa extending the definition to Muslims who espoused Marxism—especially atheism and historical materialism. Leftists were deemed to be infidels. Infidels were deemed to be unclean. And the unclean, by definition, were deemed to be pollutants, invalidating prayers. For the sake of God, the religious prisoners demanded separate living quarters, separate clothes lines, separate showers, and separate eating utensils. Hygiene specialists were brought in to advise on how to go to the toilet without inadvertently touching facilities used by unbelievers. One important religious prisoner admits that the najes issue had not bothered his predecessors and that the founder of the Fedayan-e Islam had willingly shared food and a cell with the Tudeh.[77]

This najes issue drew a sharp line between leftists and Muslims—as it was intended to do. The Mojahedin, led by Masoud Rajavi, rejected the fatwa on the grounds that it would widen the differences between the opposition while narrowing the gap between religious prisoners and guards who happened to be practicing Muslims. This position received some sympathy from Ayatollah Mahmud Taleqani, the well-known liberal cleric who was in and out of prison. But others, including

Ayatollah Montazeri and Bazargan, went along with the fatwa. One leftist remembers Bazargan quietly passing him fruit sent to him from outside but swearing him to secrecy so he would not get into trouble with his fellow believers.[78] Another remembers Montazeri refusing to shake hands with leftist inmates so as to safeguard his religious purity.

While rejecting the fatwa, the Mojahedin insisted that leftists should categorically denounce the Marxists who had recently taken over their organization as "pseudoleftists," "ultra-left opportunists," and "coup d'étatists." When, after much discussion, the majority of leftists rejected this ultimatum, the Mojahedin withdrew and formed their own separate komun. Thus after 1975 there were three separate komuns in Evin and Qasr—Chapi (Leftist), Mojahedin, and Mazhabi (Religious). The third differed from the others in two significant respects: its hierarchy was based not on elections but on religious rank; and its menial chores were not rotated but given to low-ranking members—often shop assistants from the bazaar. The Mazhabi deemed the Mojahedin touchable despite being *elteqati* (eclectic) and *enherafi* (deviant). But they deemed the Marxists untouchable, unclean, and, thereby, beyond social contact.

This najes fatwa did more than divide the komuns. It revealed the dark and often hidden side of the religious mentality. It also contained the seeds of dangers to come—namely, the bloody clashes between, on the one hand, the clergy and the Mojadedin, and, on the other, the clergy and the secular leftists. Just as people who burn books are likely to burn their authors, so people who consider others "filthy pollutants" are likely to take drastic measures to eradicate them—all for the sake of social and spiritual hygiene. Social cleansing can originate in religious as well as ethnic prejudices.

Beginnings of Public Recantations (1971–75)

The guerrilla movement posed a serious challenge to the regime precisely because it came at a time when the young intelligentsia was growing by leaps and bounds. Between 1963 and 1979, enrollment in colleges increased from 24,885 to

154,215; in foreign universities, from 18,000 to more than 80,000; and in technical, vocational, and teachers' training colleges, from 14,240 to 227,497. The number of universities grew from 4 to 16; technical schools, from 36 to more than 800; and secondary schools, from 527 to 1,714. Their graduates—like graduates the world over—wanted greater participation in politics and a larger share of the national income, especially that derived from the rising oil revenues. Moreover, the entry of working-class children into higher education radicalized the whole intelligentsia. Further, all this took place in the context of an attentive public rapidly expanding throughout the country. Literacy was growing, newspapers were increasing their circulation, transistor radios were reaching the countryside, and television was making its debut.

The challenge was compounded by the harsh reality that the Shah lacked solid legitimacy. Some felt he had forfeited it in the 1940s by violating the constitutional laws and preferring to reign rather than rule. Some felt he had forfeited it in 1953 by overthrowing Mossadeq. Some felt he had forfeited it in the 1950s and 1960s by distancing Iran from the rest of the Third World—especially over the sensitive issues of Palestine and Vietnam. Some felt he had forfeited it with his so-called White Revolution designed to glorify the pre-Islamic monarchy and thereby demean Islam. Others felt he had forfeited it in 1963 by ordering his troops to kill hundreds—if not thousands—of unarmed demonstrators. In short, the regime faced a double crisis—that of legitimacy as well as participation.

The regime tried to overcome these challenges by winning over the new intelligentsia. It created more white-collar jobs; raised salaries; awarded an increasing number of scholarships for study abroad; publicized the rising oil revenues; launched ambitious plans for industrialization, land reform, and eradication of illiteracy; created the Resurgence party with a blatantly populist program; promised to make Iran a modern Japan within a generation; and, with much fanfare, declared the Shah to be leading Iran into a New Great Civilization.

It was as part of this attempt to influence the intelligentsia and drum up support for the White Revolution that the regime hit on the strategy of televised public recantations. It seems to have hit on this strategy inadvertently. In 1971, a well-known physicist named Parviz Nikkhah serving a ten-year prison sentence for communist subversion experienced a genuine change of heart. In 1965, he, together with some recent graduates from England, had been charged with plotting to assassinate the Shah. In England, they had been active in the Confederation of Iranian Students and in the Maoist Revolutionary Organization of the Tudeh party. One of those arrested was a childhood friend of a palace guard who had tried to machine-gun the Shah. Although the assassination charges were dropped, Nikkhah and his colleagues had been given long sentences for advocating guerrilla warfare and having contacts with China. The trial had become a cause célèbre with foreign journalists' gaining access to the proceedings. Nikkhah took the opportunity to accuse SAVAK of using torture to obtain false confessions.

Six years later, Nikkhah astounded the public by coming out in full support of the regime. He argued that "true patriots" should rally behind the Shah because he was distributing land to the peasants, providing them with medical and educational facilities, developing the economy, extracting more from the exploitative oil companies, building viable state institutions, and protecting the nation from cultural imperialism. "These reforms," he argued, "have made Mao's theory of peasant war redundant and have ended Iran's era as a semi-feudal semi-colonial society."[79] The regime made sure Nikkhah's statements were circulated widely both inside and outside the country. In one of Nikkhah's many press conferences, the interviewer introduced him as "a revolutionary of yesterday and a revolutionary of today" who supports the Shah for all the "right revolutionary reasons." After his conversion, Nikkhah worked for the Radio-Television Network; some believe he also worked as a consultant for SAVAK.

Once the regime savored the Nikkhah success, it did not take it long to go one step further and "induce" other "conversions." In other words, SAVAK began to torture to get recantations as well as information. This made the nature of torture infinitely worse. With torture for information, the victims could expect eventual relief since the information was usually obsolete after the passage of time—often after twenty-four hours. But with torture for recantation, the victims could be tormented indefinitely. Their only hope was to compromise with their tormentors and produce watered-down recantations—or else convince them they preferred death to total submission. Few have appreciated the qualitative difference between these two forms of torture.

Soon after Nikkhah, eight other Confederation leaders gave similar public recantations—all in the form of radio, television, and press *mosahebeh*s (interviews).[80] They declared that they wanted to "share" their experiences so that the country would understand why they had so completely changed their views. When they had first left Iran to study abroad, the country had been backward and abysmally poor. But on their return, they had found that the White Revolution—which they had dismissed as "phony"—had successfully transformed the whole country. It had implemented land reform, eliminated feudalism, built roads, bridges, and dams, set up medical clinics and rural cooperatives, electrified the countryside, industrialized the economy, and made Iran fully independent of the imperial powers. In short, the White Revolution had accomplished everything they hoped for.

They advised students abroad not to be misled by the subversive National Front, the Tudeh, the Revolutionary Organization, or the Confederation. These groups retained an outdated view of Iran and kept their members ignorant of the true situation back home. What is more, their leaders were "selfish," "bureaucratic," "opportunistic," and "beholden to foreign powers." One claimed that the FBI and the CIA had thoroughly infiltrated the National Front. Why else would the Americans permit the Confederation to demonstrate against the Shah in the streets of the United States? They confessed they had returned to Iran with the full intention of launching a guerrilla war. But now that they had seen the reality with their own eyes, they wanted to partake in the Great Shah-People's Revolution. One stressed that he retained his former *din* (religion) of serving the masses. Another argued that he wanted to overcome his "intellectual" snobbery and study the masses firsthand. "Iran," he declared, "was neither China nor Cuba. It is endowed with its own customs, traditions, religion, history, and popular culture." One government functionary later stressed how "such statements from the highly educated profoundly affected the likes of himself who had no more than a high school diploma." To the present day, these recanters remain reticent about their experiences.

The most sensational "interviews" were given by three well-known national personalities: Parviz Qalech-Khani, a star athlete and football player; Ghulam-Hossein Sa'edi, a doctor-psychologist turned playwright; and Reza Barahani, a prominent poet, essayist, and translator. All three were highly regarded by the university educated. Their "interviews" were first aired on radio and then printed in the mass circulation newspapers.

Qalech-Khani appeared in March 1972 to explain why he had been released after being detained fourteen days for "communistic activities" (he had been caught bringing banned books into the country).[81] He explained that because he knew little about sociology he had been easily deceived by subversive propaganda: "I always searched to find fault and blamed all shortcomings on the regime." But he now knew better and appreciated the achievements of the White Revolution—especially the fivefold expansion of education: "Our pampered youth does not appreciate this major achievement." He hoped that the Shah would forgive him for not having given him due credit for all his great accomplishments.

Barahani was arrested in September 1973; his interview appeared one hundred days later. In it, he denounced terrorism, enumerated the failings of Marxism, criticized cultural imperialism, distanced himself from all oppositional groups, and stressed that Islam was incompatible with Marxism—this echoed the official line against the Mojahedin.[82] He also criticized

those who mimicked Europe, arguing that mindless Western-
ization inevitably produces social alienation—in Iran as well
as in the rest of the Third World. Although the interview was
sprinkled with Franz Fanon quotations, its whole tenor was to
reinforce the official view of the opposition.

Sa'edi's appearance in 1975 was billed as a "chitchat" (*gofteh-
gu*).[83] He took the political opposition to task for "exploiting"
his works, serving as "tools of foreign powers," misunderstand-
ing the country's culture, and refusing to credit the glorious
achievements of the Shah-People's Revolution. He denounced
the Soviets for persecuting writers and creating a "totalitarian
culture." He conceded that his own works had been depressing
but explained that they had been conceived in the bad old days
of feudalism before the Shah had implemented his Great Revolution. He ended the interview by promising to make his future works more positive and respectful of the country's
achievements, especially the nationalization of the country's
forests. He added that "Marxism has absolutely no relevance to
Iran because Islam, the White Revolution, and the monarchy
had given the country special characteristics."

None of these three ever linked their "interviews" to torture—
at least, not in public. To do so meant admitting submission,
which, in turn, meant losing self-respect and public aberu, or
reputation. In this age of revolutionary martyrdom, true heroes
were supposed to die rather than submit and compromise their
beliefs. Soon after his interview, Barahani was permitted to
travel to the United States and was vehemently denounced by
the Confederation for "collaborating" with the regime. He
wrote his prison memoirs, lectured extensively on torture, and
tried to inform the Western public about the Shah's unpopu-
larity in Iran.[84] But these prolific writings avoided the unsavory
subject of his forced interviews and the link between torture
and his unmentionable interview. On the contrary, he argued
that he had been released merely because of international pressure.[85] Thus his prison memoir reads like an incomprehensible
theater of the absurd—as if the concept of being tortured for
an "interview" is not absurd enough. In one place he touches

briefly on the issue of forced recantations—but only in the most abstract terms: "The intellectual is taken to prison, tortured and forced to recant; as a consequence of recantation he is isolated from the mainstream of the opposition and considered a traitor."[86]

For his part, Saʿedi wrote a play entitled *Honeymoon* in which an uninvited guest together with a television set, a cameraman, and thugs take over the home of a newlywed couple and proceed to play havoc with their lives. The husband is driven to drink; the wife, to spouting gibberish about nationalized forests and bejeweled marshes.[87] The uninvited guest concludes by declaring that "the best hosts are those who are happy and have nothing on their minds." A fellow writer later noted that Saʿedi had been shattered by his prison experience.[88] *Honeymoon* is the first work in Persian literature to deal exclusively with the intrusion of the state into the inner sanctuary of the home as well as of the mind. Needless to say, the work was not published until after the revolution.

In private Barahani and Saʿedi were more forthright. An American writer reported confidentially that SAVAK was using "techniques perfected in Ancient Rome and Medieval Spain as well as Auschwitz and Saigon" to produce television shows "reminiscent of the Stalinist era."[89] He also claimed that Barahani had been offered a compromise—"a statement on national television, denouncing Marxism and terrorism, in return for which his own life and those of his wife and daughter would be spared." This statement was prepared initially by Barahani himself and then revised by SAVAK before being deemed "suitable for public consumption." The report mentioned that during the broadcast a SAVAK official had been present "with a gun to attain a good performance." In his prison memoirs, Barahani mentions in passing that a genuine writer cannot possibly recant, for such an act is tantamount to the "end of his political, literary, academic, and public life, not to mention life as a human being."[90]

Saʿedi did not speak of his own prison experiences until 1984—when in Paris dying from cirrhosis of the liver. There he revealed for the first time how he had been kidnapped, taken to Evin, and subjected to days of "nightmarish tortures"—all for the purpose of extracting an "interview." He reported, "I kept pleading that if they had any charges against me they should try me in court. They kept retorting that they were interested not in a trial but in a television interview." The interrogator admitted that he wanted Sa'edi to be publicly humiliated because mere imprisonment would make him into a public hero—a mistake made with previous writers. Sa'edi mentions in passing that his body still bore the marks of these tortures. He also mentions that Nikkhah had been present as a "consultant" at the eventual filming.[91] After his release, Sa'edi had been permitted to travel to America, where he wrote a *New York Times* op-ed piece describing how one of his "patients" hated to be questioned about his prison experiences: "The psychological traumas of a person incarcerated, brutally tortured, then released, hardly heal. I knew a bookseller who had been frequently arrested. He was a man stricken by fear. He spoke with the minimum amount of words."[92]

Sa'edi was the last intellectual to be tortured into recanting. By 1975–76, the regime's human rights record was being scrutinized by numerous international organizations and foreign newspapers—Amnesty International, Sartre's Committee on Iran, the Red Cross, PEN, the International Commission of Jurists, the UN-affiliated International League for Human Rights, the *New York Times*, the *Washington Post*, the London *Times*, the *Observer*, and the *Sunday Times*. The weight of Washington was added when Jimmy Carter, running for the presidency, raised the issue of human rights in Iran as well as in the Soviet Union. The Shah tried to forestall further scrutiny by forbidding SAVAK to use physical torture—even on suspected guerrillas. Overnight prison conditions changed. Inmates dubbed this the dawn of *jimmykrasy*. Without these changes, public recantations may well have blossomed into a full industry in the 1970s under the Shah—long before they did so in the 1980s under the Islamic Republic.

Prison Politics (1976–79)

The regime did more than ban torture. It allowed the International Red Cross to make two separate visits to the main prisons. It agreed to try future political cases in civilian rather than in military courts—which broke the precedent set in 1953 and gave defendants access both to the media and to proper defense lawyers. Amnesty International was allowed to observe one such trial in 1977. The regime also began to release political prisoners—first in dribbles, later in small batches, and eventually in large groups. One batch received amnesty in 1976 with much fanfare. Some had completed their sentences. Others—mostly from the clerical opposition—had signed "letters of regret" known now as *goh-khordan nameh* (shit-eating letters). Yet others—including guerrilla sympathizers—were granted amnesty in August 1977 to commemorate the anniversary of the 1953 "glorious salvation." By April 1977, when the Red Cross made its first visit, the total number of political prisoners had been cut to three thousand. By the time the Shah left the country in January 1979, it had been further reduced to three hundred.

Prison conditions also improved. Cells got new coats of paint—some walls had graffiti from the early 1950s. Windows were washed—some for the first time since the 1960s. Rugs appeared on the floors. Food improved. Visiting hours were extended. More books and newspapers were allowed. Communal activities were more frequently granted, and Evin prisoners were allowed to visit neighboring wards. When the Red Cross came, prisoners were allowed to talk to the visitors but were warned that such foreign organizations were part of the "international conspiracy to destroy Iran's independence." SAVAK argued that true patriots would never talk to such imperialist meddlers. Few bought this argument. Meanwhile, families and friends formed the Committee for the Defense of the Rights of Political Prisoners. This committee published a bulletin and held demonstrations at Tehran University as well as outside the gates of Evin and Qasr. It also organized a large social gathering for all former political prisoners.

Conditions further improved in March 1978 when the remaining political prisoners organized a hunger strike. They demanded visiting rights for friends, removal of wire mesh in the visiting rooms, uncensored newspapers, radios, books, and improved medical facilities. The strike was initiated by fifty-three members of the seventy remaining in the leftist komun in Qasr. It soon spread to the Mojahedin komun in Qasr. By the time it ended, it brought in all the main komuns in Qasr, Evin, and Qezel Hesar. The wardens eventually conceded to all the demands—after much hesitation over the issue of radios.[93]

This relaxation brought forth the blossoming of many groups. In fact, prisons became a microcosm of future national politics: they contained the diverse groups that were to emerge in the coming years. In some ways, the future of Iran was played out in these ward komuns—especially in the lively ideological discussions around the eating mats. The heated debates included the older organizations such as the Tudeh, the Kurdish Democratic party, the National Front, the Liberation Movement, and the Maoist offshoots from the Tudeh—the Revolutionary Organization of the Tudeh, which renamed itself the Hezb-e Ranjbaran (Toilers party) in 1980, and the Marxist-Leninist Organization of Tofan, which became known simply as Tofan. (See fig.1.)

The heated debates also included the main guerrilla groups: the mainstream Mojahedin led by Rajavi; the Marxist Mojahedin, which in 1979 took the name Sazeman-e Peykar dar Rah-e Azadi-ye Tabaqeh-e Kargar (Combat Organization on the Road to the Emancipation of the Working Class), known simply as Peykar; and, of course, the Fedayi, some of whom saw Khomeini as the champion of anti-imperialism and others of whom saw him as a reactionary cleric. Soon after the revolution, the Fedayis split into two rival factions: the Fedayi Aqaliyat (Minority Fedayi), which opposed the Islamic Republic; and the Fedayi Aksariyat (Majority Fedayi), which—like the Tudeh—initially supported the new regime. Almost all the lead-

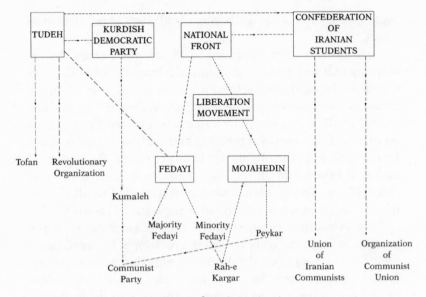

Figure 1.   Leftist Organizations

ers of these groups were fellow inmates in Evin and Qasr until the very eve of the Islamic Revolution.

The prisons also contained the seeds of other organizations that developed immediately after the revolution: the Sazeman-e Kargaran-e Enqelabi (Organization of Revolutionary Workers), composed of former Fedayis and Marxist Mojaheds who had second thoughts about the whole strategy of armed struggle (this group became known for its newspaper, *Rah-e Kargar*); Kumaleh, launched by former Fedayis and Kurdish Democrats (in 1984 Kumaleh renamed itself the Communist Party of Iran); the Ettehadieh-e Komunist-ha-ye Iran (Union of Iranian Communists), created by activists from the Confederation and the National Front; and the Sazeman-e Vahadat-e Komunisti (Organization of Communist Union), founded by Trotskyists critical of both Stalinism in the Soviet Union and Maoism in China (this group became known for its newspaper, *Rahayi* (Freedom). These small groups were to bear the brunt of the early terror unleashed by the Islamic Republic. As one prominent cleric openly admitted to a leftist prisoner as he was leaving Evin: "If we come to power we will have no choice but to eliminate all you leftists."[94]

3

The Islamic Republic

What better proof of guilt than a
confession straight from the
mouth of the guilty.
          Ettela'at, *4 May 1982*

Summary Justice (February 1979–June 1981)

In the very first days of the new regime, Khomeini set up Revolutionary Tribunals to punish prominent members of the old
regime, restore the sharia, and preserve some semblance of law
and order since the whole judiciary, including the law enforce-
ment system, was in complete disarray. In the next twenty-eight
months, the Revolutionary Tribunals executed 757 for "sowing
corruption on earth"—a term not heard in Iranian courts since
1909.[1] When one defendant had the impertinence to inquire
about its meaning, the judge retorted: "It means spreading
wretchedness; depriving people of their rights and freedoms;
and undermining the independence, security, and well-being
of the country."[2]

The tribunals also reintroduced corporal punishment, especially public flogging. The avowed aim was to "cleanse society of the putrefied vestiges of the tyrannical regime [*rezhim-e
taghuti*]." These punishments, as well as the executions, were
carried out by local komitehs and their militias, known as *pas-
dar*s (guards). The komitehs resembled the soviets and the Red
Guards of the Bolshevik Revolution—with the significant dif-

ference that the soviets had been elected from below whereas the komitehs were appointed from above by the clergy, especially Khomeini.

Those executed can be divided into political and nonpolitical victims. The latter, totaling 260, included 138 drug dealers, 47 pimps and fornicators, 20 homosexuals, 16 prostitutes, 15 rapists, 12 murderers, 7 gamblers, and 3 highway robbers. The former, totaling 497, were prominent royalists, SAVAK officials, military personnel implicated in the recent street shootings, and 125 noncommissioned officers accused of plotting a royalist coup. Among the victims were the prime minister, Hoveida; 6 cabinet ministers, including the minister of education, the only woman to have held a cabinet post, who was charged with "corrupting youth" and "favoring cultural imperialism"; the 3 surviving directors of SAVAK; 3 elderly statesmen from the secretive Freemasons; 35 generals; 25 colonels; 20 majors; the mayor of Tehran; some 90 SAVAK officials; Nikkhah, the Maoist who had become an outspoken supporter of the regime; a leading Jewish businessman; and 35 Bahais—they, as well as the Jewish businessman and the Freemasons, were accused of "spying" for Zionism and Western imperialism.

Revolutionary Tribunals were set up in the major towns with two in the capital—in Qasr and in Evin. Their presiding judges were clerics appointed by Khomeini himself. They gave final pronouncements bypassing what remained of the Justice Ministry and its appeal system. Khomeini also created a traveling tribunal for Hojjat al-Islam Khalkhali, who was known as the "Hanging Ayatollah." These judges limited trials to brief hours, sometimes minutes; found defendants guilty on the basis of "popular repute"; and dismissed the concept of defense attorney as a "Western absurdity." They also explained that the term "sowing corruption on earth" covered a host of sins—"insulting Islam and the clergy," "opposing the Islamic Revolution," "supporting the Pahlavis," and "undermining Iran's independence" by helping the 1953 coup and giving capitulatory privileges to the imperial powers.[3] With the outbreak of unrest among Kurds, Baluchis, and Turkmans, the tribunals created a new category—that of "counterrevolutionary." More than fifty prisoners were executed in 1980 under this category. Some were Marxist radicals supporting the ethnic minorities.

No time was wasted between trial and execution. Most executions were by firing squad. The first took place on the roof of a girls' school where Khomeini had taken up residence on his arrival in Tehran. Later ones took place inside Qasr and Evin. Some nonpolitical executions were done by public hanging. Khalkhali liked to hang drug dealers in soccer stadiums and public squares to give the population "a clear example ['*ebrat*]."[4] The newspapers printed photos of officials killed by firing squad to strike terror and to cater to the widespread call for revenge. In some provincial towns, traditional forms of executions were revived for moral offenses. Khalkhali declared, "Stoning provides the public with a clear example."[5]

The newspapers summarized the political trials, displaying front-page pictures of the defendants with forlorn looks— sometimes with neck placards specifying their presumed crimes. They gave prominence to the trials of two notorious SAVAK interrogators; a military judge who in the 1950s had sentenced to death the Tudeh officers and the Fedayan-e Islam leaders; the chief of staff who had helped to organize the 1953 coup; and the generals responsible for the 1963 bloodshed and the subsequent deportation of Khomeini—one was targeted for having slandered him as a "British agent." The last royal air force commander was quoted as declaring in his final testimony that he had lost all respect for the Shah when he had witnessed a visiting American general "pick him up by the nose and throw him out of Iran (like a dead mouse)."[6]

Hoveida's trial received the most coverage. The judge—unnamed and unseen by the cameras—began by declaring that the defendant epitomized the satanic regime whereas the prosecution represented the valiant Iranian people.[7] The charges included conspiring with imperialism, capitulating to foreign powers, spying for Zionism, auctioning off national resources, rigging elections, censoring newspapers, joining the Freemasons, selling drugs, converting the country into a market for

American agribusinesses, and siding with the West against Vietnam and Palestine.

Khalkhali later revealed that he had presided over Hoveida's trial. He also revealed that he had dispatched Hoveida to his execution after severing communication links between Evin and the outside world to prevent any last-minute intercession on his behalf by Mehdi Bazargan, the provisional prime minister. Hoveida had sought the opportunity to write his memoirs for posterity. In summarizing the trial, the papers described Hoveida as a notorious *kha'in* (traitor) eager to distance himself from SAVAK and the Shah. Although these trials were clearly designed to discredit the old order, the newborn regime lacked the means and the patience, and perhaps the desire, to extract recantations and public confessions. Khalkhali acknowledged that "only one prominent royalist expressed any form of remorse for his crimes."[8]

An Evin inmate writes that during the revolutionary upheavals angry crowds had dismantled the interrogation chambers. He adds that in this early period "few were tortured—unless by torture we mean detention without formal charges, trials without defence lawyers, the constant presence of death, and hasty executions after three-minute hearings."[9] Another inmate writes that immediately after the revolution, Hajj Aga Mohammad Kachouyi, the new Evin warden and himself a former political prisoner, had improved living conditions by permitting radios, newspapers, and books—even Marxist ones; upgrading the quality of food; and relying less on blindfolds and the whip. "He resorted occasionally to the fist but not to systematic torture—neither physical nor psychological."[10] The same inmate adds that in this period he never once heard the sinister terms *tavvab* (to repent), *towab* (repenter), or *tavvabin* (repenters). Some dub this the "Spring of the Islamic Revolution." Royalists—who made up the bulk of the inmates in this early period—have generalized from their limited experiences to draw misleading conclusions.[11] Consequently, Western readers of these royalist memoirs often come away with a fairly benign picture of prison life in the Islamic Republic.

The prison diary of a Peykar leader illustrates the interrogation techniques used in this early period.[12] The leader, Mohsen Fazel, was a graduate of an American university and a veteran of the guerrilla movement against the Shah. He was arrested in January 1981 on his way to Syria to reestablish contact with the Palestine resistance movement. He was placed in solitary in Evin for 139 days—most of the time in complete silence without reading materials. He preserved his sanity by exercising, tapping Morse code messages to the neighboring cells, composing poetry in his mind, and keeping a diary on orange peels and smuggled-in papers. In his diary, he often mentions he had not been "physically tortured" but had been constantly threatened with execution unless he denounced his organization in a public "interview" (mosahebeh). His ordeal did not end until June 1981, when, in the midst of the new reign of terror, he—along with many others—was dispatched to the firing squads.

The absence of physical torture and forced confessions was obvious in three highly publicized political trials—those of Taqi Shahram, Mohammad-Reza Sa'adati, and Amir-Abbas Entezam. Shahram, a prominent Maoist, was tried in 1980 for the 1974 killing of a rival guerrilla leader. Sa'adati, a Mojahed in charge of his organization's foreign contacts, was picked up outside the Soviet Embassy and accused of being a Russian spy. Entezam, Bazargan's deputy premier, was arraigned as a CIA spy after the famous student hostage-takers found documents in the U.S. Embassy describing Entezam's meetings with American diplomats and his misgivings about the course taken by the revolution. Bazargan pleaded in vain that he had assigned Entezam the task of meeting American officials and that most of his cabinet ministers had similar misgivings about the course taken by the revolution.[13]

The three were held in solitary confinement for months on end and then offered plea bargains. They would receive light sentences if they gave public interviews denouncing their organizations and political views. All three refused. The judge evicted Shahram from his own trial when the latter questioned the legitimacy of the tribunal and declared that only his peers from the guerrilla movement had the moral standing to pass judgment. Saʿadati accused the regime of trying to link the Mojahedin to the Soviet Union and argued that he, as the Mojahedin leader responsible for foreign relations, had been assigned the task of exchanging views with Soviet correspondents. The judge retorted that he had no business exchanging views with a "non-Muslim," especially one representing an "imperial power." Similarly, Entezam dismissed the charges against him as blatantly absurd and accused the regime of trying to link him to the United States.

Shahram was executed without the opportunity to speak to his family—not to mention the press. He became the first prominent leftist to be executed by the new regime. Entezam was sentenced to life; he remained in prison for more than sixteen years. Saʿadati was sentenced to ten years but served less than ten months. He was to be one of the first to be shot in the reign of terror unleashed in June 1981.

Reign of Terror (June 1981–July 1988)

The Mojahedin attempt to overthrow the regime in June 1981 set off waves of repression unprecedented in Iranian history. Between June and November 1981, the Revolutionary Tribunals executed 2,665 political prisoners—seven times the number of royalists killed in the previous sixteen months. The slain included 2,200 Mojaheds and 400 leftists—mostly from Marxist groups that had opposed the Mojahedin uprising. The government boasted it had arrested 90 percent of the Mojahedin and utterly uprooted two important Marxist groups—Peykar and the Minority Fedayi.[14]

The death toll continued to climb, reaching 5,000 by August 1983 and 12,500 by June 1985. According to a martyrs' list compiled by the Mojahedin, between June 1981 and June 1985, 12,028 lost their lives—74 percent through executions, 22 percent in armed confrontations, and 4 percent under torture.[15] The executions—with the exception of 250 hangings—were by firing squad. Only a handful were carried out in public—and these were done mostly in provincial towns. The regime found it expedient to carry out political executions out of public sight.

Of the total of 7,943 executed, 6,472 belonged to the Mojahedin; 350, to the Fedayi; 255, to Peykar; 101, to the Kurdish Democratic party; 70, to the Kurdish Kumaleh; 66, to the Union of Communists; 60, to Rah-e Kargar; 33, to the Ranjbaran party; 21, to Tofan; and 76, to smaller Marxist organizations (Red Star, Poyan Group, Union of Communist Militants, Nabard Group, Razmandegan party, Arman-e Mostazafin, and the Union for the Liberation of Labor). Another 18 belonged to Forqan, a religious but highly anticlerical group. Thus the toll taken from the left was far greater than that from the royalists. This revolution—like many others—had devoured its own children.

Those who were executed were almost all youngsters. But there were some subtle social differences between the Mojahedin and the Marxist dead. The former were mostly high school pupils, recent high school graduates, and college students. The latter were mostly college students and university graduates. Of the 4,995 Mojahedin executed whose educations are known, 1,362 (27%) were high school pupils; 1,809 (36%) were high school graduates, mostly recent graduates; and 1,290 (26%) were college students. Only 359 (7%) were college graduates. Of the Marxists whose educations are known, 132 (24%) were college graduates; 158 (29%) were college students; and 144 (28%) were high school graduates. Only 84 (15%) were high school pupils. Of the Mojahedin dead whose age is known, more than 76 percent were under twenty-six years old, and 20 percent of them were under twenty. Women constituted more than 14 percent of the Mojahedin but less than 8 percent of the Marxist victims. (See table 6.)

Shahrnush Parsipour—a prominent writer picked up for having subversive literature in her car trunk and incarcerated for four and a half years—estimates that in late 1981 the average age of her ward mates was nineteen and a half.[16] She also estimates that 80 percent were high school pupils, 15 percent

Table 6

Occupations of the Executed, 1981–85*

	Mojahedin	Marxists**
College Graduates***	359	132
Secondary school teachers	117	22
Engineers	66	41
Doctors	30	6
Civil servants	20	10
Professors	10	5
College Students	1,290	158
High School Graduates	1,809	154
Primary school teachers	279	24
Civil servants	87	6
Technicians	27	2
Seminary students	12	
Armed forces	105	5
Workers	207	30
Tradesmen	42	6
Farmers	33	3
High School Students	1,362	84
Without High School Diplomas		
Workers	81	16
Tradesmen	10	
Farmers	6	1
Armed forces	51	1
Housewives	27	1
Total	4,995	547
(Women	716	42)

* Includes those executed by firing squad and hanging, but excludes those killed in armed confrontations and under torture.
** Excludes the Tudeh and the Kurdish Kumaleh.
*** Not all occupations of college and high school graduates are known.

were university students, and the rest were young professionals—teachers, nurses, and civil servants. Those over thirty, like herself, were deemed old. She says, "June 1981 had truly been a revolt of high school kids." She adds that whereas the leftists came from urban families, the Mojahedin were the children of recent arrivals from the countryside.

The list compiled by the Mojahedin, however, is not complete. It implicitly excludes some repenters, who, despite collaborating with the regime, were nevertheless executed. It also explicitly excludes 128 Bahais, 9 Jews, and 32 Tudeh and Majority Fedayis on the grounds that they had "not actively struggled against the Islamic Republic and therefore could not be seen as true martyrs of the New Iranian Revolution." These organizations have published their own book of martyrs. Of course, none list the unknown but substantial number executed for such nonpolitical offenses as smuggling and drug trafficking.

By the time the Islamic Republic unleashed this reign of terror, it had put in place a new judiciary and an extensive prison network with an interrogation system. The judiciary was thoroughly Islamicized, undoing the work of three generations. While Revolutionary Tribunals continued to handle political and drug cases, the Justice Ministry completely revamped the criminal, civil, and family courts. Seminary training was required of all magistrates—from the Supreme Court down to the lowest local and family courts. Reza Shah had purged the clerics from the judiciary; the Islamic Republic now purged the modern-trained lawyers. The sharia was declared the law of the land, and regulations in conflict with it were to be scrapped. What is more, the new constitution set up a Guardian Council packed with clerics to ensure that all bills passed by the Majles conformed to the sharia.

The First Islamic Majles and the Guardian Council promptly codified important features of the sharia by passing two landmark bills: the Qanon-e Ta'zir (Discretionary Punishment Law) and the Qanon-e Qesas (Retribution Law). The Ta'zir Law gives judges the authority to execute and imprison those found guilty

of "declaring war on God" and "plotting with foreign powers."
It also gives them the power to mete out as many as seventy-
four lashes to those who "insult government officials," "convene
unlawful meetings," sell alcoholic beverages, fix prices, hoard
goods, kiss illicitly, fail to wear the proper *hejab* (headgear),
and, last but not least, "lie to the authorities."

The last is especially pertinent for the interrogation process.
Clerical interrogators can give indefinite series of seventy-four
lashings until they obtain "honest answers." In fact, the interrogation chambers—including the notorious block 209 of
Evin—have been renamed Otaqha-ye Ta'zir (Discretionary
Punishment Rooms). The prisoners are asked questions. If
their answers are not satisfactory, they can be lawfully whipped
for "lying." In theory, this punishment should come after a
proper law court has found them guilty of perjury. But the line
between interrogation and trial is hazy as the same clerics wear
three different turbans—prosecutor, judge, and interrogator.
According to the new law, interrogators with proper theological
credentials are entitled to lash until the guilty "confess the
truth." Playing on the multiple meanings of *hadd* (limit, extent,
and divine punishment), the prisoners dub the process "whipping until the *hadd* confession is obtained."

Meanwhile, the Qesas Law codifies other aspects of the
sharia. It subdivides crimes into hadd—those against God—
and those against fellow beings, especially other families. Some
punishments are mandatory; others, discretionary. Based on
the notion of talion, the Qesas Law calls for "an eye for an eye,
a tooth for a tooth, a life for a life"—but with the understanding
that a Muslim is more valuable than a non-Muslim, and a Muslim man more valuable than a Muslim woman.[17] Serious offenses against God—apostasy, fornication, homosexuality, and
habitual drinking—mandate death by hanging, stoning, or de-
capitation. Lesser offenses—such as theft—call for flogging,
finger amputation, and, as a concession to modernity, imprisonment. In cases of homicide, relatives can participate in the
actual execution or, if they so choose, accept monetary compensation in lieu of life.

For some capital crimes, judges need "two honest and righteous male witnesses," one such male plus two such females, or one such male and a sworn oath—which presumably could mean a "voluntary confession" from the defendant or, even more novel and ominous, a confession plus the judge's own *ʿelm* (knowledge or reasoning). Judges can reduce the sentences if they feel the criminal has "sincerely confessed" and "genuinely repented." As one secular critic has observed, the Qesas Law discriminates against women, against non-Muslims, and against the poor. It revives horrific corporal punishments. It assumes parts of the human body can be converted into money. It threatens to create an army of handicapped victims. And it "paves the way for judicial torture" by permitting the use of confessions.[18]

The new laws modify the sharia in three significant ways. First, the state retains ultimate power over life and death. Whereas the sharia—in its pure form—had given local judges final say, a new High Court reviews death sentences passed by lower magistrates. The appeals system—anathema to many traditionalists—has been accepted. The regime justifies this innovation by claiming provincial judges need yet more time to obtain proper legal training. Second, the concept of circumstantial evidence has been recognized, albeit under the rubric of "the judge's reasoning." Third, long-term imprisonment—an alien concept in traditional law—has been introduced as a legitimate form of "discretionary punishment." Diehard traditionalists, however, continue to prefer corporal punishments. As one Imam Jomʿeh argued, Islam prefers the "whip to prison" because the former deters crime whereas the latter invariably transforms petty wrongdoers into hardened criminals.[19] The same cleric continued with the ominous qualifier that "whereas female apostates should be imprisoned until they returned to Islam, males apostates should be executed without hesitation."[20] This was a portent of things to come.

While the judiciary was being Islamicized, the prison system was centralized and drastically expanded. Prisons—previously administered separately by SAVAK, the urban police, and the gendarmerie—were entrusted to a supervisory council of three clerics.[21] This council administered the main prisons with the help of wardens, pasdars, and clerical magistrates.

In Tehran, political dissidents were kept in four major prisons. Evin was enlarged with two new blocks containing six wards and six hundred solitary cells. It could now accommodate an additional 6,000 inmates. The Komiteh was renamed—not back to its Falakeh designation but to the more modern-sounding Prison No. 3,000. Colloquially it became known as the Komiteh-e Towhidi (Monotheistic Committee). Qezel Hesar, on the road to Karaj, was expanded and used mostly for political prisoners. Its gateway displayed the slogan "The Prison for Counterrevolutionaries—History's Garbage Dump." Finally, Gohar Dasht, started by the Shah, was completed as a three-floor compound with hundreds of solitary cells and large wards housing more than 8,000 inmates. It was reputed to be the largest penitentiary in the Middle East.[22] Qasr—Iran's Bastille—was now used solely for common criminals. Of course, these prisons contained separate wards for women. During the 1981 panic in Tehran, many mosques, schools, barracks, soccer stadiums, and even the Majles building were converted into temporary detention centers.

In theory, Evin was itself a detention center for those awaiting trial. After trial, those with long sentences were transferred to Qezel Hesar; those with shorter ones, to Gohar Dasht. In reality, Evin served as a regular prison as many waited years before being brought to trial. Moreover, prominent prisoners often served their entire sentences in Evin. In Tehran, political executions were carried out mostly in Evin and Gohar Dasht.

In the provinces—especially in Tabriz, Mashed, Isfahan, Shiraz, Hamadan, Sanandaj, and Kermanshah—prisoners were herded into the existing city prisons. The summer palace in Sari was transformed into a vast detention center. Tabriz was given a new city prison—built by repenters.[23] Despite the new construction, all prisons were seriously overcrowded by 1983. Komiteh, built for 500, had 1,500 inmates; Evin, built for 1,200, had 15,000; Qezel Hesar, built for 10,000, had 15,000; and Gohar Dasht, built for 8,000, had 16,000. Meanwhile, Qasr, which had housed 1,500 in 1978, had more than 6,000—all of them nonpolitical prisoners.[24]

Many of the prison wardens had themselves been political prisoners. Prominent among them was Sayyed Assadollah Ladjevardi, a former bazaar draper who had served time in Evin for trying to blow up the offices of El Al. In 1979, he was appointed the chief prosecutor of Tehran. And in June 1981, when Kachouyi was assassinated, he was given the added post of warden of Evin. He liked to be addressed as "Hajj Aqa," and boasted he was so proud of Evin that he had brought his family to live there. Some caustically remarked that SS commandants too had housed their families near concentration camps. Ladjevardi became notorious as the "Butcher of Evin." He was temporarily removed from his post in 1984, but he and his family continued to reside there to avoid assassination. Likewise, Hajj Davoud Rahmani, the warden of Qezel Hesar, was a former blacksmith from the Tehran bazaar. Before the revolution, he had served time in Qezel Hesar where he had worked as a cook.

The jailers were pasdars attached to local komitehs and the Revolutionary Tribunals. For the most part, the interrogators were young clerics and seminary students. It was rumored they had been trained by former SAVAK officials, but, in fact, there were few holdovers from the previous regime. The new interrogators did not need professional training. One—who specialized in interrogating Mojaheds—was a theology student who had seen his father, a cleric, assassinated by the Mojahedin. Another was a medical student who had participated in the U.S. Embassy takeover and had been given a crash course on theology to qualify as a religious magistrate.[25]

In the panic days of June 1981, the prison authorities readily resorted to brute force to extract information about hidden weapons, printing presses, and safe houses, as well as the identities of party leaders, members, and sympathizers. They were convinced that the regime's very existence was threatened by the fifth column allied to the all-powerful imperialists, especially the United States and the Soviet Union. The Iraqi war added further immediacy. They were also determined to forestall a 1953-style coup. As Hojjat al-Islam Khamenei declared, "We are not liberals like Mossadeq and Allende whom the CIA can easily snuff out. We are willing to take drastic action to preserve our newborn Islamic Republic."[26]

Although the initial intention was to unearth underground organizations, the regime continued to use torture well after weathering the 1981 storm. It did so increasingly to obtain public confessions, political recantations, and even ideological conversions. In the words of one former prisoner, "The regime had one overriding aim from the moment it arrested us. It was to force us to reject our beliefs and show that its lashes were stronger than our ideals."[27]

The mentalité of the interrogators readily led to this end. In their eyes, the survival of the Islamic Republic—and therefore of Islam itself—justified the means used. They could now present confessions as legal evidence. Had not Khomeini himself declared confessions to be the best proof of guilt? They considered prisoners by definition to be guilty. Why, otherwise, would they be in prison? Even if not "objectively guilty," they were "subjectively guilty" since their minds had been "contaminated" with alien "ideologies" and their hearts harbored ill will toward the Islamic Republic. One prisoner who survived both SAVAK and Ladjevardi adds that the new wardens were determined to extract recantations because they themselves in the 1970s had submitted to the Shah their own "dishonorable letters of regret."[28] The leftists had mocked these as "shit-eating letters."

Moreover, the new laws condoned judicial torture—in reality, if not in name. Even though the Constitution of the Islamic Republic explicitly outlawed shekanjeh (torture) and the use of coerced confessions, the Ta'zir Law did allow corporal punishments and voluntary confessions. The Pahlavis had used shekanjeh; the Islamic Republic forbade shekanjeh but condoned ta'zir. The new regime has often told UN delegations that ta'zir should not be equated with torture because it is sanctioned by the sharia and administered by qualified magistrates.²⁹ Victims may have trouble distinguishing shekanjeh from taʿzir; Foucault would have found the distinction highly significant.

Furthermore, "honest repentance" can lessen the punishment in this as well as in the next world. According to Ladjevardi, the Islamic Republic has converted prisons into "rehabilitation centers" and "ideological schools" where inmates study Islam, learn their errors, and do penance before returning to society. In short, prison and physical punishment can transform "deviants" into proper "human beings" (*adam*). He went on to boast that the Islamic Republic is the very first state in history to have converted prisons into universities.³⁰ Little did he know that on the eve of the Moscow trials, Vyshinsky, Stalin's chief prosecutor, had published with much fanfare a scholarly treatise entitled *From Prisons to Educational Institutions*.

Stage Preparations

By late 1981, the prison wardens had put in place a routine procedure for interrogating incoming inmates. If not overly pressured for time, they placed them in solitary cells and, providing them with paper, ballpoint, and sometimes printed questionnaires, sought information on relatives, friends, and neighbors, as well as on their own lives and political leanings. Their key question here as well as later was: "Are you willing to give us an interview [*mosahebeh*]?"

After the initial interrogation, the prisoner would be taken to the tazʿir chambers for fuller confessions of crimes—real or imagined—and, most important of all, videotaped interviews. Constraints of time and solitary cells sometimes necessitated the skipping of the initial stage. If the interrogator in the taʿzir chamber was a mere layman, he would have telephone contact with clerical magistrates authorized to mete out discretionary punishments.³¹ The issue of mosahebeh would be raised persistently throughout the whole procedure—not only by the interrogator, but also by the prosecutor, by the trial judge, and by the warden once the prisoner had completed the sentence. Some remained incarcerated even after serving their sentences simply because they declined the honor of being interviewed. One prisoner reports that his trial judge put aside his file and simply asked, "Are you willing to be interviewed?"[32] Another reports that the condemned were sometimes offered a reprieve if they provided the interview.[33] Yet another says that in the taʿzir chamber his interrogator kept on repeating throughout his torment, "This *hadd* punishment will continue until you give us a videotaped interview."[34]

The techniques used in the taʿzir chambers resembled those of SAVAK. They included whipping, sometimes of the back but most often of the feet with the body tied on an iron bed; the qapani; deprivation of sleep; suspension from ceilings and high walls; twisting of forearms until they broke; crushing of hands and fingers between metal presses; insertion of sharp instruments under the fingernails; cigarette burns; submersion under water; standing in one place for hours on end; mock executions; and physical threats against family members. Of these, the most prevalent was the whipping of soles, obviously because it was explicitly sanctioned by the sharia.

The torture techniques included two innovations: the "coffin" and the compulsory watching of—and even participation in—executions. Some were placed in small cubicles, blindfolded and in absolute silence, for seventeen-hour stretches with two fifteen-minute breaks for eating and going to the toilet. These stints could last months—until the prisoner agreed to the interview. Few avoided the interview and also remained sane. Others were forced to join firing squads and remove dead bodies. When they returned to their cells with blood dripping from their hands, their roommates surmised what had transpired. In the summer, newcomers to Evin—including women—had to pass the main courtyard and view rows of hanged prisoners.[35]

The new interrogators differed from their predecessors in other subtle ways. Contrary to common belief, they avoided sexual organs. They shied away from the iron helmet, the metal prod, and the electrified chair; such mechanical devices were deemed too Western. They kept their victims blindfolded throughout the whole procedure, often even in the trial chamber; most never obtained even a glance of their interrogators. SAVAK officials had been less shy. The new interrogators even blanketed the heads of women being whipped. Some were prudish enough to refuse to help lift women who had fainted. Women interrogators were rarely used on the grounds that they were not strong enough to administer the whip. The ta'zir chamber was one place where the strict codes of gender segregation were freely overlooked.

Entezam—Bazargan's former deputy—described conditions in Evin in a series of letters smuggled out during 1994–95.[36] He vouched that over sixteen years he had personally witnessed "hundreds" die and be driven insane. "For months on end, prisoners were put in small 50 x 80 x 140 cm coffins. In 1984, 30 were in such coffins. Some went mad." Although he himself had escaped the worst, he had been deprived of sleep, food, soap, medicine, visitors, and reading materials. On three separate occasions, he had been taken blindfolded to the execution chamber—once he had been kept there two full days while the Imam contemplated his death warrant. He had been placed in solitary for 555 days, and in an overcrowded cell for two and a half years. The cell had been so overcrowded that inmates took turns sleeping on the floor—each person rationed to three hours of sleep every twenty-four hours. He suffered permanent ear damage, skin disease, and spinal deformities. He added that prisoners were deprived not only of lawyers but also of such basic information as the charges against them and even their eventual sentences; some remained incarcerated not knowing how many years they were to serve. "Islam is a religion of care, compassion, and forgiveness. This regime makes it a religion of destruction, death, and torture."

The interrogation became a perverse form of bargaining. On one side, the interrogator knew that dead prisoners were of little use—even potential embarrassments. One survivor writes that by 1984 doctors were invariably present in the ta'zir chambers to prevent unwanted deaths.[37] The interrogator also knew that the interview had to be believable to be marketable; unexpected crimes and uncharacteristic language would make the recantation unbelievable and thus unusable. Each recantation had to fit the specific recanter. Consequently, he was willing to let victims write their own confessions. On the other side, the prisoners realized that their interrogator wanted a recantation—not a dead body. They also realized that they could face the death penalty if they pinned themselves down to specific high crimes. What is more, if they went overboard in their groveling, they risked losing completely their self-respect, reputation, public credibility, and future political career—that is, they would be committing political suicide.

Despite these unstated guidelines, fatal mistakes sometimes occurred. The martyrs' list compiled by the Mojahedin names 460 killed under torture in the period between June 1981 and June 1985.[38] Some may have committed suicide. Among the 460 were 397 Mojaheds, 9 Fedayis, 7 Peykaris, 5 Kurdish Democrats, 2 Kurdish Kumalehs, and 13 from smaller Marxist groups. This list excludes for political reasons another 9 Bahais and 13 Tudeh activists who had died under similar circumstances in this same period.

Many resorted to modesty to avoid the obligatory interview. Raha, a young woman incarcerated nine years because of her leftist brother, pleaded that "it made no sense for her to appear before the cameras since she was a nobody."[39] A Mojahedin sympathizer offered a "letter of regret" instead of the interview on the grounds that he had never been a full member and had to protect his honor and reputation: "I work in the bazaar and have to think of my wife and children."[40] E.A., a university student imprisoned in Evin during 1981–83 for possessing left-wing literature, writes that almost all prisoners began by pleading that "they were nobodies and not significant enough even within their own small organizations to feature in such national interviews."[41] Such modesty rarely worked.

Once the bargain was reached, the interrogators provided their victims with a standard introduction and conclusion but left the main text for them to fill in. This gave the victims the opportunity to make their recantations nebulous, full of double meanings, and, most important, long on generalities but short on specifics. They chose each word, each metaphor, each argument carefully, knowing well that their lives and their reputations were at stake—especially if the recantations were earmarked for newspapers and prime-time television. Of course, they could not choose the headlines under which their recantations would appear.

The standard introduction hailed Khomeini as the Imam (Infallible Leader), the Rahbar-e Kaber-e Enqelab (Great Leader of the Revolution), the Rahbar-e Mostazafin (Leader of the Oppressed), and the Bonyadgozar-e Jomhuri-ye Islami (Founder of the Islamic Republic). This signified submission to the authorities and the acceptance of their legitimacy. The introduction also emphasized that the "interview" was entirely voluntary and that the speaker had come forth willingly to warn others of the pitfalls awaiting them if they deviated from the Khatt-e Imam (Imam's Line). The speaker invariably included a biographical sketch stressing his importance within the pertinent political organization.

The standard conclusion thanked the wardens for the opportunity to study, discuss ideas, and see the light. It beseeched forgiveness and sought a second chance to work for the Islamic Revolution, the Islamic Republic, and the Iranian people. It hoped that the sincere repentance and the Imam's compassion would pave the way for forgiveness, redemption, and reacceptance into the community. If, however, the Imam chose not to forgive, that too would be understandable in light of the enormity of the crimes. Absolution—but not retribution—was to be credited to the all-compassionate authorities. Orwell could not have phrased it better.

Whereas the beginning and the end were positive propaganda for the regime, the central text contained negative propaganda against the opposition in general and the recanter's own organization in particular. It echoed—and thus "confirmed"—the official accusations against that organization.

Sometimes the accusations involved "treason," "espionage," and "foreign subversion." At other times they involved "terrorism," "eclecticism," "religious deviation," and "ideological contamination." Most used such terms as "counterrevolution" and "fifth column"—both of distinct European origin. In short, the regime waged a propaganda war not so much by raising new charges against its opponents as by forcing its opponents to articulate in their own words and their own logic the official charges against themselves. It was propaganda by self-denunciation.

This lent an aura of authenticity to the whole exercise. The language of a royalist would differ from that of a student activist. That of a Mojahed would differ from that of a Marxist, a Liberal, or an ex-Khomeinist. That of a Tudehi would differ from that of a Maoist or an anti-Soviet communist. Of course, that of a Bahai would differ drastically from all the others. Although Bahais were subjected to the same torture process, they were rarely forced before the television cameras. Instead, they were compelled to place announcements—often no longer than one short paragraph—in the daily papers paying allegiance to Shi'i Islam and disassociating themselves from the "bombastic," "cruel," and "Zionist Bahai organization." The regime insists that the Bahais are suspect not because of their "religious beliefs" but because "their organization by its very nature is a Zionist-imperialist conspiracy"—that is, they are suspect not because of their own beliefs but because they belong to an organization whose beliefs inevitably make them into "spies," "plotters," "troublemakers," and "apostates."[42] No doubt, the victims appreciate this fine distinction.

Typical of the recantation shows were weekly two-hour programs aired through the autumn of 1983 on prime-time television.[43] These were billed as *mizegerd*s (roundtable discussions), *goftogu*s (conversations), and *monazereh*s (debates), as well as mosahebehs, or interviews. They were also broadcast over the radio and their transcripts circulated widely through newspapers and pamphlets entitled *Karnameh-e Siyah* (Black Report Cards). The shows were filmed within Evin in its large two-story auditorium recently renamed the Hosseiniyeh (Religious Lecture Hall). The audience was composed of prisoners, with women and men sitting on separate sides of the floor. The walls displayed a thirty-foot mural of Khomeini, pictures of recently assassinated clerics, and a Koranic inscription urging believers to be vigilant against unbelievers. They also displayed such slogans as "Death to the Soviets," "Death to the United States," and "Death to the Unbelievers and Those Who Fight God."

Ladjevardi, the prison warden, chaired the programs. He began with the conventional "In the Name of God the Merciful, the Compassionate." He saluted the Imam of the Muslim Community (Imam-e Ummat) and the Leader of the Oppressed (Rahbar-e Mostazafin), as well as the Martyr-nourishing Community of Iran (Ummat-e Shahidparvar-e Iran). He thanked the clergy for leading the long struggle against the imperialists from the time of the 1892 Tobacco Crisis through the Constitutional Revolution to the recent Islamic Revolution. He then introduced the twenty-nine participants as "guests representing the *goruhakhha-ye zedd-e enqelabi* [counterrevolutionary mini-groups]." He explained that these "volunteers" were eager to take questions from the floor and discuss the dangers of *enheraf* (deviation), *elteqat* (eclecticism), *mohareb* (warring against God), and *gerayesh beh gharb va sharq* (leaning toward either the West or East). This set the tone for their presentations.

The twenty-nine included thirteen from the Mojahedin, five from Peykar, five from the office of former President Bani-Sadr, three from the National Front, and another three from the Minority Fedayi. Lumping them together as "counterrevolutionaries," the regime labeled the Mojaheds "terrorists," the National Frontists and the Bani-Sadr supporters "liberals," and the Peykaris and Fedayis "American Marxists" (Marksistha-ye Amrikayi). It argued that since the latter groups were vehemently anti-Soviet, they must logically be pro-American—covertly, if not overtly. None were women. Although women were forced to recant, the regime rarely televised their recantations.

When it did, it depicted them as misled wives and sisters—not as political activists in their own right. One female prisoner argues that the recantations of women were rarely televised because the regime was reluctant to publicly admit even the existence of independent-minded women activists.[44]

These Evin programs have been perceptively described by E.A.—the university student imprisoned for collecting left-wing literature.[45] He likened them to "high drama," "battlefields," and "gladiator matches." On one side were Ladjevardi, the interrogators, and the repenters. On the other side were those in the audience who had not been broken. Recanters had to stand up and prove their sincerity by vehemently denouncing former beliefs, colleagues, and leaders. Those not vehement enough were subjected to death taunts. These "nightly shows," he writes, were staged as "ideological theater" to break down morale, turning "prisoner against prisoner," "friend against friend," "comrade against comrade," "Mojahed against Mojahed," "leftist against leftist," even "self against self." E.A. adds that although he did not know the origin of these "nightmares," he could see that by late 1983 they had become an integral feature of prison life.

Raha—the young woman incarcerated because of her leftist brother—considers the compulsory attendance at these recantations to be as painful as physical torture itself. She writes that they were forced to watch wives denounce their husbands, children their parents, friends their friends.[46] Similarly, Parsipour—the prominent writer imprisoned because of the literature found in her car—narrates that these Hosseiniyeh shows took a heavy toll from the audience as well as the participants. She describes one recanter whose personality literally split into two. One part—adopting the Muslim name Fatemeh—meekly submitted and vehemently denounced her former beliefs. The other—retaining her pre-Islamic name Azita—remained true to her beliefs and her executed communist husband. She eventually became stark-raving mad.[47]

These tense shows could easily be subverted into carnivals—at least, by those willing to risk death. E.A. recounts that a teenage boy was invited to the podium by Ladjevardi to explain why he was in Evin. He explained that he had first joined the Tudeh but had left it once he discovered that the party supported the Islamic Republic. He had looked around for a party to his liking but, finding none, had formed his own organization with a total membership of one—himself. At that point much of the audience was smirking, for it was clear that he was in Evin simply because he did not like the regime. Raha recounts how one daring woman from the audience asked a prominent recanter the whereabouts of his former colleague, knowing perfectly well that he had died under torture. The recanter huffed and puffed, claiming lack of knowledge. A Mojahed relates how Ladjevardi ordered a Forqan member to explain why they had assassinated Khomeini's prized disciple.[48] Instead of reciting the expected litany about eclecticism, the Forqan member set off a commotion by declaring: "We did it because we had studied the Holy Koran." Of course, such scenes were not televised.

Also, overly tragic scenes remained on the cutting room floor. A teenage girl stood up at a recantation session and beseeched the wardens to take her life because she had no relatives left to return to: "You have executed my mother and one brother. Another brother you have given a life sentence. My father died of a heart attack when he heard of the executions. It is a pity you executed my fifteen-year-old brother. If you had not, maybe he too would be here on his way back to true Islam."[49] A sixty-year-old man who had spent months in a "coffin" punctuated his recantation with periodic weeping and hysterical laughter. It was clear he had lost his sanity.[50] Similarly, a sixteen-year-old girl cried and laughed hysterically while pleading with her listeners to seek redemption through repentance. The warden interrupted, declaring that she was living proof that those who "strayed from Islam" risked losing their sanity.[51]

Mojahedin

The majority of the recantations in 1981–83 came from the Mojahedin—at the time the main threat to the regime. Since the leading Mojaheds had escaped abroad or died in shoot-outs, the regime had to settle for rank-and-file recanters, who they billed as important "cadres" and "militant activists." It also published two sets of multivolume signed affadavits. One, entitled *Shekanjeh* (Torture), described in vivid detail how the Mojahedin had "physically tormented innocent pasdars and their families." The other, entitled *Karnameh-e Siyah* (Black Report Card), carried the subtitles *E'terafat* (Confessions), *Monazareh-e Zendaniyan-e Evin* (Debates among Evin Prisoners), *Chehreh-e Nafaq* (The Face of Discord), and *Chehguneh Teroryist Showdam* (How I Became a Terrorist).

These recanters started with the traditional "In the Name of God the Merciful, the Compassionate"—not with the Mojahedin-coined opening "In the Name of God and the Heroic People of Iran." This symbolized submission to official Islam. They also referred to themselves as the Monafeqin (Hypocrites)—the official term for the Mojahedin. The Koran uses this term to describe those in Medina who had pretended to be good Muslims while conspiring with the pagans in Mecca. The Prophet had pronounced "a *monafeq* [hypocrite] to be worse than a *kafer* [unbeliever]." This became a government slogan. According to the regime, Imam Ali had warned the faithful to be on guard against hypocrites who deceive, deviate, dilute religion, consort with the Devil, and resort to *teroryism*.[52] Obviously, foreign terminology heightened the danger.

The Mojahedin recanters directed their attacks at their former leaders—especially Masoud Rajavi—accusing them of hypocrisy and terrorism.[53] These leaders had supposedly ordered the murders of not only prominent clerics and revolutionary guards—which was common knowledge—but also countless ordinary and defenseless citizens, including women, children, and old folks. They had ordered Molotov *koktel*s (cocktails) to be thrown at stores, private homes, city buses, schools, public libraries, ambulances, and even kindergartens. They had also sabotaged the economy and the war effort by blowing up bridges, power stations, railways, hospitals, and medical clinics. They had ordered militants to commit suicide rather than be taken prisoner. They had placed children—especially young girls—at the forefront of their armed demonstrations. "Our leaders," declared one, "place no value whatsoever on human life." These were confessions of "embellished terrorism."

They declared that their terrorism was outdone only by their hypocrisy. They pretended to be devout Muslims but, in fact, were secret Marxists. Like the Babis of the Constitutional Revolution who had pretended to be good Muslims, they were wolves in sheeps' clothing. They waxed eloquent about Islam-i Towhidi (Monotheistic Islam) but contaminated true religion with alien ideologies—especially atheistic materialism. They proclaimed themselves committed believers but in truth were opportunists (*oportunistha*) and pragmatists (*peragmatistha*) sacrificing principle on the altar of political power. They hailed themselves as working class but in reality had little public support and often set up safe houses in middle-class neighborhoods—especially in the Armenian districts of Tehran. They outdid others in radical talk but secretly supported the *liberalha* (liberals)—first Bazargan and his Provisional Government, later President Bani-Sadr. They made much ado about democracy but demanded "blind acceptance" of Rajavi's "cult of personality." They pretended to champion the oppressed masses (*mostazafin*) but were confined to the narrow circles of the privileged intelligentsia (*rowshanfekran*). They wrapped themselves in the national flag but, in reality, were a "fifth column" in the pay of foreign powers—of the Soviet Union, the United States, and Iraq. Their true aim was not to fight imperialism but to overthrow the Islamic Republic. "To work for Satan one does not have to be a card-holding member of the CIA or the KGB. One can help imperialism by simply undermining the Islamic Republic."

One Mojahed thanked both the pasdars, for saving him from an angry crowd, and the wardens, for showing him the road to true Islam. He cut short his recantation pleading that the mere memory of his crimes choked him with tears. Another confessed to being a *jasous* (spy) and to publishing confidential information gathered from the ministries. He ridiculed the rumor that prisoners had been tortured to death, insisting that some had committed suicide to embarrass the authorities. He also argued that he felt freer in prison because in the outside world his organization had pressured him into "self-censorship" (*khod sansour*). Yet another claimed that he had been ordered to throw bombs at schools, kidnap pasdars, decapitate old ladies, and practice such "medieval tortures" as gouging out eyes and cutting off hands. Such gory confessions had some effect—at least on those predisposed to distrust the Mojahedin. Raha writes that she never imagined that a political organization could resort to such "mafia-like methods."[54]

The regime produced its first and only Mojahed leader in 1989—a few months after the organization had made an abortive incursion into the country from its military base in Iraq. The captured leader, Sa'id Shahsavandi, was a veteran activist. He had been sentenced to life imprisonment in 1973, ran for the Majles in 1980, and recently directed the organization's radio station in Iraq. The Mojahedin promptly tried damage control, announcing that he was a mere rank-and-file member.

In a series of television interviews, open letters, and university lectures, Shahsavandi expounded on the "hypocritical nature" of the Mojahedin.[55] He declared that from the very beginning there had been a major discrepancy between what the Mojahedin espoused and what they believed in. He claimed that his former colleagues paid lip service to Islam but were more interested in Lenin, Che Guevara, Ho Chi Minh, and Mao Tse-tung. They talked about "true Islam" but in actual fact showed no interest in what thousands of religious scholars had written over the last thirteen centuries. They had paid allegiance to the Islamic Republic but in the meantime had prepared for a *kudeta* (coup d'état). They waved the Iranian flag but secretly consorted with King Hossein, the Saudis, and Saddam Hossein—not to mention the CIA and the KGB.

Shahsavandi claimed that nothing remained of the Mojahedin within Iran; that Rajavi imprisoned, tortured, and executed disobedient followers; that untrained youngsters had been rushed from Paris, London, and New York to take part in the ill-fated military incursion; and that the exiled organization was riddled with suicides, desertions, factionalism, and dis-illusionment. He did not explain why the regime could not produce other prominent defectors. After these interviews, Shahsavandi left for Europe to elaborate on these same themes. When asked why he had been permitted to live and leave, Shah-savandi answered that he had been "saved from Ladjevardi by influential friends," that he was more useful to the regime alive than dead, and that he no longer advocated armed struggle.[56] Some suspect that relatives in Iran guaranteed his good behav-ior. Whatever the truth, Shahsavandi traveled widely repeating the regime's propaganda salvos against the Mojahedin. But coming from a former leader, they were far more effective.

The Left

In 1982 the media aired recantations from most leftist organ-izations—except from the Tudeh and the Majority Fedayi, which continued to support the Islamic Republic until 1983. As with the Mojahedin, the regime had to make do with minor figures as these small groups had few prominent leaders.

One of the few was Hossein Ruhani, a Peykar leader and a prominent veteran of the early guerrilla movement. Born into a clerical family in Mashed in 1941, Ruhani had a traditional religious upbringing before entering Tehran University to study agriculture. There he had been active in Bazargan's Liberation Movement and had been one of the first to join the Mojahedin. He soon headed its ideological committee; served as its liaison with the PLO and the Shi'i guerrillas in Lebanon; and, most important of all, in 1972–74 headed its delicate negotiations with Khomeini in Najaf. At the time, the Mojahedin needed clerical endorsement to raise funds for its activities, and Kho-meini needed contacts to expand his network in the Arab world and among Iranian students in Europe.

When in 1974 the Mojahedin split into rival Muslim and Marxist factions, Ruhani was prominent in the latter. He helped to write its first *Manifesto* explaining why they had jet-tisoned Islam in favor of Marxism-Leninism.[57] He argued that whereas the former was a "petty bourgeois ideology designed to sedate the masses," the latter held the secrets for the "liberation of the working class." Whereas the former was "unrealistic," "utopian," and "incapable of understanding social change," the latter was a true science, like physics, revealing the iron laws of historical change. Whereas the former diverted attention from this world to metaphysics and the soul, the latter focused human energies on action, social change, and the engineering of the good society in this world. The essence of Marxism was liberation; that of Islam was prayer, devotion, and, at best, charity.

After the split, Ruhani served as the Marxist Mojahedin's chief representative in Europe and the Arab world. During the early stages of the revolution, he returned to Tehran to set up underground factory cells. Immediately after the revolution, when the Marxist Mojahedin renamed itself Peykar, he ran as its Majles candidate in Tehran. As such he received extensive press coverage. He also caused a major scandal in 1980 by divulging for the first time the secret Mojahedin negotiations with Khomeini.[58] In doing so, he depicted Khomeini as a "medieval obscurantist" less interested in the armed struggle than in the question of whether the body would reconstruct itself on Resurrection Day. This was the very first time a left-wing organization had personally criticized Khomeini. Peykar was also vocal in denouncing the regime as "reactionary," "fascistic," and tied to the "petty bourgeois bazaaris" as well as to the "capitalist imperialists." It even argued that the term "revolution" could not be applied to February 1979 because the fall of the Shah had not brought about fundamental changes. Although Peykar did not support the Mojahedin in its June 1981 uprising, its members were arrested and executed en masse.

Ruhani appeared on television in May 1982, becoming one of the first leftists to recant.[59] He had already appeared in the Hosseiniyeh, but that video had been unusable because he had partly retracted his recantation when challenged by a daring woman in the audience. He also reappeared in the 1982 program of the Evin twenty-nine. He began his May 1982 recantation with "In the Name of God the Merciful, the Compassionate"—a strange opening for a Marxist. He sprinkled his presentations with Koranic quotations and religious declarations—equally strange as few Marxist leaders became born-again Muslims in prison. That would have been too unbelievable for the public, especially for their own particular constituency. The bulk of his recantation, however, freely used Marxist terminology and leftist arguments.

After thanking the authorities for the press conference, Ruhani praised the Imam for providing the Muslim world with its first true leadership since the departure of the Holy Prophet: "Our Imam represents Islam." He declared that his two-month stay in Evin had produced in him "qualitative changes" that he wished to share with the general public and his former communist comrades. He added that he felt freer inside Evin for in the outside world he had always been "stifled by dogmatism, false ideologies, and self-censorship." In short, prison was freedom; the outside world was a prison.

Ruhani devoted much of his allocated time to attacking the Mojahedin and the Marxist opposition. He acknowledged that in his conversations with the Imam in Iraq, the latter had correctly diagnosed the main disease of the Mojahedin to be "eclecticism"—a term he used no less than a dozen times. He admitted that at the time he himself had not recognized this disease. "But then," he continued, "eclectics rarely recognize their own ailment." He claimed he had written the handbooks the Mojahedin had circulated as the works of their most revered martyrs. He also claimed that the 1975–76 fighting between the Muslim and the Marxist Mojahedin had left a much higher toll than generally acknowledged.

The rest of the recantation was directed at the Marxists. He faulted them for smearing the Islamic Republic as *erteja'yi* (reactionary) and *zedd-e enqelabi* (counterrevolutionary). He said, "Prison has shown me that this is a truly anti-imperialist people's regime [*rezhim-e mardomi*]." By not supporting the regime, the left had "deviated" from the true path. "Marxism is deviationism in the same way the Mojahedin is eclecticism." He argued that since the essence of the revolution had been Islam, revolutionaries need to accept Islam as the country's true ideology. He urged the left to follow the Imam's Line on the grounds that the imperialists were using all means available to undermine the revolution—cultural, military, economic, and political. The last included the ethnic minorities, the liberals, and the left. Withholding support for the regime was tantamount to collaborating with the United States. This reinforced the argument that the Marxists who were not "linked" to the Soviets must inevitably be linked to the Americans.

Ruhani continued with a multipronged attack on the left. He harped on recent fighting that had broken out in Kurdestan between Peykar, Kumaleh, and the Kurdish Democratic party. He warned that the Tudeh was undermining the revolution because it was "revisionist" and tied to the Soviet "Social Imperialists." He argued that the revolution had been made by common folk, not by the mini-guerrilla organizations. He added that the theory of "armed struggle" had been cooked up by the intelligentsia to play down the role of the masses. He stressed that the left was "cut off from the people" whereas the Islamic Republic enjoyed their enthusiastic support: "The Left refuses to accept objective reality because it suffers from subjectivism." He dwelled on factional infighting within leftist organizations, arguing that all these groups were led by "selfish power-hungry would-be dictators lacking any principles." "They believe that the end justifies the means and they can use any means available to eliminate personal rivals." He concluded with the hope that he could have an audience with the Imam and additional press conferences to further elaborate on these important topics.

These recantations had a profound demoralizing effect on Peykar in particular and on the left in general. In the words of Raha—by no means a supporter of Peykar—these Evin *shous* (shows) were "surprising," "amazing" and "hard to believe."

Here was a militant leader and veteran of twenty-five years struggle claiming that in a mere two months he had completely converted from Marxism to Islam. . . . I could not fathom what I was seeing with my own eyes. Was it real or a bad dream? Ruhani was Ruhani in the flesh. Ladjevardi was Ladjevardi in the flesh. For us in the audience, the whole show was depressing and painful—as painful as observing an actual death. For the same reason that show was a joyous occasion for Ladjevardi and his cohorts.[60]

E.A. writes that the recantations of Ruhani and other Peykar leaders had a profoundly "upsetting effect"—even on leftists outside Peykar: "The night Ruhani went to the microphones something snapped inside all of us. We never expected someone of his reputation to get down on his knees. Some commented it was as revolting as watching a human being cannibalize himself." E.A. was also intrigued that these recanters continued to use such "leftist terms as class struggle, petty bourgeois, sectarianism, colonialism, and imperialism."[61]

Ruhani continued to feature in the Hosseiniyeh meetings for the next three years—until he was quietly and inexplicably executed. He became a nonperson; even Peykar refused to list him as a martyr. His recantations, however, set the tone for other Marxists—with the significant difference that few others professed conversion to Islam.

The other Marxist recanters in 1982–83 included activists from the Minority Fedayi, Rah-e Kargar, Kumaleh, the Union of Iranian Communists, and the Union of Militant Communists. They argued that their criticism of the regime had been misplaced; that the regime was the true representative of the working class; and that opposition to the regime was equivalent to supporting capitalism, feudalism, and imperialism.[62] One cited Lenin as saying: "To recognize your friends look and see who the enemies of your friends are." Another contrasted the "medieval SAVAK torturers" to his "considerate" wardens who had turned the "prisons into genuine universities." Yet another argued that he had joined the left because he opposed imperialism, but in prison he had discovered that the true bulwark against imperialism was the Islamic Republic: "Infantile leftists are puppets of Zionism, Iraqi Baathism, and American imperialism."

Liberals

According to the regime, those who favored secularism and political pluralism were "liberals." And those who were "liberals" were by their very nature "linked to the West"—despite their own vehement denials. The two most prominent recanters fitting the "liberal" category were Taher Ahmadzadeh and Sadeq Qotbzadeh. The former had worked closely with Bazargan for four decades. The latter had served as Khomeini's English-language translator in Paris.

Ahmadzadeh had been active in the opposition to the Shah since the early 1950s. He had to helped found the Liberation Movement and had spent ten years in prison—a rare feat for a religious intellectual of his generation. Meanwhile, his son—a founding member of the Fedayi—had been executed. Immediately after the revolution, he had been appointed governor of Khurasan and his family had been praised for refusing to compromise their principles with the hated Shah. But by June 1981, he had fallen out of favor, having openly criticized the clergy for monopolizing power.

Ahmadzadeh featured prominently in the 1983 "roundtable discussions" from Evin.[63] He began with a Koran reading and salutations to the Imam—"the Revolutionary Sun that illuminates and invigorates Iran." He hoped his confession would reach the "Honorable People of Iran" and would be accepted by God and the Imam, the "most important person in Islam since the days of the Holy Prophet." He stressed that months of contemplation, reading of the Koran, and scrutiny of the evidence had persuaded him to reevaluate his whole attitude toward the government—especially his previous complaint that pasdars had killed innocent citizens. He now realized his negative attitude had been wrong, his complaints against the pasdars had been unjust, and the government was on the road mapped out by Imam Ali.

He confessed that he had been influenced by "hypocrites" who had persuaded him to try to escape to the West: "I stand before you guilty of helping imperialism as well as betraying Islam and Iran." Having heard the previous confessions, he now realized that the "hypocrites" were a bunch of "terrorists," "torturers," and "power-hungry maniacs" linked to fascism and imperialism. He also realized that the Imam was the true representative of the people, the Koran, and Islam. He hoped that he would be permitted to rejoin the "caravan of progress on its passage to God." He concluded with "Long Live the Holy Martyrs of Islam, especially the Martyrs of the Islamic Revolution. Long Live the Imam, Our Dear Leader and the Champion of the World's Oppressed Masses."

This recantation was one of the very few to be subjected to critical analysis. Abdol-Karim Lahiji, his old friend and now a human-rights lawyer in Paris, wrote that only indescribable forms of torture could explain outlandish statements from such a steadfast person as Ahmadzadeh—"the symbol of heroic resistance against SAVAK."[64] Comparing the recantation to the Moscow trials, Lahiji argued that the new regime was extracting phony confessions by threatening family members, even small children. This was the first—and a rare—article to appear anywhere in Persian discussing the whole subject of public recantations and forced confessions. Ahmadzadeh was released four years later after having taken a vow of silence about his prison experiences. He has kept his vow.

Qotbzadeh was even better known. He had been active in the National Front, the Liberation Movement, and the Student Confederation. He had accompanied Khomeini on his triumphant return to Iran. After the revolution, he first headed the National Radio-Television Network from which he purged royalists, women, and leftists. He then headed the Foreign Ministry and tried unsuccessfully to resolve the American hostage crisis. Having antagonized the hard-line clerics, he resigned and promptly lost access to Khomeini.

Qotbzadeh appeared before the cameras in early 1982 to "reveal" that he had participated in a pro-Western military plot.[65] The plot involved bombing the Imam's residence and killing him if necessary. To finance the venture, he had contacted a Paris-based Argentinian arms merchant; the Saudi government; and, most important of all, Grand Ayatollah Shariatmadari whom many revered as their main spiritual guide. In fact, many Azerbaijanis felt that Shariatmadari outranked Khomeini in scholarship and clerical seniority. During the revolution, Shariatmadari had favored the restoration of the 1905 Fundamental Laws and had criticized Khomeini's theory of Islamic Government. After the revolution, Shariatmadari had supported Bazargan in the hope of stopping Khomeini. Qotbzadeh concluded his confession by pleading for prompt judgment—either forgiveness or execution. He had no wish to remain in prison.

Qotbzadeh was accompanied to his "press conference" by Hojjat al-Islam Mohammad Reyshahri, the chief judge of the newly created Military Revolutionary Tribunal. Reyshahri emphasized the utmost gravity of the plot, insinuating that Qotbzadeh was also linked to a recently uncovered royalist conspiracy to launch a military coup from Hamadan.[66] To explain the plots, the chief judge presented an elaborate chart full of boxes and arrows linking Qotbzadeh and the royalist officers, on one side, to the "feudalists, the leftist mini-groups, and the phony clerics," and, on the other side, to the "National Front, Israel, the Pahlavis, and the Socialist International." The last four were then linked to the CIA. Ironically, the State Department had for years denied Qotbzadeh an entry visa into the United States on the grounds that he was a Soviet agent. Qotbzadeh himself suspected his clerical judges of being Soviet agents.[67]

Qotbzadeh's final appearance was before the Military Revolutionary Tribunal.[68] In the dock with him were three colonels and three clerics, including Shariatmadari's son-in-law. Pleading allegiance to the Imam, the Revolution, and the Islamic Republic, Qotbzadeh admitted receiving money from abroad.

But he modified his earlier statements, arguing that he had hoped to detain, not kill, the Imam, and to change, not overthrow, the government. Although one officer denied the existence of any plot, one of the clerics confessed to conveying messages from Qotbzadeh to Shariatmadari, to the Saudis, to the European Socialists, and to West German businessmen. This convinced the judge that Qotbzadeh deserved no pity. A friend of Qotbzadeh claims that on the eve of his execution, Ahmad Khomeini, the Imam's son, offered him clemency if he publicly groveled for his life.[69]

Qotbzadeh's arrest led to Shariatmadari's "confession"— probably to save his own son-in-law. Appearing on television, Shariatmadari apologized for failing to report rumors of the plot to the proper authorities. He had dismissed them as ridiculous hearsay. "Besides," he said, "I presumed the authorities themselves had heard these widespread rumors."[70] The chief prosecutor—echoed by the press—billed this as a "Confession of Guilt."[71] One editorial asked rhetorically, "What better proof of a plot than confessions from the mouths of the plotters themselves?"[72] Hojjat al-Islam Rafsanjani, then the Imam Jom'eh of Tehran, declared that anyone who had been privy to such a "heinous plot" should not enjoy public respect.[73] One of Shariatmadari's sons pleaded in vain from Europe that according to the sharia all coerced statements were null and void.[74]

The regime used the "Shariatmadari confession" to launch a full-scale campaign against him. It depicted him as a "liberal" linked to SAVAK, the royalists, the Saudis, and the West. It published U.S. Embassy documents describing him as a moderate. It insinuated that he liked luxury and wanted to separate Azerbaijan from Iran. It surrounded his home with demonstrators clamoring for his death. It questioned his religious credentials, claiming that the Shah had elevated him to the position of ayatollah; to support the latter claim, it reprinted a 1946 photo of him in the presence of the Shah. Finally, in an unprecedented act, it defrocked him, declaring that he no longer held the title of ayatollah and therefore could no longer collect religious dues. He was confined to his house until 1986 when he died of natural causes. In short, his destruction had been brought about by his so-called confession.

Royalists

In April 1987, General Hossein Fardoust—the elusive but famous childhood friend of the Shah—appeared before the television cameras for the very first time in his long public career. In his own words, Fardoust had been "the second most powerful man in the fallen regime."[75] For ten years, he ran the day-to-day affairs of SAVAK by serving as its deputy director. For twenty years, he headed the Special Intelligence Bureau—a form of SAVAK within SAVAK. Immediately after the revolution, it was rumored that he defected to the other side, handed over crucial files, and transformed SAVAK into SAVAMA, a new secret service organization. His television appearance took the form of an undated video "interview." It was his last—as well as his first—television appearance. Three weeks later the government announced he had died from "old age and other natural causes."

Fardoust's interview reinforced public perceptions of the Pahlavis—especially their rampant "corruption" and foreign "dependency." Fardoust began with an autobiographical sketch stressing his long friendship with the former Shah: his childhood in the palace; his years with the princes at the exclusive Le Rosey School in Switzerland; his training with the crown prince at the military academy; and his thirty-eight-year service to the palace and in the security forces. These years, he stressed, had given him an intimate insight into the inner workings of the old regime.

Having established his credibility, Fardoust dwelled on the old regime's corruption and foreign dependency. He argued that the elite was so greedy, so money-grabbing, and so plundering that the Special Intelligence Bureau would have needed at least 10,000 full-time investigators just to keep tabs on the grand larcenists alone. "There was no way of keeping track of lesser crooks." He also "revealed" that the British had arranged the marriage as well as the divorce of the Shah to Princess Fawzieh of Egypt and had planted a young valet named Ernest Perron in Le Rosey School to befriend the crown prince and return to live with him in the royal palace. Furthermore, he revealed that the Shah had daily meetings with Sir Jay Reporter—the supposed MI6 head in Tehran. He claimed that the latter's true name was Shahpour J. and that he was an Indian-born Zoroastrian pretending to be the local correspondent of the London *Times*.

These two themes were further developed in a posthumous book entitled *Khaterat-e Arteshbod-e Baznesheshteh Hossein Fardoust* (The Memoirs of Retired General Hossein Fardoust). This was also serialized in newspapers in the course of the next three years—and yet again in 1998.[76] This long, meandering, and repetitive book dwells on how the former elite had "plundered the country" through commercial kickbacks, weapons contracts, real estate speculation, market controls, gambling, outright expropriations, and heroin trafficking. The distinct impression is given that the only honest person in the old regime was the author himself. This tale of corruption includes much court gossip—especially about the Shah's insatiable desire for "prostitutes, chatterboxes, loose women, and other men's wives." At times, Fardoust traces the collapse of the regime to gossiping, greedy, and back-biting women—including the Shah's wives and sisters. Fardoust writes that he had sent his own wife off to the United States to free himself of her constant nagging. The book was clearly designed to reinforce the notion that the regime's interest in women was part and parcel of its moral decay.

The second theme was developed even further. According to the book, the imperial powers, especially Britain, dominated Iran through direct and indirect means—through embassies, military missions, secret agencies, privileged families, and political parties. They cultivated elite families—"many of whom were their paid agents." They nourished the Freemasons—"most politicians belonged to this secret conspiracy." They also nourished the Bahais—one of whom, General Ayadi, the court doctor, was the Rasputin of Iran. They relied on Jews who controlled "not only Israel but also the United States." The British ordered Perron to set up a homosexual clique within the palace. The British also pulled strings through such secular organizations as the Tudeh and the National Front. In fact, Mossadeq had always favored the British and his campaign to nationalize the oil company had been inspired by the "British themselves." The Tudeh was controlled by the British as well as by the Soviets. The book declares:

> All seeking power tried to curry favor with London and Washington. Certainly those with the best foreign links, especially with secret agencies, had the best chance of promotion. Personal attributes also helped—attributes such as dishonesty, charlatanry, and flattery. If the agent was a woman, she would get her desired job through illicit sex. Of course, the same applied to men.

The book devotes much space to internal security—Fardoust's own specialty. Apparently it was Queen Elizabeth's personal suggestion that had led to the creation of the Special Intelligence Bureau and the dispatch of Fardoust to London to receive training in how to compile succinct and logical reports. The training left much to be desired. Preferring "scientific methods of interrogation," Fardoust had sent SAVAK personnel to MOSSAD because the CIA continued to favor "cruder methods." He also mentions that MI6 surpassed the CIA in its knowledge of Iran.

Fardoust concludes by trying to explain how he had survived the revolution. As director of the Special Intelligence Bureau, he could see that the regime was too corrupt to weather the upheaval. He could also see that only the Imam could provide the country with much-needed law and order. He had thus thrown himself at the mercy of the Imam. "But," he claimed, "the Tudeh and the royalists together are spreading the malicious rumor that I am working for new security services."

Obviously, many—including Khomeinists—must have been wondering why Fardoust had survived while lesser men had perished.

Ex-Khomeinists

If Fardoust was used to discredit the former regime, the equally sensational television appearance of Hojjat al-Islam Sayyed Mehdi Hashemi was designed to send a clear and loud message to any believers tempted to stray from the official path. Hashemi was well known in clerical circles. He was the brother-in-law of Ayatollah Montazeri, Khomeini's designated heir. His brother administered Montazeri's office and helped him make influential appointments. Their father had taught Montazeri and treated him as a member of his family. Hashemi himself sat on the ruling Council of the Revolutionary Guards and served as the chair of its Ideological Committee as well as the director of its International Division. In the latter capacity, he funneled arms and money into Lebanon and Afghanistan.

Hashemi had become a cause célèbre first in 1977 when SAVAK arrested him for the vigilante murders of prostitutes, homosexuals, and drug traffickers. He had also been accused of murdering a conservative cleric who had publicly insulted Ayatollah Montazeri. At the time, the opposition defended Hashemi as an innocent victim and accused SAVAK of scheming to tarnish the reputation of the clerical establishment. He came out of prison in 1979 a religious hero.

The new regime arrested Hashemi and forty associates in May 1986. The immediate reason was his opposition to the regime's secret dealings with the United States and Israel. He had organized a street demonstration in downtown Tehran to protest the arrival of Robert McFarlane, President Ronald Reagan's secret emissary. He had also leaked news of the whole venture to a Lebanese newspaper, thereby triggering what became known as the Irangate scandal.

A month after the arrest, Khomeini assigned the case to Reyshahri, the former judge of the military tribunals who had just been appointed minister of intelligence. This new ministry had taken over the functions of SAVAK as well as those of the Second Bureau. Reyshahri's *Political Memoirs* provide a rare—albeit oblique—insider's picture of the whole investigatory process.[77] He boasts that this was his hardest case to crack as influential patrons were protecting the prisoner from his interrogators: "The monthlong investigation had come to a dead end. All they had obtained was a taped interview in which the wise guy had cleverly planted deviant ideas." Another factor made this case especially hard. As a militant Muslim, Hashemi could not be tarnished with the imperial brush. The left could be linked to the Soviets. The royalists and liberals could be linked to the West. But by no stretch of the imagination could Hashemi be linked to either the West or the Communist Bloc.

Before questioning Hashemi, Reyshahri consulted Khomeini and the Koran. Khomeini told him to treat the prisoner as he would any "grocer"—even though, as a sayyed, Hashemi was presumably a descendant of the Holy Prophet. The Koran, opened at random, produced this verse: "And [as for] those who believe and do good, We will most certainly do away with their evil deeds and We will most certainly reward them for the best of what they did." In short, the end justifies the means. Reyshahri goes on to claim that this brief exchange paved the way for the eventual "confession":

> I said: "Are you not afraid of God?"
> He said: "Yes."
> I said: "God knows what type of person you are and what you have done. You yourself know. Why don't you tell us everything?"
> He said: "I already have."
> I said: "Have you told us everything?"
> He said: "No."
> I said: "Tell us everything."
> He said: "Fine. I will tell you everything."

These memoirs, however, leave much between the lines. Reyshahri ordered his "brother investigators" to interrogate

Hashemi "thoroughly." At one point, he found him guilty of lying and, as discretionary punishment, gave him seventy-five lashes. He extracted "damaging confessions" from his forty accomplices, including his own brother. What is more, he spent a full eight months and made three different tapes before getting a satisfactory confession. Khomeini himself, as well as a select audience, previewed the final tape before having it aired on national television.

The press headlined Hashemi's confession as "I am Manifest Proof of *Monharef* [Deviation]."[78] He began with salutations to Imam Khomeini, Grand Ayatollah Montazeri, the Imam-e Zaman (The Messiah), the Victory of Islam, and the Sacred Struggle to Liberate Karbala and Jerusalem. He insisted he had initiated the interview to show fellow Muslims the dangers of straying from the narrow and straight path. Prison had given him the opportunity to reflect on his many mistakes.

Hashemi divides his mistakes into pre- and postrevolutionary categories. The former included extremism, immaturity, scholastic ignorance, eclectic thinking, and hyperactivity (*amalzadegi*). The latter included storing weapons, forging documents, criticizing the government, and sowing dissension among seminary students as well as among revolutionary guards. He had done these knowing well that the United States was determined to undermine the Islamic Republic.

> Deviation is my ultimate sin. This is why I now stand before you. I began my career with minor infractions, gradually strayed from the correct path, continued with larger mistakes, then to major sins, and ultimately to the worst sin possible—that of heresy, apostasy, and treason against the Imam, the Community, Islam, and the Islamic Revolution. I have to ask myself what was the root cause of my downfall?

His answer—sprinkled throughout the confession—is that "carnal instincts" (*nafsaniyat*) had enticed him into "illicit relations" (*ravabat*) with SAVAK and Satan. "Nafsaniyat"—a term he uses no less than eight times—means self-centeredness as well as earthly desires such as power, property, and physical pleasure. Satan here plays the same role as that of the imperialists in the previous recantations. For the secular mind, Satan is a metaphor; for the religious mind, Satan is very real. Carnal instincts had tempted him away from the seminary. Carnal instincts had led him to kill. Carnal instincts had lured him to cultivate ties with SAVAK—especially after his 1977 arrest. Carnal instincts had caused him to sow dissension among the revolutionary guards. And carnal instincts had induced him to misuse Montazeri's office. He writes, "I now realize that despicable sinners like myself had no business inside the heir-designate's office. I thank God that I have been removed from that office." Hashemi ends by pleading for forgiveness so that he can devote the rest of his life to God, the Imam, and the people.

> I would like to plead with my former colleagues and friends who shared my deviant ideas to return to the correct path, relinquish their false notions, reform themselves, unite against imperialism, and overcome the carnal instincts that can lead them toward having relations with Satan and his representatives.

Immediately after the confession, Reyshahri announced that Hashemi would be tried by a Special Clerical Court.[79] Montazeri had tried to prevent the setting up of such a court outside the normal appeals system. Reyshahri also announced that the formal charges were even more serious than those admitted in the confession. Hashemi had aided and abetted the Mojahedin. He had an ongoing relationship with SAVAK. He had smuggled opium from Afghanistan. His activities had caused considerable loss of life in Afghanistan and Lebanon as well as Iran. He had illicit relations with foreigners—these foreigners turned out to be Syrians, Libyans, Lebanese, Koreans, and Afghans. He had wished the death of the Imam so that the heir-designate would take over. To top it all, he had eliminated one of Montazeri's rivals by "inducing the spread of cancer through his body." Reyshahri claimed that years earlier the Imam had

predicted that Hashemi would some day become a "deviant."
Reyshahri also took the opportunity to dispel the "insidious
notion" that Hashemi was being punished because of his opposition to the McFarlane visit. "Those spreading this false rumor are helping the Black House [White House]."

Hashemi's trial took place in August 1987—a full fifteen
months after his initial arrest. The chief prosecutor used the
televised confession to charge him with "waging war on God,"
"sowing corruption on earth," "inciting sedition [*fetnah*]," "succumbing to Satan," and "desecrating the martyrs of the Islamic
Revolution."[80] He explained Hashemi had committed these heinous sins because of his "weak character," his "relationships
with Satan," and his "disease of eclecticism" (*bimari-e elteqati*).
In his final statement, Hashemi again pleaded guilty, congratulated the authorities for saving youth from him, and sought
forgiveness from the Imam and the "martyr-producing people
of Iran." But, he added, he would willingly accept the verdict
of the court.[81]

Hashemi was executed before the verdict was publicly announced. Reyshahri admits he rushed to preempt Montazeri's
intervention.[82] During the proceedings, Montazeri had written
to Khomeini dismissing the charges as unfair:

> I have known him inside-out since our childhood. He is a
> devout Muslim, a militant revolutionary, and a great ad-
> mirer of the Imam. He speaks well, writes well, and in
> terms of learning and organizational skills is superior to
> the head of the revolutionary guards and the Intelligence
> Minister. He is no less committed and pious than they.
> But in one respect he differs from them. He is not willing
> to obey orders blindly.[83]

Ahmad Khomeini, Reyshahri's ally, responded that Montazeri was a "poor judge of character" as the defendant himself
had testified to his crimes, his "character flaws," and "his relationships with Satan." "These confessions come out of his
own mouth."[84] Reyshahri mentions in passing that Montazeri
had not been invited to the screening of the video confession

on the grounds that he would have dismissed it as the products of "torture."[85] Despite the extremely serious nature of the charges, only one Hashemi associate was executed. The others were pardoned or given light sentences. In announcing the executions, Reyshahri declared that Hashemi had made a full confession to "purify himself before meeting his Creator." This would have been understood by the Spanish Inquisition.

Prison Life

Prison life was drastically worse under the Islamic Republic than under the Pahlavis. One who survived both writes that four months under Ladjevardi took the toll of four years under SAVAK.[86] Another writes that one day under the former equaled ten years under the latter.[87] What made it worse was the intense ideological pressure—especially for public recantations.

Prisoners were incessantly bombarded with propaganda from all sides—from the Hosseiniyeh recantations; from similar programs aired on radio and shown on closed-circuit television (television sets had been installed in October 1981 in most rooms); from loudspeakers blaring into all cells, even into solitary cells and the "coffins"; from sermons broadcast over radio and television; from ideological sessions led by repenters and visiting seminary students; from "educational television" shown every morning; from compulsory Friday prayers, Ramadan fasts, and Moharram flagellations; from pressure to vote in national elections (those refusing to participate were required to give written explanations); and from government newspapers and officially sanctioned publications such as the collected works of Ayatollahs Khomeini, Mottahari, and Dastgheib.

Secular works, including those by Shariati, not to mention Western novelists, were strictly forbidden. Secular celebrations, such as May Day and Constitutional Day, were also strictly forbidden. Ladjevardi even banned Nowruz as "a pagan Zoroastrian festival."[88] Prisoners had to observe najes rules and avoid physical contact with leftists as well as Bahais on the grounds that they were all unclean unbelievers. Women had the additional burden of having to observe the increasingly onerous dress code. They first had to wear "modest headgear"— the scarf, then the full chador, eventually the full black chador. In short, prisons became indoctrination centers; Gohar Dasht had the most sinister reputation because it was officially designated a "reformatory."

What is more, prisoners were closely watched by repenters ever eager to win privileges and their freedom. Not surprisingly, prisoners detested these *kapos* and *antenns* (antennas) on the lookout for incriminating information. Raha writes that in prison one found the worst as well as the best of humanity— those willing to betray friends and relatives, and those prepared to die for their beliefs and comrades.[89] The wardens set up a Repenters' Society, a newspaper called *Payam-e Tawabin* (Repenters' Message), and special wards named Bandeh Jehad (Crusaders' Wards). They offered them incentives—more generous rations, lighter sentences, even amnesty, and access to the prison workshops, where women could earn pocket money as garment workers and men could earn pocket money as metal workers. They also encouraged women repenters to marry eligible guards. This fueled the rumor—mostly unfounded—that they condoned sex between guards and prisoners.

To intensify the ideological pressures, prisoners were given little access to the outside world. Only official publications were permitted. Visits were restricted to ten minutes every two weeks for family members only. The conversation had to avoid prison conditions and had to be in Persian so that the listening guards could understand. Local dialects, as well as Azeri, Kurdish, and Baluchi, were strictly forbidden. Some were deprived of even these family visits. For example, Raha spent six months in Qezel Hesar away from Evin without her relatives knowing. They presumed the worst.

Other factors worsened the situation. The Iraqi war caused shortages of food and medicine. Wardens dismissed food complaints with the retort that a nation on short rations could not afford "sumptuous meals" for its internal enemies. Similarly, prison doctors withheld medicine on the grounds that the frontline troops were more deserving.

The mass arrests of 1981 turned the wards into "sardine cans."[90] In Evin, rooms initially built for fifteen contained thirty-five by early 1981 and seventy-five by late 1981. In Qezel Hesar, those built for eighteen housed forty-eight. In Gohar Dasht, those built for twelve housed ninety. At the height of the panic, thousands were jammed in the corridors, and to prevent breakouts were kept totally blindfolded around the clock. In winter, the cells were freezing. In summer, they were sweltering. Overcrowding also placed a sharp limit on time allowed in the courtyards; Evin prisoners were given no more than ten minutes per day. By early 1982, many suffered from vitamin D deficiencies. Ironically, overcrowding made solitary confinement a punishment the wardens could ill afford. Only the very important were kept in total solitary. The "coffins" were probably designed to ease this housing problem. Parsipour calculates that the twelve "solitary cells" in her wing of Qezel Hesar contained as many as 180 inmates.[91]

Mass executions turned prisons into morgues. Whereas less than 100 political prisoners had been executed between 1971 and 1979, more than 7,900 were executed between 1981 and 1985. At night inmates would count the gunshots, and the next morning compare their count with the list published in the official newspapers. Often hooded repenters stalked the wards looking for former colleagues to send to the scaffold. In Raha's words, the danger of execution constantly hovered over their heads like Damocles' sword.[92] In the prison literature of the Pahlavi era, the recurring words had been "boredom" and "monotony." In that of the Islamic Republic, they were "fear," "death," "terror," "horror," and, most frequent of all, "nightmare" (*kabos*). To further impress the prisoners, the wardens often took them to survey dead bodies. For example, when Musa Khiabani, the second in command of the Mojahedin, and Ashraf Rabii, the spouse of the first in command, were killed in a shoot-out, prisoners were bused in to Evin from Gohar

Dasht and Qezel Hesar to view their bullet-ridden bodies. National television broadcast the macabre scene together with Ladjevardi cuddling Rabii's infant son.

The harsh conditions were further compounded by the social gap between inmates and the authorities. Whereas most prisoners, particularly leftists, were children of the modern middle class, the religious magistrates came from clerical families, the wardens from the lower levels of the bazaar, and the guards from rural backgrounds—especially from the Persian-speaking Shi'i regions of central Iran. This drastically reduced social empathy. Not surprisingly, prisoners often bore the brunt of class hostility. One Fedayi writes that his warden fancied himself to be a seminary "philosopher" and harbored a "visceral hatred" for the university educated.[93] Another writes that the guards "willingly obeyed orders to mistreat them since they were rural, illiterate, and semi-educated."[94] For their part, the prisoners mocked the wardens behind their backs—especially after Ladjevardi gave a sermon denouncing that "notorious Marxist named Mr. Anti-Duhring." Ideological intensity added to the problem as many revolutionary guards—in contrast to the policemen of the bygone era—were too committed to be malleable and bribable. Modernity had worsened prison conditions in more ways than one.

Harsh conditions took their toll. Some committed suicide. In fact, those forced to recant on national television were invariably put on around-the-clock suicide watch. The chador made suicide much easier for women. Some lost their sanity. Each ward had inmates who were either clinically depressed or had lost all sense of reality. The guards—like their counterparts in nineteenth-century Europe—often brutalized them, claiming they were feigning and a sound thrashing would bring them back to reality. Prisoners often pleaded with the wardens to hospitalize the hopelessly insane—especially those who had lost control of bodily functions. One inmate who had been forced to watch the hanging of a close relative compulsively smeared feces along the cell walls. Another incessantly bleated like a sheep. Another barked like a dog. Yet another—a former teacher—constantly taught an imaginary class. One woman wore a heavy coat and full Islamic dress at all times—in the summer and even in the shower. Another—who had to be placed in solitary—refused to wear a stitch of clothing even in midwinter.

The prisoners developed various strategies to keep intact their bodies and minds. When possible, they exercised by pacing around the wards, cells, and courtyards. A few practiced yoga. They lent moral and practical support to comrades. They expanded their social networks, retaining old friendships and establishing new ones—but invariably within their own political circles. They treated all forms of sex as taboo. Parsipour writes that during the many years she spent in prison she heard of only one case of inmates having sexual relations—this despite the long sentences, the physical proximity, and the youth of most prisoners.[95] Similarly, a leftist who had spent five years in Evin told me that he had heard of only one incident of sexual misconduct. These political prisoners, like their predecessors, stressed the importance of sexual abstinence. Victorians did not have a monopoly over "Puritanism."

The prisoners made full use of the available books, newspapers, and television hours. In addition to the obligatory programs, they watched soaps, Hollywood movies, and sports—especially soccer matches. Women, however, were not allowed to watch the latter because the players wore short pants. They also improved their Arabic and English by reading the Koran and the government-published U.S. Embassy documents. On the whole, the presence of television and the absence of serious literature made these prisoners far less book-oriented than their predecessors.

When out of sight of the repenters, the prisoners practiced various forms of "passive resistance." They recited poetry; drew pictures; narrated the plots of old films and novels; and taught each other languages, especially Azeri, Kurdish, English, and French. They made fun of the religiously sanctioned books—especially Khomeini's and Dasgheib's discussions of sex. They quietly commemorated birthdays, secular holidays such as

Nowruz and May Day, and special anniversaries—especially
the martyrdom of loved ones. They also secretly learned songs
and tribal dances and played chess with homemade sets. Music
was deemed un-Islamic. Chess was banned on the grounds that
it had pagan associations and sexual connotations.

Most important of all, like-minded prisoners lived together
and jealously guarded their territory. The Mojaheds, the Bahais, the royalists, the Tudeh and the Majority Fedayi, and the
other leftists, especially the Minority Tudeh, Peykar, and
Rah-e Kargar, lived in the same wards or sections of large
wards. They ate together, shared chores, nursed their tortured
and sick colleagues, and pooled their money, cigarettes, and
even clothes. Only the royalists refused to pool their resources.
In fact, these groups formed their own komuns even though
the authorities had explicitly banned that leftist term.

Ironically, the najes rules helped demarcate the lines between Marxists and non-Marxists, repenters and nonrepenters,
Muslims and non-Muslims. Prisoners entering Gohar Dasht
were sorted out after being asked, "Do you pray or do you not
pray—like the Jews?"[96] Those with positive answers were sent
to the northern wards; those with negative answers, to the
southern wards. By 1987, blocks 2 and 12 were reserved for
Mojaheds with short sentences; 3 and 4, for Mojaheds with
more than ten-year sentences; 5, for Marxists with short sentences; 6, for Marxists with longer sentences; 7 and 8, for Marxists with sentences up to ten years; 8, for Bahais; 9, for
repenters; 11, for prisoners transferred from Kermanshah; 20,
for the Tudeh; and 13, for the mellikesh—those who had completed their sentences but had not been released because of
their refusal to give the obligatory recantations.

In most prisons, the wards administered themselves. They
elected "leaders" as well as "officials" to portion out meals, pour
tea, distribute reading materials, administer pocket money,
procure goods from the prison shop, allocate shower time,
choose the day's workers (kargars), and assign them cleaning
chores. They used the term "kargar" even though it, along with
the term "komun," had been forbidden. The elected officials

also allocated sleeping space for the night, and, to ward off lethargy and depression, prevented inmates from taking naps during the day. Moreover, the prisoners channeled all communications with the guards through their elected leaders. Violators of this code were mercilessly ostracized. E.A. explains that the code was designed to hide internal differences from the authorities.[97] Furthermore, the wards held lengthy discussions and arrived at majority decisions whenever particularly divisive issues arose—issues such as whether to allow smoking or buy foods with few vitamins, such as watermelons, what television programs to watch, how much to open the windows during winter nights, and, in the women's wards, whether to risk lice infestations by permitting long hair.

Parsipour notes that leftists and the Mojahedin—despite their ideological differences—managed to live together amicably when thrown into the same wards. E.A. describes the wards as "egalitarian and democratic." He equates the ward leader to a democratically elected president; the officials, to similarly chosen ministers, governors, and mayors. He relates how at one point the largest ward in Evin had so many issues to resolve that it convened a two-day *kongereh* (congress). The issues reflected differences between Mojaheds and Marxists, between intellectuals and nonintellectuals, between political and nonpolitical prisoners, and between poor and better-off inmates reluctant to pool their resources. Such activities helped to create a sense of solidarity within the nightmarish context.

The few who managed to survive with body and mind fully intact did so because of special circumstances. For example, Raha was deemed fairly harmless since she had been picked up because of her brother. She had a healthy and insatiable interest in others—even those from rival political groups. She—like most other women who have written prison memoirs—was determined to survive to bear witness and "to remember everything and forget nothing about the martyred." She also had family connections. Her father, a bazaar merchant, had been a devout Muslim; another relative had served in the first postrevolutionary cabinet. Her judge, who had studied theology with her father, treated her more as a wayward daughter in need of guidance than as a dangerous revolutionary. He was more than eager to release her—of course, on condition she produced the obligatory recantation. Such factors help to explain the intriguing phenomenon of why women have produced much of the recent prison literature. There is also another factor: whereas the men—invariably full party members—could not publish their memoirs unless instructed to do so by their organizations, the women, often only sympathizers, were free to record their personal experiences.

Prison conditions improved—albeit briefly—in mid-1984 when Montazeri, Khomeini's designated heir, supplanted Ladjevardi's cohorts with his own. Montazeri was rumored to have been outraged when shown photos of the "coffins." The new wardens received UN and Majles delegations. They stopped demanding religious observances and public recantations—instead they asked for short "letters of regret." They released many repenters and those who had completed their sentences. This immediately diminished the watchful eyes of the repenters, emptied Qezel Hesar of political prisoners, and alleviated the overcrowding problem in Evin and Gohar Dasht.

They were also more generous with family visits, food rations, soap, warm showers, courtyard time, and cigarettes— each prisoner, including women, was given three cigarettes a day. This was the first time women were permitted to smoke. They allowed language classes, writing materials, chess, Nowruz celebrations, and social calls to neighboring cells. They turned a blind eye to komun activities and quiet May Day celebrations. They permitted political discussions and group recreation, including volleyball, soccer, and early morning gymnastics. At first they insisted on appointing the gym leaders but relented when the prisoners demanded to elect them. They even allowed the reading of some nonreligious books, including Mowlavi, Sa'di, Pavlov, Freud, *War and Peace,* and *Les Miserables.* Somehow a work by Stalin—with his picture on the cover—circulated in the women's wards in Evin. Raha writes,

"In those days we leftists did not yet consider Stalin to be a dictator."[98]

The prisoners settled down to a daily routine. They woke up at 6.30 A.M.; had breakfast at 7.30; and from 8:00 until lunchtime attended classes. Some prepared for high school and college exams; some studied languages, especially English. The "workers" aired beds and cleaned out the cells. A few wasted time watching television. In the women's wards, some tended to their children—indeed, mothers without suitable relatives were allowed to nurse infants and raise toddlers in their cells. After lunch and the accompanying siesta, the prisoners exercised, gardened, or played team sports. Those in need of pocket money spent time in the prison workshops. After dinner, they watched television, socialized, read, and held komun meetings. Lights out was at 11:00 P.M. Parsipour, allowed to write her novel on condition she did not mention incarceration, stresses that in this period "prison conditions improved 180 degrees."[99]

By mid-1986, prisoners were openly challenging the wardens. Political prisoners in the largest Evin ward organized a successful hunger strike to remove all repenters and common criminals from their midst. Others organized another hunger strike demanding that the authorities deliver food to their doorsteps—not to the bottom of the stairs. They argued that if they picked up food at the bottom of the stairs, they would have to do endless chores throughout the prison. These chores were usually done by either repenters or Afghan prisoners. Others confronted the Evin warden on the sensitive najes issue, wanting to know how he—a German-educated engineer—could have observed such rules while living for years in Europe. They also wanted to know how dignitaries such as President Khamenei could travel throughout the world—including the communist countries—observing these "senseless rules." The warden was taken aback. Meanwhile, relatives held meetings in Luna Park demanding better prison conditions and information on those who had disappeared.

This mild period, however, ended as abruptly as it had begun. In mid-1986, most prisons were taken out of Montazeri's control and transferred back to Ladjevardi and his associates. Unbeknown to their victims, this laid the groundwork for the worst horrors yet to come—the mass executions of 1988. For the survivors, their worst "nightmares" came not in 1981–84 or in June 1981—but in the summer of 1988.

4

Tudeh Recantations

> I am Nuraldin Kianuri, the
> Chairman of the Tudeh Party. . . .
> I am not the same person I was
> when I entered prison a few
> months ago. I would like to thank
> the authorities for the opportunity
> both to study history and to
> present here my findings to the
> public, especially to the party
> youth.
> *"Kianuri Exposes Half-Century of*
> *Treachery by the Soviets, the*
> *Marxists, and the Tudeh Party,"*
> Ettela'at, *28 August 1983*

May Day 1983

On May Day 1983, television viewers were startled by the unscheduled appearance of two Tudeh leaders confessing pro-
fusely for having committed "treason," "subversion," and
miscellaneous "horrendous crimes." In the next twelve months,
eighteen others made even more sensational "revelations" in a
series of "interviews," "press conferences," and "roundtable discussions." Negating their whole lives, they recanted their beliefs, their party, their colleagues, and their own pasts. The
Tudeh protested that their leaders had been "brainwashed"
with "mind-altering drugs" provided by MI6, MOSSAD, and the

177

CIA.[1] It was as if the Tudeh could not admit—even to itself—that its leaders could have succumbed to torture. True revolutionaries were supposed to die rather than betray their ideals.

These Tudeh recantations received more publicity than all the others put together. The reasons are obvious. The regime considered Marxism the main ideological rival of Islam. Unlike liberalism, nationalism, and monarchism, it challenged religious metaphysics, held out a utopian future, and offered a comprehensive view of the past and the present. In short, it was a total ideology. Moreover, the Tudeh—despite its Soviet associations—was reputed to be the most experienced and organized of the leftist parties. Unlike the others, it could not be dismissed as a mere university mini-group. Furthermore, it contained "stars"—celebrities, established writers, veteran prisoners, and recent parliamentary candidates. These recantations, writes Parsipour, had "historic significance" for many members of the Iranian intelligentsia had at one time or another supported the Tudeh party.[2] Similarly, E.A. writes that many leftists at first gloated over the Tudeh crackdown but soon found the television recantations bewildering: "They had trouble believing their eyes and ears."[3]

Two months before these May Day recantations, some two hundred Tudeh organizers, including thirty members of the central committee, had been arrested. There has been much speculation about these arrests. Some claim that the defection of the Soviet vice-consul in Tehran to Britain led to the uncovering of a vast Tudeh "espionage" network. But in his memoirs, the vice-consul denies any link between his defection and the arrests. He also reveals profound ignorance of the Tudeh party and stresses that the KGB had explicit instructions to keep away from local communists because they were deemed to be security risks: "Every intelligence officer in the KGB knows that the Central Committee of the Soviet Communist Party categorically forbids the KGB to approach members of other communist parties."[4]

The likelier reason for the arrests was the party's increasing criticism of the regime—especially after the government closed down its newspaper, purged its members from the ministries, jettisoned some radical legislation, especially land reform, and, most serious of all, made the fatal decision in mid-1982 to take the war into Iraqi territory after the liberation of Khorram-shahr.[5] Urging acceptance of a UN peace offer, the Tudeh warned that the continuation of the war would "play into the hands of the imperialists." It also warned that the Hojjatieh Society—a highly conservative group started in the 1950s as the Association to Combat Bahaism—was infiltrating the regime to sidetrack the revolution.[6] Just before these arrests, the Tudeh had published in a Soviet paper articles criticizing the regime on these issues as well as on the sensitive question of women's rights.[7] According to the vice-consul, the Soviet government had predicted the Tudeh crackdown knowing well that the clergy, like the Bolsheviks, had no intention of tolerating rivals.[8]

The May Day program was shared by Kianuri and Behazin—two figures well known throughout Iran. Kianuri was dubbed the "Communist Ayatollah" both because he was the grandson of the famous Shaykh Fazlallah Nuri and because he had often appeared on television vociferously praising the Islamic Republic as the best bulwark against U.S. imperialism. He had been elected party chairman on the eve of the revolution after a bitter struggle with his predecessor, Iraj Iskandari, who had hoped to stem the rise of Khomeini by allying with the secular National Front. Iskandari had lost the struggle when the National Front leader himself had submitted to Khomeini.

Iskandari had disliked Kianuri ever since the early 1940s. He labeled him a "post-Stalingrad Tudehi"—that is, a newcomer who had not belonged to the Fifty-three. He associated him with his brother-in-law Kambakhsh, whom he held responsible for the arrest of Arani and the Fifty-three. What is more, he distrusted him as a dangerous adventurer who had advocated foolhardy policies and permitted Rouzbeh to carry out unauthorized actions. During Iskandari's tenure as chairman, Kianuri—as well as his wife, Maryam Firuz—had been forced out of party politics into semiretirement in East Germany. Ironically, this enmity saved Iskandari from the recantation shows. Continuing to criticize Kianuri and the Islamic Republic, he was soon forced to return to Western Europe where he died in 1991—thus becoming one of the last survivors of the Fifty-three.

Behazin, who shared the podium with Kianuri, was well known as the president of the Writers' Association. He had made his literary debut in 1941, when, as a wounded war hero, he had published a collection of short stories. Over the years, he had published more short stories and essays, translated Balzac and Sholokhov, and written an account of his 1970 prison experiences. He had also been very much in the news during the last months of the old regime when he had been rearrested for launching a pro-Tudeh paper and reviving the Writers' Association. Soon after his 1983 arrest, his wife complained to Ayatollah Montazeri that she had not been permitted to see her husband and that her son too had been arrested. "My son," she said, "is being used as a pawn against his own father."[9]

Kianuri and Behazin turned their recantations into long history lessons.[10] Surveying the last hundred years, they focused on flash points when the left had supposedly "betrayed" the people of Iran: the Constitutional Revolution of 1905–9; the Jangali Revolt of 1917–21; the rise of Reza Shah in 1921–25; the Kurdish and Azerbaijan uprisings in 1945; the Soviet oil demand and the Tudeh participation in Ahmad Qavam's government in 1946; and the campaign to nationalize the oil industry in 1951–53. Historians cannot complain that the Islamic Republic does not take the past seriously. They might, however, find its methods of revising history somewhat unorthodox. Like most ideological regimes, it harbors an unhealthy interest in history.

Behazin kicked off the program. He argued that throughout history leftists with "alien ideologies" had "betrayed" the Iranian masses. To illustrate this, he reached back to the Constitutional Revolution when secular Democrats had helped the government disarm those allied with the clerical Moderate party. As he put it, "This was our first deed of betrayal." He continued with a long list of crises in which the left had failed to stem the rightists—especially the 1953 coup and the White Revolution. "What better proof of treason than the simple fact that in 1960s the Tudeh called not for a revolution but for the establishment of a constitutional monarchy." Behazin held himself "personally responsible" for these "treasonable offenses"—some of which had occurred long before his birth. He said that Marxism had no future in Iran both because it offered nothing but empty slogans and because Islam in general and the clergy in particular had deep social roots going back "one thousand years" and concluded, "Marxism has hit a cul-de-sac. What is more, Islam with its policy of 'Neither East Nor West' can shield Iran from imperialism."

Kianuri's recantation was equally long on generalities but short on specifics. He conceded that the party had been insincere when it mouthed the slogan "Neither East Nor West": "Because of our historical links to the Soviets we did not really believe in this slogan." "This," he argued, "was the mother of all our other infringements [*takhallof-ha*]." He claimed that his recent confinement had given him the opportunity for the very first time in his life to reflect on history and understand why Islam—in contrast to Marxism—had such an attraction for the masses, especially recent migrants into the cities.[11]

As a result of intensive study, Kianuri had come to the conclusion that the communist movement had persistently erred because it was afflicted with four fatal *bemari-ha* (diseases): *vabastegi* (dependency); *idolouzhi-ye beganeh* (foreign ideology); *khodparasti* (self-worship); and *nashenakht-e Iran* (not knowing Iran). The first made the Tudeh ideologically, politically, and organizationally dependent on the Soviet Union: "We were subjects rather than comrades of the Soviet Communist party." The second gave it an alien worldview: "We tried to solve the problems of Iran with Marxism—an irrelevant ideology." The third racked the party with personal rivalries, jealousies, and power struggles: "Our party leaders, like the rest of the Iranian intelligentsia, were corrupted by egoism and selfishness." The fourth disease made communists ignorant of their nation: "We knew more about Europe than about Iran. We had no idea how our workers and peasants thought because we had not bothered to study our own history." Academics may be flattered by this equation of ignorance with "high treason." One wonders how many politicians would pass such tests.

These diseases explain the most "treasonable mistakes." In 1944, the Tudeh had supported the Soviet demand for an oil concession even though, according to Kianuri, "we had much misgivings on this issue and two months earlier had vehemently opposed the granting of a similar concession to the Americans." "This demand caused as much consternation as the Tobacco Crisis had done in 1892." In 1945, the Tudeh had supported the Soviet-sponsored revolts in Kurdestan and Azerbaijan even though their preparations had been hidden from the party itself. "Our leaders had been kept totally in the dark." In 1946, it had entered Qavam's coalition government although "it is now perfectly clear that this gentleman was an American tool." "Our entry into the coalition cabinet is clear proof of treason [*khiyanat*]." In 1948, Rouzbeh had tried to destabilize the government by assassinating the anticourt journalist Massoud. Here Kianuri mentions in passing that the "party itself was not involved in the assassination." In 1951, the Tudeh had failed to support Mossadeq, and instead had accused the oil nationalization campaign of being "dependent on the Americans." "This treacherous act was highly unpopular among the party rank and file." What is more, the four "fatal diseases" account for why the party had remained passive throughout the 1953 coup.

These maladies continued after the 1953 coup. In 1953–54, the Tudeh had "shown signs of weakness." "Some leaders even collaborated with the regime." In 1953–55, it had assassinated four police informers. In 1954, its military branch had been uncovered with disastrous consequences. "This, in effect, terminated party activities within the country." In 1963–64, it had done little to oppose the White Revolution. "Instead of forthright opposition, we said yes to reform, no to dictatorship." "This was another proof of treason as it is now clear that the sole purpose of the White Revolution was to turn Iran into a

large market for American goods." During the 1978–79 mass
protests, it had made no significant contribution to the revolution. "Our party membership inside Iran was no more than
a handful." This was yet another proof of treason. Kianuri was
embellishing errors and shortcomings into wrongdoings and
misdemeanors—then wrongdoings and misdemeanors into
treason and high crimes.

After the revolution, Kianuri continued, the Tudeh "ungrate-
fully" exploited freedom to undermine the Islamic Republic. It
pretended to support the war effort, even sending volunteers to
the front, but in reality favored the UN peace offer. "We committed treason because we did not sincerely believe in the slogan 'War, War Until Victory.' " It also pledged support for the
Islamic Republic but, at the same time, looked toward a post-
Khomeini era when it would seek more influence—even power.
"We hoped to exploit the future, especially if Iran experienced
a major socioeconomic crisis."

Kianuri described some "shameful deeds" for which he, as
party leader, took "full responsibility." After the revolution, he
instructed some party members to keep their pistols. "This was
especially serious since our frontline troops were in dire need
of weapons." He obtained from the Soviets one thousand tons
of paper—"a scarce and lucrative commodity at the time." He
recruited military personnel in clear violation of the Imam's
decree ordering all political parties to stay clear of the armed
forces. He encouraged party members to work hard and obtain
promotions in the ministries and universities. He tried to escape from the country when it became clear that the party
could no longer function. He also gave the Soviet Embassy
handwritten reports on the national and international situation. "Others members of the central committee may have had
their own lines of communication with the Soviets. But the
investigators would know more than me about this."

Kianuri went out of his way to emphasize that his appearance was voluntary and that Islam was superior to Marxism.
He ridiculed rumors "spread by foreign officials" that he had
been subjected to drugs and chemicals. "I would like to thank

the authorities for their humane treatment." He also emphasized that his intensive research into history had shown him
that Marxism was divorced from reality whereas Islam, especially the true version espoused by the progressive clergy, had
always enjoyed strong roots among the Iranian masses—from
the time of the Tobacco Crisis and the Constitutional Revolution, through the Mossadeq-Kashani era, into the Islamic Revolution. And, finally, he said,

> I would like to conclude by telling the youth, especially
> the party youth, that the mother of all our deviation and
> treason has been our links with foreign ways of thought.
> I beseech you to study Iranian society and history. . . . If
> you study diligently you will see that imperialism poses a
> serious threat to Iran. At present the threat comes in the
> form of the Iraqi aggression, but in future years it could
> come in the shape of plots and conspiracies hatched by
> the imperial powers. This is why it is the duty of all Ira-
> nians—even nonreligious ones—to rally behind the Rev-
> olution.

Although Kianuri and Behazin avoided the subject of espionage, government newspapers gave these recantations such
sensational headlines as "Tudeh Confessions of Spying for the
Soviet Union and Plotting to Overthrow the Islamic Republic";
"Kianuri Exposes Half-Century of Treachery by the Soviets, the
Marxists, and the Tudeh Party"; "Two Tudeh Leaders Make
Sensational Confessions of Spying and Plotting to Overthrow."[12] Throughout their television appearances, the two kept
their hands hidden under the table. Kianuri's hand had been
broken during his stage preparations. Behazin's had been in-
jured in World War II. In her protest letter, Mrs. Behazin complained that the authorities were trying to force her husband
to "commit ideological suicide" as well as to smear himself as
a "traitor" even though he had sacrificed his hand for his country.[13]

Immediately after Behazin and Kianuri's appearance, the
government outlawed the Tudeh on the grounds it had "spied

for foreigners," "infiltrated the ministries and the armed forces," "incited factory strikes," "stored arms to overthrow the Islamic Republic," and "established contact with groups warring against God"—this probably referred to the Mojahedin or the Hashemi group.[14] The regime ordered party members to turn themselves in. Some one thousand party members were apprehended.[15] The same was soon done to the Majority Fedayi on the grounds that it was closely identified with the Tudeh. The same was also done to a small anti-Tudeh Trotskyist group.

In an evenhanded denunciation, Khomeini pronounced both the Bahais and the Tudeh to be "foreign spies" and declared that the Tudeh leaders themselves had "come forward to expose their own pasts": "These gentlemen are in prison not because of their views but because of their espionage activities."[16] In a long series of editorials entitled "Confession," *Ettela'at* declared these disclosures to be "unprecedented in world history" and to be "living proof of Islam's strength":

> No one else has been able to obtain confessions revealing such a large spy network—not even the Shah with all his foreign experts, surveillance equipment, modern police tactics, and up-to-date interrogation methods. Under the Shah, such criminals would spend years in prison without confessing their crimes. But under the Islamic Republic, they are willing to make full disclosures after a few brief months. What better proof of Islam's moral superiority.[17]

The chief prosecutor claimed that the confessions showed the Tudeh had "declared war on God" and was so despicable that it had "betrayed" even the Soviet Union as well as the Islamic Republic. He added that according to the sharia the eventual punishment for those who had declared war on God could be lightened if they came forward willingly and repented before their trials began. "Late repentance will not lessen the retribution. The sharia has strict rules against those who war against God."[18] Ayatollah Janati, the Imam Jom'eh of Qom, declared that the arrests were more important than the takeover of the "U.S. spy den" on the grounds that the Tudeh had been trying to "steal our youth" and spread "corruption" (*fasad*) and "unrest" (*fetnah*) throughout the land.[19] Ayatollah Taheri, the Imam Jom'eh of Isfahan, congratulated the government for saving youth from such a "filthy and corrupt organization."[20]

Hojjat al-Islam Hojjati-Kermani, a former Bani-Sadr supporter, was even more laudatory. Without any sense of irony, he "congratulated the Imam and the community for their great ideological victory," arguing that the confessions buried once and for all the corpse of "historical materialism" and showed to all the towering superiority of Islam. "The leaders of the Fedayan-e Islam—unlike these atheists—died rather than give up their ideals. No doubt, some communists will try to escape the proscribed fate for apostates by claiming to have been born Jewish."[21] Hojjati-Kermani considers himself to be a modern-thinking cleric.

Equally revealing were the comments that poured forth from émigré intellectuals, exiled newspapers, and rival political parties. Like the Moscow trials, the confessions generated much heat but little analysis. Few linked them to torture and prison brutality. Most cited them to reinforce their own predispositions toward the Tudeh. In other words, even enemies of the regime used the occasion to blame the victims—not to scrutinize the regime itself. For example, the Mojahedin claimed that the show had been staged to mislead the public into thinking the real opposition was the Tudeh. It added that the Tudeh deserved to end up on "Khomeini's dungheap" because it had "opportunistically supported—even spied for—his medieval bloodthirsty dictatorship."[22] The royalists argued that the Tudeh leaders were playing a "clever game" so as to continue propagating their antimonarchist propaganda.[23] This echoed their bizarre claim that the Islamic Republic was a front organization for the Kremlin. They also argued that the confessions merely confirmed the common knowledge that the Tudeh was nothing more than an "espionage network." One royalist even contrasted the recanters with their 1950s' predecessors such as Rouzbeh who had chosen to die for their beliefs.[24]

The Minority Fedayi declared the recantations to be a major defeat not for Marxists but for foolish "revisionists" who had refused to heed their warning that Khomeini was out to create a "bourgeois dictatorship."[25] To support their point, they reprinted a secret 1981 government memo outlining plans to round up all leftists, including those supporting the regime. The Liberation Movement, the party closest to Western liberalism, declared that the confessions confirmed what it had been saying about the Tudeh for the last forty years—that it was inherently a "treacherous organization." It added that the Tudeh fate was predictable for those who had taken the trouble to read the Holy Koran.[26]

Even those familiar with the Moscow trials failed to place these confessions in their context. Jahanshahlu, a member of the Fifty-three who had recently broken with the Tudeh, completed his two-volume memoirs by declaring that these "traitors" were merely "spilling the beans about their Russian masters."[27] Iskandari, the former party chairman, argued that the likes of Kianuri had already moved so close to the regime that a "small nudge" was enough to get them to produce such ridiculous statements.[28] Hajj Sayyed-Javadi—a veteran Maleki supporter—wrote that these recantations confirmed that the Tudeh knew nothing about Marxism and that Maleki had been right in his denunciations of Stalinism.[29] Bahman Bakhtiari, a professor of political science in America, managed to write a whole article on the crackdown without dwelling unnecessarily on such unseemly subjects as torture and prison brutality.[30] Similarly, Professor Sephr Zabih—the in-house expert on Iranian communism at the Hoover Institution—treated these "pathetic" confessions as confirming the well-known truths about KGB-Tudeh links.[31] He speculated that the Tudeh leaders had given these history sketches to "flatter Khomeini" and "cultivate favor with the Islamic Republic." Presumably those who had ascended to the auto-da-fé had done so to "flatter" the Inquisition.

Television Confessions (May–September 1983)

Immediately after the Kianuri-Behazin show, eight other members of the central committee made their own separate television appearances. Their statements were equally ambiguous, the newspaper headlines equally sensational: "Members of the Central Committee Confess to Spying for the KGB"; "Tudeh Created for the Sole Purpose of Espionage"; "Tudeh Leaders Confess to Treason"; "Confessions Unprecedented in World History."

Ghulam-Hossein Qaempanah, an army officer who had escaped to the Soviet Union in 1950, gave the longest of the eight statements. He began by admitting that during his twenty-nine-year exile he had "some dealings" with the KGB.[32] It would be hard to imagine a political exile in the Soviet Union for so long without some such dealings. He then digressed into another history lesson, starting with the early 1920s, going through the 1940s, and ending with the Soviet invasion of Afghanistan in 1979. "Our policies over these years," he said, "prove that we are linked to the Soviets." He added that the Soviet Communist party gave financial assistance to the Tudeh and monitored its important central committee meetings. "What better evidence of treason than the closing down of our radio station in 1961 to facilitate the Soviet rapprochement with the Shah?" He further added that after the revolution party cells began their weekly meeting with an exchange of news and information. Significant information was then passed to the central committee. Kianuri, in turn, passed some of this information to the Afghan and Soviet embassies. "Sometimes one needs a sudden shake to wake up from deep sleep. I woke up in prison, opened my eyes, and saw that over the years I had fallen into a treacherous quicksand."

Rafat Mohammadzadeh, a gendarmerie officer who had participated in the sensational 1950 escape from Qasr, seems to have hardly spoken. The press published a two-sentence summary of his supposed acknowledgment that "he had joined the KGB as soon as he had reached the Soviet Union in July 1951."[33] In fact, the KGB had not come into existence until March 1954. Like many others, Mohammadzadeh had spent much of his long exile working for a doctorate. He had also helped to edit the party's journal *Donya* and contributed social science articles to it.

Gagik Ovanessian, a printer who had spent much of the 1960s in prison, was equally taciturn, merely stating that after the revolution he often hand-carried reports from Kianuri to the Soviet Embassy.[34] No relative of Ardashir Ovanessian from the Reza Shah period, Gagik Ovanessian was now the only Tudeh leader with a Christian background. He was a childhood friend of the Kianuris from Qazvin. Maryam Firuz considered him "her elder brother."[35]

Mohammad-Ali Rasadi, another army officer who had lived in exile for thirty-three years, admitted that while in Baku Soviet officials had at times consulted him about the internal workings of the Tudeh party. Again the newspaper summary claimed that he had admitted to being recruited "into the KGB in 1951."[36] In 1945, Rasadi and two dozen officers in Khurasan had launched an ill-fated mutiny without even consulting the Tudeh party.

Kiamars Zarshenas, who had joined the party in 1961 as a university student and still headed the youth branch, declared that history, especially Qavam's 1946 coalition cabinet, proved that the Tudeh was linked to the Soviet Union. "After the revolution we tried to undermine the regime by substituting the slogan 'Independence, Freedom, and the Islamic Republic' with 'Independence, Freedom, and Social Justice.' "[37]

Manoucher Behzadi, a party member since his law school days in 1943, had emigrated in 1954, received a doctorate in economics from East Germany, and returned in 1979 to edit the party organ *Mardom*. He argued that the Tudeh had a minimum and a maximum program.[38] The former was to win over the public by glossing over the differences between Islam and Marxism and by demanding land reform, workers' councils, and student organizations. The latter was to overthrow the regime by inflaming class hatreds and aggravating internal differences among the clergy. He added that the first time he learned of these sinister goals was in prison—after his arrest.

Reza Sheltouki, an air force officer imprisoned from 1954 until 1978, declared that "he had no choice but to confess to treason."[39] You may well ask, he said, why someone like himself, who spent twenty-four years tortured in the Shah's prisons, should now come forward and make a voluntary confession. The answer, he continued, is simple: we either confess our crimes or else remain forever banished from the revolutionary movement. He added that one should distinguish between SAVAK and the present wardens who are "considerate," "fruits of the masses," and "use plain everyday language to explain the importance of repentance." Without actually acknowledging espionage, he declared that *jasousi* (spying) was one of the most shameful words in the whole language: "It is so repugnant that I have trouble bringing myself to say the word."

Finally, Amoui—famous for his twenty-four-year imprisonment—declared the party to be "replete with treason."[40] While pledging support, it had tried to subvert the Islamic Republic. It had submitted to the government an incomplete list of its central committee. It had not really believed in "Neither East Nor West." It had created an armed underground organization. And it had been linked to the Soviets from the very beginning. "The best proof of this is the simple fact that in 1942 the Tudeh established its first cells in the Soviet-occupied zone." He concluded by thanking the authorities for dissolving such a "treacherous" organization. Hojjati-Kermani commented that of all the recantations Amoui's was the most sensational: "I know Mr. Amoui from prison. He was a true believer in Marxism. He considered the Tudeh to be his whole life—his family, his father, his mother, his wife, his child. . . . His recantation signifies the total triumph of Islam over Marxism."[41]

Once these appearances were over, *Ettela'at* published an article by a Tehran University professor proclaiming that these confessions proved beyond doubt that the Tudeh was linked not only with the Soviet Union but also with the United States. For the Tudeh and the United States, he argued, have the same long-range goal—to contain and roll back the Islamic movement sweeping across the whole world. "This is why we should consider the Tudeh to be the conspiratorial weapon of both East and West."[42] The United States must have more friends than it realizes.

Roundtable Discussion (October 1983)

These solo performances were followed in October with a "roundtable discussion" of seventeen top leaders. This was televised in three ninety-minute segments; and then their transcripts were circulated widely through newspapers, journals, even pamphlets with color illustrations.[43] Meanwhile, videotapes of the whole event were repeatedly shown in Iranian consulates throughout the world. This was video recantation par excellence, both in production and in distribution.

The event was staged in the Evin lecture hall. Its high walls were decked for the occasion with large banners declaring "Death to the Soviets," "Death to America," "Neither East Nor West," "We don't accept as Iranians those who sacrifice their Islamic and national values for the U.S. and the USSR." The seventeen sat cowed under the banners looking repentant and forlorn. But they had in front of them microphones and water cups—as if at an academic meeting or a press conference.

Among the seventeen were seven who had already appeared—Kianuri, Behzadi, Qaempanah, Amoui, Rasadi, Sheltouki, and Ovanessian. The other ten were all members of the central committee. Some were well-known nationally, having run recently for the Majles or the Assembly of Experts. Dr. Hossein Jowdat, the oldest, was the Sorbonne-educated physicist who had escaped from Qasr in 1950. His elder brother, an army officer who had joined the Azerbaijan revolt, had been executed in 1946. He himself had lived in exile since 1955.

Abbas Hejri, another army officer, had spent twenty-five years in prison together with Amoui and Sheltouki. Mohammad Pourhormozan and Mehdi Kayhan, two survivors of the 1945 Khorasan mutiny, had lived in exile from 1946 until 1979. Ali Galavij, originally from the Kurdish Democratic party, had fled to the Soviet Union after the collapse of the 1946 Kurdish revolt. He had joined the Tudeh in 1960 while studying for a doctorate. Similarly, Anushirevan Ibrahimi, who had a doctorate in history, had made his way to the Soviet Union in 1946 after the collapse of the Azerbaijan government. His elder brother had been the justice minister in that government and had been executed in 1946. Their father had been a founding member of the Communist party and had been killed in the Jangali Revolt.

Farajollah Mizani, another recent returnee from the Soviet Union, had joined the Tudeh in 1945 while studying at Tehran University. He had escaped to the Soviet Union in 1957 where he had obtained a doctorate in Persian literature while helping Noshin reinterpret the *Shahnameh* as a radical antiroyalist epic. He had also headed the party's clandestine radio station *Payk-e Iran* (Iran's Messenger), which had been located first in East Germany and then in Bulgaria. He was a regular contributor to *Donya* under the pen name F. M. Javanshir.

Assef Razmdedeh, a factory worker, had been arrested in the early 1970s for organizing illegal unions and had been kept in Qasr even after completing a seven-year prison sentence. Finally, Mehdi Partovi and Shahroukh Jahangeri, both former Fedayis, had joined the party while in prison, and during the revolution had been instrumental in setting up an underground armed network for the Tudeh. Although modest in size, this network had played a role in the final February 1979 confrontation with the royalist forces. Partovi and Jahangeri were the only members of the seventeen who were under forty years of age.

These seventeen reflect the social composition of the top Tudeh leadership in the 1980s. Their average age was fifty-six. Jowdat was seventy-five; Kianuri, sixty-eight. Seven were former military officers—three of them had each spent twenty-four years in prison. Fourteen had graduated from institutions of higher learning—seven from military academies, six from the Soviet Union, and two from Western Europe. Fifteen came from the salaried middle class. Only two were workers—a typesetter and a factory worker. In terms of ethnicity, the group contained eight Azeris, seven Persians, one Kurd, and one Armenian. Like the early communist movement—but unlike the early Tudeh party—the Azeri component was pronounced. (See table 7.)

Some prominent members of the central committee were conspicuous by their absence from the roundtable. Behazin had disappeared from public view after the May Day program. He spent the next few years in prison translating Roman Rolland's epic novel *Jean-Christophe*, which he renamed *The Free Spirit*. Ehsan Tabari—the party's main theorist—had suffered a stroke and was being nursed for a later appearance. Taqi Keymanash, another officer who had spent twenty-four years in prison, had died during his interrogation. So had thirteen others.[44] Maryam Firuz, the head of the women's branch and Kianuri's spouse, was also absent despite her well-known name— she had recently run for both the Majles and the Assembly of Experts. It is not clear whether her absence was due to clerical sensitivity about women participating in such shows—especially at the same table as men—or due to the fact that her interrogation had left her ear and spine permanently impaired. She had trouble hearing and sitting.[45]

The roundtable discussion reads like a parody of public recantations. Amoui—respected because of his twenty-four-year imprisonment—chaired. He opened and closed the meetings but otherwise said little. His introduction saluted the Great Leader of the Revolution, the Founder of the Islamic Republic as well as the Heroic and Honorable People of Iran, and the generous volunteers fighting the Baathist invaders from Iraq. He sought forgiveness for all the participants, arguing that these discussions proved beyond doubt that the Tudeh had "links with the Soviets" and that Marxism had "failed to find roots among the Muslim masses." He concluded, "You viewers, like us, must put yourself at the service of the Imam."

The others opened with similar salutations, sketched their own political careers, and insisted that their presence was entirely voluntary. Kianuri ridiculed the rumor that he had been executed and repeated that he had changed his views not because of coercion but because of "confronting the truth in prison." Ovanessian joked that the rumor of this death was much exaggerated. Mizani dismissed reports that he had been subjected to drugs supplied by MOSSAD: "Our discussions with

Table 7

Tudeh Roundtable Discussants, October 1983

Name & Dates	Profession	Higher Education	Place of Birth	Past	Fate
Kianuri, Nuraldin (1915–)	Professor-architect	Germany	Mazandaran	Exile 1955–79	Prison 1983–
Behzadi, Manoucher (1927–88)	Journalist	Tehran Univ. & USSR Ph.D.	Tehran	Exile 1954–79	Executed 1988
Jowdat, Hossein (1908–88)	Professor of physics	France	Tabriz	Exile 1955–79	Executed 1988
Qaempanah, Ghulam (1923–)	Officer	Academy	Tabriz	Exile 1951–79	Prison 1983–
Amoui, Mohammad (1923–)	Officer	Academy	Kermanshah	Prison 1954–79	Prison 1983–
Sheltouki, Reza (1926–85)	Officer	Academy	Kermanshah	Prison 1954–79	Died in prison
Hejri, Abbas (1922–88)	Officer	Academy	Mashed	Prison 1954–78	Executed 1988
Rasadi, Ahmad (1915–88)	Officer	Academy & USSR Ph.D.	Rasht	Exile 1946–79	Executed 1988
Pourhormozan, Mohammad (1920–88)	Officer	Academy & USSR Ph.D.	Tehran	Exile 1946–79	Executed 1988

Name	Occupation	Education	City	Status	Fate
Kayhan, Mehdi (1915–88)	Officer	Academy & USSR Ph.D.	Mashed	Exile 1946–79	Executed 1988
Ibrahimi, Anushirevan (1927–88)	Teacher	USSR Ph.D.	Astara	Exile 1946–79	Executed 1988
Ovanessian, Gagik (1920–88)	Printer	None	Qazvin	Prison 1954–64	Died in prison
Mizani, Farajollah (1925–88)	Engineer	Tehran University & USSR Ph.D.	Tabriz	Exile 1957–79	Executed 1988
Razmdedeh, Assef	Worker	None	Ardabel	Prison 1965–79	Executed 1988
Galavij, Ali	Teacher	USSR Ph.D.	Kurdestan	Exile 1946–79	Prison 1983–
Jahangeri, Shahroukh (1948–84)	Teacher-taxi driver	Tehran University	Rasht	Fedayi	Executed 1984
Partovi, Mehdi (1948–)		Tehran University		Fedayi	Amnestied

our prison guards convinced us that the revolution had made great strides for the masses—especially for the recent migrants into the cities." Sheltouki declared that in prison he had realized that all these years he had been reading the wrong type of books: "The simple fact is that Iran and Marxism-Leninism are diametrically different in all aspects—in ideology, thought, psychology, sociology, and way of life."

Kayhan declared that the guards had psychologically disarmed him with their deep and sincere respect for the toiling masses: "Prison woke us up and made us conscious of the enormity of our crimes. . . . Prison gave us the lash of truth [*shalaq-e haqayeq*]." Behzadi declared that he was there to bear witness to the young generation and to show what happens when one wanders from the narrow and straight path. Partovi thanked the wardens for their humanitarian consideration, and argued that history proved torture could never change the convictions of the truly committed. Jowdat described his prison experiences as "highly educational" and thanked the mothers of his guards for having brought into the world such "upright, honest, and considerate human beings." It is not clear how many viewers caught the irony.

In presenting negative propaganda against themselves, they reiterated the litany of historical episodes when the left had supposedly "betrayed" the nation—again beginning with 1905 and ending with the war against Iraq. In doing so, they observed a vague division of labor, with each focusing on his own field of party expertise.

Kianuri repeated more or less his earlier history lesson, stressing that lack of intellectual sophistication had led the Tudeh to persistently "betray the nation." He also "revealed some historical secrets." The Soviets had apparently "created" the Fifty-three. The Tudeh had contemplated supporting Shariatmadari against Khomeini. The central committee had eliminated from Rouzbeh's last testament any reference to his assassination exploits—especially those of Massoud and Lankrani. "We wanted to portray Rouzbeh as a revolutionary martyr with no blemishes whatsoever." Little of this was either new or proof of treason.

Meanwhile, Jowdat went over the Lankrani murder. Ibrahimi insinuated that Pishevari had hatched the Azerbaijan revolt because of his personal disputes with the Tudeh and because of his failure to get elected to the first party congress. Galavij claimed that imperialists wanted to create a united Kurdestan and that the Tudeh had done its best to woo members away from Kumaleh and the Kurdish Democratic party. Pourhormozan complained that whereas the Tudeh had persistently supported the Soviets, the Soviets had equally persistently failed to help the Tudeh.

Qaempanah claimed that "the KGB began recruiting from the Firqeh and the Tudeh as soon as these parties fled to the Soviet Union." "They wanted information on our internal working and were particularly fearful of Maoism." Partovi acknowledged that after the Islamic Revolution the Tudeh had retained some weapons and refused to disband its underground network. Rasadi stated that the Soviets were eager to obtain information on the political situation in Iran—especially on such politicians as Bani-Sadr. Kayhan admitted working for the Voice of the Iranian People, a Soviet-financed radio station. He added that this station had supported the invasion of Afghanistan, the arming of Saddam Hossein, and the White Revolution—the last would have been news to the Shah. He further added that the Tudeh—presumably unlike the Islamic Republic—had a "cult of personality" and believed in "blind obedience to its leader." Finally, Hejri thanked the authorities for dissolving the party and declared that during his twenty-five-year imprisonment he had never once imagined he would end up in his present predicament.

Although these presentations used such loaded terms as KGB, *khiyanat* (treason), *beganeh* (foreigners), *jasousi* (espionage), *fetnah* (sedition), *touteh* (conspiracy), *barandakhtan* (overthrow), and *vabasteh-e khareji* (foreign dependency), they contained nothing earthshaking. It was common knowledge that the Tudeh advocated Marxism; failed to forestall the 1953 coup; communicated with the Soviets; and consistently supported the Soviet Union, which support sometimes put it on a collision course with the nationalists. But it is unlikely that they considered these "proofs of treason"—unless, of course, one drastically stretches the definition of treason. In which case, many others, including Khomeini, would be vulnerable to the charge of treason. After all, he—like most clerics—had failed to support Mosaddeq against the Shah and the CIA.

The only hard evidence presented at the roundtable were acknowledgments by Partovi, Ovanessian, and Qaempanah that they had hand-carried sealed reports from Kianuri to the Soviet Embassy. But it was not clear whether these contained top secret military information—as the government claimed— or merely Kianuri's views on the political situation—as Kianuri himself insisted. Whatever the truth, they formed the linchpin of the forthcoming tribunal against 101 defendants—most of them from the armed forces. In later years, Kianuri explained that two of his many reports had discussed military matters: one had dealt with American F14 planes; another with a Soviet submarine that had sunk in the Persian Gulf before the revolution. But he did not consider this "espionage" because these reports affected the security of the United States—not that of Iran. Kianuri reminded his audience that the Imam himself had described the United States as "the main enemy of Iran."[46]

These seventeen were to meet different fates. Kianuri, Amoui, and Qaempanah remained incarcerated for over a decade. Kianuri and Amoui survived to publish their memoirs— of course, leaving out their recent prison experiences. Kianuri's memoirs were even published under the auspices of the Islamic Republic. Ovanessian and Sheltouki soon "died" in Evin. Partovi was pardoned and given a publishing house. Jahangeri was executed in 1984. The others—Hejri, Behzadi, Rasadi, Pourhormozan, Kayhan, Ibrahimi, Mizani, Razmdedeh, and the eighty-year-old Jowdat—perished in the 1988 executions.

Military Trials (December 1983–January 1984)

The 101 were brought before a Military Tribunal in late 1983. Their judge was Hojjat al-Islam Reyshahri—Mehdi Hashemi's chief interrogator. Although the press gave extensive coverage, it never revealed the tribunal's location. The court walls displayed a well-known Khomeini quotation: "America Is Worse than Britain. Britain Is Worse than America. The Soviets Are Worse than Both." The defendants were charged with "sowing corruption on earth," "spying for a foreign power," "stockpiling arms," "plotting to overthrow the Islamic Republic," and "violating the edict against political activities in the armed forces."[47] The press portrayed the trial as one of espionage. But the court itself focused on subversion—especially plotting to overthrow the Islamic Republic.

The defendants included a number of stars: Admiral Bahram Afzali, the commander of the victorious navy in the Gulf War; Colonel Houshang Attarian, a special assistant to the war minister; Colonel Bezhan Kabiri, a decorated field commander from the war front; Colonel Hassan Azarfar, a professor at the Military Academy; Colonel Seifallah Ghiasund, a medical doctor who had also recently returned from the front; and Colonel Abul-Qassem Afrayi, a gendarmerie officer who had been decorated for his refusal to shoot into the crowds during the revolution. Most of the others were young officers, sergeants, and air force technicians.

The prosecutor presented Kianuri and Partovi as "state witnesses." Throughout the proceedings, Kianuri spoke in generalities about how the Tudeh had always depended on the Soviets, failed to study history, and aspired to reach power some day. He also stressed that he, as party chairman, was willing to take full responsibility for all mistakes. Partovi, however, was a cooperative witness, detailing how Kianuri had created an armed underground organization and sent reports to the Soviet Embassy. His evidence helped to seal the fate of some of his colleagues—including that of his younger brother.

Before the trial started, the military prosecutor declared that the earlier television confessions had already established the fact that Tudeh was guilty of "treason," "espionage," and "subversion." The newspaper headlines declared: "Tudeh Leaders Confess to Spying"; "Tudeh Plotted to Turn Iran into Another Afghanistan"; "Tudeh Gave the Soviets Information About Iran's Secret Missiles"; and "Authorities Uncover the Largest Spy Network in the Whole World."

Despite extensive preparations and exclusion of foreign reporters, the trial was not as well managed as the previous television recantations. The numbers involved made it somewhat unwieldy. Instead of providing the media with videotapes, the regime published summaries of the proceedings in the main newspapers. These summaries give inklings of the problems involved in stage managing such a large cast.

At first glance, the defendants appear to be acknowledging the serious charges. They use such terms as "treason," "treachery," "sins," "crimes," "guilt," "betrayal," "shame," "dishonor," "subversion," and "deserved punishments." They submit to the regime, thank the wardens, recognize the legitimacy of the tribunal, and praise the ultimate wisdom of the Imam. They beat their chests, beseech forgiveness, and seek a second chance to serve the people, the revolution, and the Imam. One defendant hoped that Imam Khomeini would continue to live until the reappearance of the Hidden Imam. Another declared that he had full trust in the tribunal because he knew it had given fair hearings to previous defendants. Yet another pleaded to be sent to the war front so he could die there and thus remove from himself and his family the stain of being a "traitor" and a "spy"—"the two most shameful words in our language."

Closer scrutiny, however, reveals ambiguities, hidden meanings, and double entendres. Those—including Western scholars—who read only the headlines came away convinced that the defendants had pleaded guilty to the charges. Those who read beyond the headlines are less sure. Some defendants retracted their signed confessions. Others diluted them with so many qualifications and explanations as to make them harmless. One refused to participate in the proceedings. At one point, the judge abruptly recessed the proceedings on the pretext that the electrical system had failed. At other points, the judge and the prosecutor cut off the defendants in the middle of their statements because they had clearly wandered from the expected script. Some managed to drop the information that their wives and daughters had also been arrested. Others proclaimed that "their eyes had been opened in court" and that "the first they had heard of espionage was in prison."

On the whole, the confessions were big on mea culpa but small on incriminating facts. Kianuri admitted that he had instructed the Tudeh underground to hide some two hundred handguns. He himself had purchased from a foreign engineer eight pistols and a radio receiver. And he had sent memos to the Soviet Embassy. But he drastically qualified each admission. The memos dealt with political—not security—issues. The underground organization was designed to forestall a royalist coup—not to overthrow the Islamic Republic. "The 1953 fiasco had to be avoided at all cost." The radio receiver and pistols were to facilitate escape in case of a military crackdown. He added that two hundred pistols could hardly threaten the powerful Islamic Republic. He further added the Tudeh hoped to come to power some day—but only if the Islamic Republic had already collapsed. "The Tudeh—like any real political party—intends to come to power some day." For some, this was a confession of subversion. For others, it was a self-evident fact of political life.

Admiral Afzali implicitly ridiculed the notion that a small organization could overthrow the mighty Islamic Republic. He acknowledged talking to Kianuri about the sunken Soviet submarine but added that this had no military significance as the accident had occurred two years earlier. He acknowledged other conversations with Kianuri but added that these dealt merely with politics and Bani-Sadr's "detrimental policies." He declared that he had joined the Tudeh to "help the country, the revolution, and the people of Iran." He added that he had not concealed his pro-Tudeh sympathies as he had been an active party member in the early 1950s. He denied spying, adding cryptically that the "very first time he heard of such activities was after his arrest." He beseeched the judge to undertake the task of defending him because he himself had no legal training. Of course, none of the defendants had legal counsel.

Colonel Attarian conceded that he had joined the Tudeh in violation of the Imam's edict. But he categorically denied spying and plotting against the state. He admitted that he had compiled reports for the central committee but explained that he had relied only on public sources such as newspapers—not on military documents. At this point, the prosecutor interjected to explain that the definition of "espionage" was not the passing of "confidential" information but of any information. "The definition of spy is someone who passes to foreigners any information whatsoever." This brief interjection spoke volumes.

Colonel Kabiri declared that he would accept any verdict the judge handed down but denied the charges and stressed that he had never hidden his sympathies for the Tudeh—even when fighting at the front. Colonel Azarfar denounced himself as a "traitor" on the grounds that he had had reservations about continuing the war into Iraq. "I realize now that I must support the government wholeheartedly." Colonel Ghiasund confessed that he had written a report on war casualties, but in doing so had merely used data published in the daily newspapers. He categorically denied that the party had asked him for secret data. Likewise, retired Colonel Afrayi argued he had no secrets to give and asked why the authorities had not banned the Tudeh earlier if it was such an evil "anti-Islamic organization." Another colonel pleaded that he had given money to the Tudeh not realizing it true nature. At this point, the prosecutor exclaimed: "How can an educated person like you claim you are ignorant of the atheistic nature of the Tudeh party. Only uneducated simpletons could think that Marxism is compatible with Islam." This belied the official claim that the defendants were being prosecuted for espionage and subversion—not for political beliefs.

Many managed to smuggle in pro-Tudeh propaganda. Most

stressed that they had joined the Tudeh because it was the only party supporting the revolution and the republic. Some repeated the claim that the party had created the secret organization for use only against a possible royalist counterrevolution. The regime could hardly dismiss this as absurd as it claimed to live in permanent fear of such a counterrevolution. Some declared that the money collected from membership dues went to feed the unemployed. One noted that Admiral Afzali had sold family lands in Qom to aid those who had lost their jobs. Another argued that he had no intention of "defending" himself because he did not consider the party to be an enemy of the Islamic Republic. Yet another declared that he had joined the Tudeh because it was the only party at the time to "champion the rights of the peasantry."

The tribunal handed down uneven sentences. It condemned ten to death; six to life imprisonment; twelve to terms ranging from fifteen to thirty years; nineteen to terms ranging from eight to fourteen years; eight to seven years; thirty to five years; and thirteen to less than five years. The condemned—including Admiral Afzali as well as Colonels Attarian, Kabiri, and Azarfar—were executed in February 1984. Nineteen others—including two who had completed their sentences—perished in the 1988 executions.[48]

At a press conference convened to announce the ten executions, Reyshahri declared that he had been lenient with some despite the enormity of their crimes because their cooperation and recantations had proved the sincerity of their repentance.[49] When a French reporter asked if the government had more evidence than that presented in the newspapers, he answered in the affirmative, adding that some of the proof was too sensitive to show in open court. When a Japanese correspondent asked why the numbers of those sentenced did not tally with those originally brought to trial, he hedged—it was rumored some had died during their interrogation. When an Iranian reporter noted that some foreign correspondents were intrigued about why so many diehard communists would repent their sins, he replied that he too had been "surprised." But he added that psychologists could understand why even hardened "materialists" repent when confronted by "upright Islamic officials":

> One of the revolution's greatest assets is the ability to get criminals to look at their own nature and discard the veils of deception that cover their eyes. As many of the defendants have admitted, they had been blind before their arrest, but in prison they have seen the light. In short, to answer your question, one has to know something about psychology.

Koestler's Ivanov too had flattered himself as an amateur psychologist.

Tabari's Recantations

The grand finale of the Tudeh recantations came in May 1984. It came in the shape of Tabari—the party's main theoretician—making a television appearance. He began by explaining that he was reading his statement and speaking with a slur because he had recently suffered a stroke.[50] He then gave a biographical sketch stressing both his clerical lineage and his fifty-year leftist experiences—beginning with his acquaintance with Arani and the Fifty-three; continuing with his role in the founding of the Tudeh and his 1944 election to the central committee; and ending with his thirty-year exile in Eastern Europe where he had edited *Donya* and written books on Marxism, Iranian history, Persian literature, and Islamic philosophy.

Tabari declared that his recent confinement had exposed him for the very first time to the works of great Islamic thinkers, especially Ayatollah Motahhari—Khomeini's favorite "martyred" disciple. Giving a reading list of Motahhari's works, he argued that these books had led him first to question his own convictions and eventually to repudiate the works he had written over the past forty years. He now realized that his entire life's work was "defective," "damaging," and "totally spurious" because it had all been based on unreliable thinkers—Freemasons nourished by the Pahlavis; secularists such as Ahmad Kasravi; Western liberals and Marxists linked to "imperialism and Zionism"; and, of course, Soviet Marxists wedded to the notion that Iran had experienced feudalism. "Marxism is not applicable to Iran for the simple reason that our country has a history of oriental despotism—not of feudalism." Presumably feudalism—but not oriental despotism—was a Marxist notion.

Tabari also argued that he now realized that historical materialism was not an exact science, as Marx and Engels had claimed. On the contrary, it was a form of dogmatic Machiavellianism subscribing to the amoral notion that the "end justifies the means." Motahhari, however, had proved that Islam was the exact opposite, and that the Marxist paradigm of economic base and ideological superstructure is wrong because ideas and religions are as important as matter, economics, and the mode of production. "Historical materialism—unlike Shi'ism—cannot explain phenomena such as Spartacus and Pugachef." Tabari's prison experiences must rival those of Saul on the road to Damascus.

In addition to repudiating his own works, Tabari repeated the long history lessons presented by the previous Tudeh leaders—especially Kianuri and Behazin. The Iranian left, he argued, had failed because it had not appreciated the importance of religion and had dismissed clerical leaders such as Kuchek Khan, Modarres, and Kashani as "reactionaries," "petty bourgeois," and "representatives of the landed classes." He also stressed that the "confessions" he had seen on television had convinced him that the party had "plotted" to overthrow the Islamic Republic and had always served as a "Soviet spy network." "These confessions prove the Tudeh has no future in Iran. It leaves behind nothing but a black mark."

Tabari's recantation is conspicuous by its frequent references to religion. While the others had applauded the clergy for mobilizing the masses against imperialism, Tabari praised Islam for its "great spiritual strength." He opened with "In the Name of God the Merciful, the Compassionate." He ended with the Koranic verses "God helps those who follow the right path" and "God the merciful forgives those who repent, reform, and proclaim the truth." He sprinkled his presentation with references to the Twelve Imams and Islamic thinkers—notably Farabi, Tousi, Avicenna, Mulla Sadr, and, "most important of all, Motahhari." He also praised Islam for its "spirituality," "mystical values," "high ideals," and "purification of the soul through confessions." He concluded by seeking pardon for his sins and urging youth to read Motahhari instead of Marx. Clearly, the regime wanted the main party philosopher to "return to Islam"—not to just beat his breast about "political mistakes."

Tabari spent the next five years in solitary confinement. But the government-controlled press left readers with the distinct impression that he was living at home giving frequent press interviews. Besides these interviews, he published numerous articles and two books entitled *Kazh Raheh: Khaterati az Tarikh Hezb-e Tudeh* (The Crooked Road: Memoirs from the Tudeh Party) and *Shenakht va Sanjesh-e Marksism* (The Epistemology and Evaluation of Marxism). These books were also serialized by the main newspapers.[51] They did against Marxism what Fardoust's memoirs had done against monarchism. The press hailed the memoirs as "the most important book to have ever appeared on the history of the Iranian Left."[52] It also hailed the work on epistemology as one of the first critiques of historical materialism to come from "inside the walls of Marxism."[53]

Tabari explained that he had subtitled his autobiogaphy "an anti-memoir" because it was designed not as history but as "anti-history" to reveal the dangers of deviation from the right path. It was an "anti-memoir" in other ways. It supposedly described his intellectual return to Islam after a long tortuous detour through Marxism. In fact, it reveals nothing new of his life or of the Tudeh party. It reads like a cut-and-paste job from previously published memoirs. It rehashes the stock history of the left since 1905, dwelling on internal conflicts but shying away from political issues. It explains these conflicts simply in terms of personal jealousies. His own role recedes into an occasional reference—invariably in the third person. The book concludes by claiming that the Tudeh had stopped supporting the war against Iraq because it wanted to preserve Saddam Hossein. "History shows that the Tudeh has a long record of treachery, murder, lying, deception, and subservience to the West as well as to the East." Thus the main Tudeh theoretician confirmed the regime's claim that the Tudeh was part of the communist-capitalist conspiracy against Iran and Islam. The official press hailed the book as an invaluable *'ebrat nameh* (cautionary letter). Despite the nature of this "memoir," one former colleague in Iran took it seriously enough to publish a whole book pointing out its erroneous facts—of course, without mentioning Tabari's own writing environment.[54]

In his salvos against Marxist thought, Tabari used a grab bag of well-known arguments: James Burnham's theory of the managerial class; Talcott Parsons's concept of structural-functionalism; Newton's and Einstein's belief in God; the anarchist influences on Lenin; the Soviet failure to create a good society; the crimes committed by Stalin; the Lysenko fiasco; and the supposed assistance given by the Soviet Union to British and American imperialism. He also argued that Islam was more scientific than Marxism because whereas the former took into account the laws of cause and effect, the latter denied the existence of the Supreme Being and could not explain the "big bang"—or why meteors were "cold matter." As a clincher, he referred to a certain American scientist named Sinnott who had proved beyond doubt that "God directs living organisms." All this went to show that the great Islamic philosophers—especially Mulla Sadr and Motahhari—were correct in believing that "life is the realization of God's will in the organisms."

> In the past I was prejudiced against Islamic philosophy. I now realize that Islamic philosophy has moved way beyond dialectical materialism and contemporary Western thought. Nothing remains for me but to pursue a detailed study of this vast literature and thus recompense for my wasted life.[55]

According to some, Tabari had become a born-again Muslim. According to others, he had recanted either because of torture or, like Galileo, at the mere sight of the rack. Whatever the truth, Tabari remained not only incarcerated but also in total isolation—even from his own family. One prisoner describes seeing him drag his partly paralyzed body to the Hosseiniyeh podium in Evin to read a long convoluted paper on the weaknesses of Marxism and the strengths of Islam—especially the fact that the world now contained over one billion Muslims. When Ladjevardi asked him to deny outright the rumor that he had cast himself into the role of a "Galileo," Tabari gave another long convoluted response that further befogged the audience.[56]

When Tabari died in 1989, the government-controlled press eulogized him as an intellectual genius who had rediscovered Islam after mastering ten languages, rubbing shoulders with luminaries, studying with the main Soviet Iranologists, and attaining fame as "one of the greatest Marxist theoreticians in the whole world."[57] Tabari had become world famous—at least in the Islamic Republic.

5

Mass Executions of 1988

> These mass executions . . . violate
> the fundamental principles of
> Islam, of the Holy Prophet, and of
> our Imam Ali.
>
> *Ayatollah Montazeri*, "Letter to
> Imam Khomeini," 31 August 1988

The Inquisition

In the early hours of Friday, 19 July 1988, the regime suddenly, without warning, isolated the main prisons from the outside world. It slammed shut their gates; canceled scheduled visits and telephone calls; banned all newspapers; cleared the cells of radios and televisions; refused to accept letters, care packages, and even vital medicines; and forbade relatives from congregating outside the prison gates—especially in Luna Park outside Evin. What is more, the main law courts went on an unscheduled vacation so that concerned relatives would not gather there seeking information. Some panic-stricken families rushed to Qom in search of Ayatollah Montazeri—who was still the heir-designate.[1]

The wardens isolated not only the prisons from the outside world but also each cell block from other cell blocks in the same prison. Inmates were confined to their cells. Communal places, such as lecture halls, workshops, infirmaries, and courtyards, were closed down. Guards and Afghan prison workers were instructed not to speak to inmates. In effect, the political prisoners were completely isolated from the nonpolitical ones, the Mojahedin from the leftists, the repenters from the nonrepenters, those with long sentences from those with short ones, and those who had just started theirs from those who had completed theirs. One ingenious inmate assembled a wireless set to find out what was happening only to discover that the radio stations were not reporting news about the prisons. They were observing a news blackout. Thus began an act of violence unprecedented in Iranian history—unprecedented in form, content, and intensity. It even outdid the 1979 reign of terror. The curtain of secrecy, however, was so effective that no Western journalist heard of it and no Western academic discussed it. They still have not.

Just before the executions—we do not know exactly when—Khomeini had issued a secret but extraordinary order—some suspect a formal fatwa, or religious decree—setting up Special Commissions with instructions to execute Mojaheds as moharebs (those who war against God) and leftists as *mortads* (apostates from Islam). The Tehran commission—totaling sixteen—contained representatives from the Imam himself, the president, the chief prosecutor, the Revolutionary Tribunals, the Ministries of Justice and Intelligence, and the administrations of Evin and Gohar Dasht. Its chair, Ayatollah Eshraqi, had two special assistants—Hojjat al-Islam Nayeri and Hojjat al-Islam Mobasheri. In the next five months, this commission shuttled back and forth from Evin to Gohar Dasht by helicopter. It was to be dubbed "the commission of death." Similar commissions were set up in the provinces.

The Tehran commission began with the Mojahedin and their repenters. It prefaced the proceedings by assuring them that this was not a trial but a process for initiating a general amnesty and separating the Muslims from the non-Muslims. It then asked their organizational affiliation. If they replied "Mojahedin," the questioning ended there. If they replied "monafeqin" (hypocrites), the commission continued with such questions as "Are you willing to denounce former colleagues?" "Are you willing to denounce them before the cameras?" "Are you willing to help us hunt them down?" "Will you name secret sympathizers?" "Will you identify phony repenters?" "Will you go to the war front and walk through enemy minefields?"

The prisoners in Evin remained blindfolded throughout the proceedings. But those in Gohar Dasht were permitted to see the commission members. The questions were clearly designed to tax to the utmost the victim's sense of decency, honor, and self-respect. Raha writes that not a single one of the fifty Mojaheds in her ward returned from the investigation.[2] Another eyewitness writes that 195 of the 200 Mojaheds in block 2 of Gohar Dasht did not return.[3] Yet another writes that Hojjat al-Islam Nayeri was determined to take as large a toll as possible whereas Ayatollah Eshraqi made a halfhearted attempt to moderate.[4]

The Mojahedin who gave unsatisfactory answers were promptly taken to a special room where they were ordered to write their last will and testament. They were also ordered to discard such personal belongings as rings, watches, and spectacles. They were then led blindfolded to the gallows. The gallows in Evin were in the secluded Hosseiniyeh lecture hall. Those in Gohar Dasht were in the enclosed amphitheater and the adjacent box-making factory. The victims were hanged in batches of six. Some took fifteen minutes to die—the traditional method of hanging in Iran involves stringing up the victim by the neck rather than dropping him down a trapdoor. After the first few days, the overworked executioners requested firing squads. These requests, however, were rejected on the claim that the sharia mandated hanging for apostates and enemies of God. Probably the real reason was the need for absolute silence and secrecy.

The leftists were told that the Mojahedin were being transferred elsewhere. But a few in Gohar Dasht suspected something was amiss when they saw freezer vans and masked guards moving in and out of the amphitheater—unbeknown to them masks were being used because the morgue freezers had broken down. One guard claimed that they were merely "cleaning out the prison and that every new regime sooner or later needs to clean out its prisons." The prisoners did not get the double meaning until later. One Afghan worker delivering food made ominous signs around his neck. But again the prisoners did not get the meaning until later. Some thought he was trying to indicate that Khomeini had died. It was hard for them to imagine mass slaughter at a time of national rejoicing—Khomeini had just ended the eight-year war by accepting the UN peace offer. As with concentration camp inmates, familiarity with death did not necessarily prepare them for the worst. One survivor admits that he thought he was being processed to be released in time for the forthcoming peace celebrations.[5]

After August 27, the commission turned its attention to the leftists. Assuring them that it merely sought to separate practicing Muslims from nonpracticing ones, it asked them: "Are you a Muslim?" "Do you believe in God?" "Is the Holy Koran the Word of God?" "Do you believe in Heaven and Hell?" "Do you accept the Holy Mohammad to be the Seal of the Prophets?" "Will you publicly recant historical materialism?" "Will you denounce your former beliefs before the cameras?" "Do you fast during Ramadan?" "Do you pray and read the Holy Koran?" "Would you rather share a cell with a Muslim or a non-Muslim?" "Will you sign an affidavit that you believe in God, the Prophet, the Holy Koran, and the Resurrection?" "When you were growing up did your father pray, fast, and read the Holy Koran?" Few grasped the lethal significance of the last question.

Like the medieval Inquisition, the commission was posing loaded questions—especially for college students ignorant of esoteric theology. Such questions bewildered Iranians as much as they would their Western counterparts. They had never been raised before in Iranian courts—if ever in the Middle East. It was an inquisition in the full sense of the term—an investigation into religious beliefs rather than into political and organizational affiliations. Conspicuously absent from them were the issues that had concerned the preceding tribunals—issues such as "subversion," "treason," "espionage," "terrorism," and "imperialist links." As one Fedayi commented, "In previous years, they wanted us to confess to spying. In 1988, they wanted us to convert to Islam."[6] Another Fedayi admitted that he was bewildered by the fact that his interrogators seemed completely uninterested in his political activities, political affiliations, and political stands.[7]

The first leftists to go before the Evin commission were those with light, and even completed, sentences. This gives the death list the appearance of a random lottery. Some who perished on the first day were serving short sentences; some who survived in the following days were serving long, even life, sentences. The discrepancy can be explained. At Gohar Dasht, a leftist prisoner who had at one time attended a seminary quickly grasped the theological significance of the questions. He spent the night of August 30 sending Morse code messages to other cells pointing out their hidden dangers. He warned that refusal to answer on grounds of "privacy" could itself be taken as an admission of "apostasy." More important, he pointed out that technically one was not an apostate unless one had been raised by a Muslim father who regularly prayed, read the Koran, and observed Ramadan. Nominal Muslims not raised in proper Muslim homes first had to be exposed to true Islam before they could be deemed apostates deserving death. According to Qom, apostates came in two forms: *mortad-e fetri* (innate apostates) and *mortad-e melli* (national apostates). The former deserved death; the latter deserved a second chance.

Those on the leftist wards spent the night discussing what position to take toward the questionnaire. Some determined to die, and, in preparation, put on their best clothes. One even wore a necktie as a flagrant symbol of cultural resistance. But others decided to give *pasokh-ha-ye taktiki* (tactical answers). One such answer was to say that one's parents had not been observant Muslims. Of course, this was only tempting for those whose parents had passed away. One informed the commission he had been raised in the atheistic Soviet Union. Another remembered that his father—a strict secularist—had threatened to discipline him if he ever caught him praying. Another "tactical answer" was to say that they had lapsed in their religious observances not because of ideological objections but because they had been too busy earning a living. Yet another "tactical answer" was that they were not Marxists but leftists who believed in God, the Prophet, and the Resurrection. One told the commission that he could be both a Muslim and a full-fledged Tudeh member because the party program did not discriminate against religion: "The party is against capitalism, not against God."[8] Ironically, one of the very first casualties was a Tudeh militant who happened to be a devout Muslim. He refused to respond to the questions on the grounds that the state had no business asking him "personal questions." By contrast, almost everyone in Evin's block 6—reserved for Tudeh members with fifteen-year sentences—survived by voting to give tactical answers.[9] On the whole, Ayatollah Eshraqi was willing to accept such answers at face value.

These investigations continued for three months. In Evin and Gohar Dasht, they were carried out in the main courtrooms. Some prisoners were given oral investigations; others, typed questionnaires. Some could see their interrogators; others were separated from them by high platforms. Those giving acceptable answers were shown to the doors on the right. Those with unacceptable ones were shown to the doors on the left. The former were returned to their cells, ordered to perform their daily prayers, and given ten lashes for each one they refused to perform—totaling fifty lashes per day. Those who failed the test were taken to the gallows with a brief stopover to deposit their personal possessions and write their last will and testament. In the commotion, a few survived by being sent to the wrong doors. Two survivors remember taking this talk of last testaments as a joke because they could not imagine such a questionnaire sealing one's fate.[10]

The treatment meted out to women was somewhat more complicated. Whereas Mojahedin women were promptly hanged as "armed enemies of God," leftist women—even those raised as practicing Muslims—were given another "opportunity" to reconsider their "apostasy." In the eyes of the magistrates, women were not fully responsible for their actions, and

disobedient women—including apostates—could be given discretionary punishments to mend their ways and obey their
male superiors. After the investigation, leftist women were systematically given five lashes for every prayer missed—half that
meted out to the men. After a while, many agreed to pray. One
admitted ten years later that she still had recurring nightmares
in which she saw herself praying and thereby betraying her
whole persona. Some went on a hunger strike—refusing even
water. One died after twenty-two days and 550 lashes. The authorities certified her death as suicide—after all, it was "she
who had made the decision not to pray."[11]

Real suicides also occurred in increasing numbers—in
men's as well as women's wards. Some got the distinct impression that the authorities were intentionally leaving razor blades
around to facilitate suicides.[12] In an article entitled "Life after
1988," one survivor describes characteristics that can be identified as typical posttrauma symptoms: inability to accept the
calamity, terror that it would be repeated, deep depression,
acute survival guilt, and refusal to admit—even to themselves—
that they had given "tactical answers." He describes the scene
as a Kafkaesque nightmare and adds that the survivors vowed
to write down their experiences to "bear witness" for those who
had perished.[13]

The full scope of these executions remains unknown. We
have few eyewitness accounts from the provinces. All we know
for certain is that Isfahan was the only major provincial capital
to escape them. The Isfahan prison was still administered by
Montazeri supporters. What is more, the regime in 1988—unlike 1979 and 1981—released no lists. On the contrary, it insisted—and still does—that no such executions took place.

Raha places the death toll in the "thousands."[14] Another eyewitness puts it between 5,000 and 6,000—1,000 from the left
and the rest from the Mojahedin.[15] Yet another estimates it in
the "thousands," with Gohar Dasht alone having as many as
1,500.[16] A recent study using scattered information from the
provinces places the figure at 12,000.[17] Amnesty International
estimates that the national total is more than 2,500 and

describes the vast majority of the victims as "prisoners of con-science" as they had not been charged with actual deeds or plans of deeds against the state.[18] Whatever the exact figures, the total outdid 1979 when the casualties had included some who had been shot in armed confrontations. In 1988, they were all killed in cold blood.

The Majority Fedayi has published the names of 615 victims, giving, where possible, organizational affiliation and place of execution.[19] But this list is by no means complete as it is con-fined to specific blocks within Evin and Gohar Dasht. Of the 615, 137 were from the Mojadehin; 90, from the Tudeh; 108, from the Majority Fedayi; 20, from the Minority Fedayi; 21, from other Fedayi offshoots; 30, from Kumaleh; 12, from Rah-e Kargar; 3, from Peykar; and 12, from other leftist groups. The political affiliations of the other 182 remain unknown.

The Tudeh has published obituaries for eighty of its mar-tyrs.[20] They include 20 former military officers, 4 of whom had been imprisoned by the Shah for twenty-four years; 14 engi-neers; 12 technicians; 12 workers; 11 full-time party function-aries, many with college degrees from the Soviet Union; 8 teachers; 5 university students; 2 medical doctors; 2 accoun-tants; and another 2 civil servants. Thirty—including 10 from the 1983 "roundtable"—were members of the central commit-tee. In terms of region, 17 had been born in Tehran; 16, in Azerbaijan; 15, in the Caspian provinces; 14, in the central provinces; 9, in Kurdestan; and 7, in Khorasan. In terms of age, 11 were in their twenties; 23, in their thirties; 14, in their for-ties; 10, in their fifties; 19, in their sixties; 5, in their seventies; and 1, in his eighties. This inquisition was no respecter of age.

Some victims had been in prison since 1983. Some had com-pleted their sentences. Some had not yet been tried. But almost all had been arrested for relatively minor offenses. Those with serious charges had already been executed. The 1988 slaughter resembled the "disappearances" of contemporary Latin Amer-ica—but with one ironic difference. In Latin America, inqui-sitional methods were not used despite the Catholic tradition.

But in Iran, they were used even though the country lacked such a tradition. The medieval Inquisition had made its debut in modern Iran.

Relatives were not officially informed of the executions until well after November 25. To prevent public gatherings, they were informed in separate groups in the course of many weeks. They were explicitly ordered not to observe the traditional forty-day mourning period. Some were told by telephone. Most were summoned to neighborhood komitehs—a few to Evin— to collect the personal possessions as well as the last will and testament of the deceased. Only innocuous last wills were handed over.

Relatives feared the worst long before November. They had seen unmarked graves appearing in Behesht-e Zahara, the main cemetery, and, in Khavarestan, a new one opened next to the Bahai graveyard in eastern Tehran. Behesht-e Zahara was reserved for Muslims; Khavarestan, for Muslim apostates. The Mojahedin—being Muslims—could be buried in Behesht-e Zahara. But the Marxists—being unbelievers—had to be segregated. Najes rules applied in death as in life. The regime had even transferred from Behesht-e Zahara to Khavarestan some Fedayi victims of SAVAK. The authorities dubbed the place *kaferestan* (land of unbelievers) and *lanatabad* (the land of the damned). The bereaved, having planted rose beds there, called it Golzar-e Khaveran (Eastern Flower Fields). In contemporary Iran, cemeteries are potent signifiers in more ways than one.

Even now, a decade later, the motives behind the 1988 massacres remain unclear. Some speculate that the regime was either reacting to hunger strikes in Evin or was trying to ease the prison overcrowding problem. In other words, the executions were a form of "housecleaning." Some speculate that they were designed primarily to silence the opposition and strike terror into the public. Others link them to Khomeini's acceptance of the UN peace offer—an act he equated with "drinking poison." According to this theory, he launched the executions to deflect anger from the costly war that he could have ended six years before when Iran had liberated Khorramshahr. Yet others link them to a military offensive the Mojahedin launched into western Iran as soon as Khomeini accepted the ceasefire.

These theories, however, do not withstand careful scutiny. The prisons were less crowded in 1988 than at any other time in the previous eight years. In fact, Qezel Hesar had been emptied of all political prisoners. Besides, the regime could have solved any overcrowding problem by simply releasing the repenters and those who had completed their sentences. The hunger strike in Evin had been resolved long before the Special Commission convened. The secrecy shrouding the whole event belies the notion that it was designed to strike fear into the public. If the intention was to create public terror, the regime should have publicized the executions to the hilt—as it had in 1979 and 1981.

The armistice may have been "poison" for Khomeini, but for the rest of the country, especially for those in uniform, it was relief sent from God. Similarly, the Mojahedin incursion, which was a complete fiasco from its inception, may possibly explain the Mojahedin executions; but by no stretch of the imagination can it explain the others as the leftists opposed the Mojahedin and were not accused of "warring against God." Likewise, the regime could not have been resorting to such drastic measures out of a sense of insecurity as it had just ended the war and crushed the Mojahedin incursion. In fact, many leftists went before the investigatory commissions expecting to receive amnesty for the peace celebrations.[21] Thus these executions appear to have been the product, not of fearful panic, but of calculated planning.

The real answer may lie elsewhere—in the regime's internal dynamics. Peace with Iraq brought Khomeini the realization that he had lost the most valuable glue holding together his disparate followers—some of whom were moderates, others radicals, some reformers, others conservatives, some dogmatic fundamentalists, others pragmatic populists. He also realized that his ailing health would soon remove him from the scene and thus leave his followers without a paramount leader. He

further realized that the regime contained influential personalities, such as Hojjat al-Islam Rafsanjani, who probably hoped
someday to mend bridges with the West as well as with more
moderate elements in the opposition.

To forge unity, Khomeini came up with a two-pronged strategy: the Salman Rushdie fatwa and the mass executions. The
Rushdie fatwa would not only further isolate the country but
would also raise formidable—if not insurmountable—obsta-
cles in the way of any future leader hoping to initiate a détente
with the West. Even more important, the bloodbath would test
the true mettle of his followers. It would weed out the halfhearted from the true believers, the wishy-washy from the real
revolutionaries, the weak-willed from the fully committed. It
would force them to realize that they would stand or fall together. It would silence them on the issues of human rights and
individual liberties. It would also sever once and for all the
religious radicals within his movement from the secular radicals outside. In fact, Tudeh organizers had been tortured in
1983–84 to confess to having secret ties with radicals within
the regime—especially with the labor minister. In short, the
slaughter would serve both as a baptism of blood and as a self-
administered purge.

It accomplished exactly that—forcing Ayatollah Montazeri
to resign as the heir-designate. In the course of the previous
year, Montazeri had taken issue with the diehard cleric on a
number of subjects—the Hashemi trial, the antihoarding campaign, and the special courts, as well as the appointment of
judges, seminary teachers, imam jom'ehs, prison wardens, and
parliamentary committees to investigate prison conditions.[22]
But these conflicts had remained behind closed doors. Outsid-
ers, even prisoners, had no inkling of what was going on behind
the scenes. In the words of one prisoner, "We leftists failed to
distinguish between the pro- and the anti-Montazeri wardens
and clerics. We did not realize our mistake until much later."[23]

The mass executions turned out to be the last straw for Montazeri. He rushed off three public letters—two to Khomeini,
one to the Special Commission—denouncing in no uncertain

terms these "thousands of executions." He began by reminding
the recipients that he had suffered more than they at the hands
of the opposition as the Mojahedin had assassinated his son.
He then took the Special Commission to task for violating Islam by executing repenters and minor offenders who in a
proper court of law would have received a mere reprimand. He
also took the commission to task for putting intolerable bur-
dens on prisoners—even demanding they should walk through
minefields. "In addition to alienating many citizens, these unlawful executions can provide our enemies abroad with valuable propaganda ammunition to hurl against us."[24] Montazeri
concluded by requesting relief from the "heavy responsibility"
of being the future Supreme Leader.

Khomeini promptly obliged, replying cryptically that "the responsibility requires more endurance than you have shown."[25]
To protect his own political infallibility, Khomeini claimed that
he had always harbored reservations about Montazeri's com-
petence and that it had been the Assembly of Experts that had
insisted on naming him the future Supreme Leader. "I," declared Khomeini, "expressed reservations when the Assembly
of Experts first appointed you."

In the following months, the regime circulated a selection of
letters exchanged between Khomeini and Montazeri. The
avowed aim was to explain the latter's resignation. But the selection dealt only with the Hashemi affair and scrupulously
avoided the mass executions—thus observing the official line
that these executions never took place.[26] Likewise, ten years
later, when Montazeri dared to renew his criticism, the regime
took him to task for "deviating" on a number of issues—but
failed to mention the unsavory subject of mass executions.[27]
Immediately after his resignation, Montazeri became a nonperson—much like the late Ayatollah Shariatmadari. His pictures were removed from public places. His office was closed.
His name disappeared from the mass media. What is more, he
was physically confined to Qom. Thus when Khomeini died in
June 1989, he could feel confident that he was leaving behind
a regime free of weak-kneed and halfhearted supporters. Those

who remained had proved their mettle either by endorsing or by participating in the mass executions. Khomeini's creative genius should never be underestimated.

Once the task had been accomplished, the regime ended the mass executions—thus further disproving the notion that they had been triggered by panic. It wound down the Special Commission, reopened the prison doors, and permitted bereaved families to gather at the cemeteries. It even turned a blind eye when Mojahedin and leftist families exchanged visits at Behesht-e Zahara and Khavarestan. Some families formed the Society for the Support of Political Prisoners and mimeographed a newsletter called *Band-e Raha'i* (Cry of Freedom). This carried news about prisons as well as biographies of those executed. The society drew support from the Mojahedin and the Minority Fedayi, as well as from the Tudeh, the Majority Fedayi, Rah-e Kargar, Kumaleh, and the Kurdish Democrats.

The regime also permitted Galindo Pohl, the UN Special Commissioner on Human Rights in Iran, to make two separate visits to Iran—even to Evin. Ladjevardi welcomed Pohl to Evin with a band concert—oblivious to the fact that similar concerts had routinely greeted the Red Cross at Auschwitz. What is more, Ladjevardi and other wardens stopped whipping those who refused to pray and perform religious rituals. They also stopped insisting on public recantations, and instead sought short "letters of regret" and promises not to discuss their prison experiences. Finally, Ladjevardi announced with much fanfare a broad amnesty, implying that most political prisoners would soon be released.

In early 1989, the television networks featured a large Friday prayer meeting in downtown Tehran involving former royalists, Mojahedins, and well-known leftists from diverse Marxist groups. One former prisoner relates how one morning, without warning, he was ordered to put on his best clothes, and then was bused to this meeting where he was given a placard to carry.[28] The media gave the impression that these "repenters" were about to be pardoned because they had been "forgiven." One paper headlined the story as the "Morning of Freedom for those Returning to the True Light."[29] One participant was quoted as saying that some of those returning to Islam had resisted SAVAK for years without forsaking their Marxism. This all went to prove the superiority of Islam.

The End of Television Recantations

The recantation shows, which had peaked in the mid-1980s, gradually dwindled in the late 1980s and became a rarity by the early 1990s. This, however, did not mean the end of political repression. On the contrary, arbitrary arrests, secret executions, and even summary ones proceeded—although at a reduced rate. The number of political prisoners remained high despite the 1989 amnesty. According to the UN, in 1994 Iran still had more than 19,000 political prisoners.[30] Jewish and Bahai leaders continued to be shot as "foreign spies." Exiled politicians were increasingly assassinated. Dissidents inside Iran began to "disappear," die suddenly of "natural causes," and be targeted by government propaganda—especially by a new television program called "Hoviyyat" (Identity). This program specialized in naming intellectuals as "hired agents" of the Bahais, Zionists, Freemasons, British, Americans, and even Germans. For obvious reasons, the Soviets had disappeared from the litany.

Moreover, the prison authorities continued to torture to obtain videotaped confessions and ideological recantations—even though they no longer aired them on national television. In 1994, the UN reported that the regime had reverted to the practice of not releasing political prisoners until they had recanted before the videocameras.[31] Similarly, Amnesty International noted that the use of torture to obtain recantations and self-incriminating confessions had returned by the mid-1990s.[32] But these videos were now used solely for internal consumption—especially for trials held in camera. Like Stalinist Russia after 1939, the regime ceased broadcasting such confessions but continued to use them in closed trials. The judicial system had routinized forced confessions.

The regime stopped televising recantations not because it had become more respectful of human rights but because it realized that the viewing public—especially the attentive public—had grown more sophisticated on the issues of forced confessions and foreign conspiracies. Many had tired of hearing the incessant call that "the country is in danger." Some were discussing—even taking gibes—at the paranoia mood that had gripped the country in earlier decades. Paradoxically, the regime's own survival had helped to diminish the mood. By the 1990s, few felt that omnipotent external powers were on the verge of taking over the country. After all, Iran had survived the hostage crises as well as the Iraqi war; the Soviet Union had collapsed; and the United States had been unable to alter the course of the revolution. What is more, the call sounded hollow in light of Irangate and the regime's own dealings with Israel and the United States. Had not Khomeini himself coined the famous slogan "America Cannot Do Much"?

Even more important was the increasing awareness among the attentive public of the stage preparations needed to produce recantation shows. By the late 1980s, all the opposition groups—not only the UN and Amnesty International—had published reams of eyewitness accounts documenting the use of torture to extract recantations and confessions. This contrasted sharply with the earlier reticence to discuss the whole subject. In letters faxed to the UN, Entezam, Bazargan's deputy, documented the pressures exerted on fellow prisoners to give false confessions.[33] Similarly, in an open letter to Montazeri, an imprisoned surgeon described these tortures and declared, "You once said that the use of torture for forced recantations is as great a sin as committing adultery in the Ka'aba."[34] Likewise, Kianuri in his prison cell described to Galindo Pohl how he and his wife had been tortured to give false confessions. As evidence, he held up his badly set broken arm.[35] Pohl added that Maryam Firuz had difficulty hearing, swallowing food, and sitting down because of beatings suffered eight years earlier.[36]

References to tortured recantations even crept into the official media—albeit in roundabout ways. In 1991–93, Kianuri—

now in "house imprisonment"—was interviewed extensively by *Kayhan* and *Jomhuri-ye Islam*.[37] Although the interviews were ostensibly on the collapse of the Soviet Union, Kianuri used the occasion to set the "record straight." He categorically denied that he and his colleagues had confessed to espionage. He rejected the charge that the Tudeh had ever committed "treason." He took issue over the claim that there was a religious revival in the world and made fun of Tabari for claiming to have become a "born-again Muslim." He vociferously defended the "unprecedented achievements" of the Great October Revolution and "the heroic struggles of the Soviet people" and blamed the recent debacle in Moscow on such "Judases" as Gorbachev and Yeltsin. In short, he remained an unreconstructed Stalinist—despite seven years of prison indoctrination.

Kianuri took Stalin to task on two significant issues, however. Stalin, he stressed, had "executed patriotic and well-trained military officers who would have been useful in the war against the foreign invaders." Even worse, he had used "medieval inquisitional methods to extract false confessions." "At the time people believed these confessions. They did not discover the truth until years later." One does not need to be a trained Kremlinologist to realize that Kianuri's real target was not Stalin but someone closer to home. In these interviews, Kianuri did not try to explain how he had managed to survive—probably because he, like many others, had signed a vow promising not to discuss his prison experiences.

This rising awareness about torture led many to be more understanding of recanters—even to empathize with them. This again contrasted sharply with the past. Traditionally, the term *e'terafat* (confession, recantation) had connoted betrayal and defection. By the late 1980s, it could mean no more than a measured response to unbearable pain. Similarly, the term *towab* (repenter) originally had the associations of active collaboration. But by the 1980s, it could mean no more than passive and limited submission. The prisoners themselves sharply differentiated between "tactical" and genuine "repentances," between halfhearted and full-hearted recantations, between harmless and deadly confessions, and between those "broken" into passive submission and those induced into active collaboration.

Raha writes that prisoners carefully scrutinized the confession shows to figure out which speakers had capitulated without much resistance and which had resisted to their utmost.[38] She describes how when Mehdi Hashemi—no friend of the Marxists—appeared on television she and her fellow leftists spontaneously said to themselves, "He must have suffered unbearable tortures."[39] She adds that one should not bandy about such loaded terms as *kha'en* (traitor).[40]

Another prisoner writes that one should distinguish between those giving perfunctory "confessions" and those actively tormenting fellow inmates. He argues that the term "repenter" should be reserved for these tormenters.[41] Another argues that one should recognize the large gray area between "treason" and "resistance," distinguish between various degrees of collaboration, and think carefully before labeling someone a "tavvab."[42] The Majority Fedayi argued that as far as the wardens were concerned a true "repenter" was one willing to go all the way—spying for them, whipping fellow prisoners, and taking part in executions.[43] The Minority Fedayi reported that by 1988 so many Mojahedin had given "tactical recantations" that these "tactical repenters" controlled whole wards and used their positions to undermine the wardens and help fellow prisoners.[44] Clearly, the recantation by itself no longer had the lethal ability to destroy the victim's aberu (honor, reputation, and self-respect). Without this ability, the recantation show had lost much of its lethal potency.

Instead of destroying the victim, public recantations now threatened to discredit the regime itself. Pohl reports that by 1990 television confessions "aroused considerable scepticism." They not only lacked "spontaneity and authenticity" but also inevitably raised a host of questions about "prison practices."[45] Other visitors to Iran, as well as readers of Persian publications inside and outside the country, were struck by the increasing interest shown in Galileo, Bukharin, Joan of Arc, the medieval

Inquisition, Arthur Miller, Koestler, and, most noticeably, Orwell. Those who in the past had dismissed Koestler's *Darkness at Noon* and Orwell's *Nineteen Eighty-four* as cold war propaganda were now—for the first time—taking them seriously.[46] In other words, Iranian intellectuals—like their counterparts in the West—had grown more sophisticated on the whole subject of public confessions. They no longer associated them with truth, penance, and redemption. Instead, they linked them to torture, brutality, and state terror.

The regime—always sensitive to public perceptions—was observant enough to realize that such shows were now counterproductive. Three well-publicized cases illustrate this. In 1990, the Intelligence Ministry announced that eight colleagues of Bazargan, including a ninety-year-old friend, had confessed before the videocameras to forming an American "fifth column."[47] The ministry promised to try them in open court and televise their confessions so that all would see how they had forged ties to a certain Iranian woman in America who was linked to the Voice of America, which, in turn, as everyone knew, was linked to the CIA. In sharp contrast to the previous decade, much of the opposition—including the Tudeh, Bazargan's bête noire—promptly declared that such confessions were worse than worthless because they were the products of horrendous tortures.[48] Without any confessions being televised, the eight were given short sentences by a closed court.

In 1994, the Intelligence Ministry announced that the prominent author Ali-Akbar Sa'idi Sirjani had confessed on camera to having indulged in drink, drugs, gambling, sex, especially homosexuality, and "spying for a foreign power" and "receiving money from the West, Israel, the royalists, and the Freemasons."[49] Before his arrest—prompted by a poem satirizing the Supreme Leader—Sirjani had been known for supporting Islam, the revolution, and Imam Khomeini. When a delegation of writers petitioned on his behalf, the Intelligence Ministry offered to show them his videotaped confession. But they declined with the retort that in recent years they had seen enough such confessions. Nine months later, the government announced that Sirjani had succumbed to "a heart attack." His videotaped confession was never televised.

Similarly, Faraj Sarkouhi, the editor of the left-wing *Adineh* (Friday), was kidnapped by security officials in December 1996. He had managed to publish his journal all these years by avoiding controversial issues. But just before his disappearance he had signed a petition against censorship and published an article critical of the new television program "Hoviyyat." After a forty-seven-day absence, Sarkouhi reappeared and succeeded—through relatives—in faxing out of the country an open letter describing his kidnapping. He wrote that he had been tortured to "make and remake" videotapes confessing to being a "foreign spy" and giving outrageous lies about his own and his colleagues' sex lives. Comparing his experience to Orwell's *Nineteen Eighty-four*, Sarkouhi concluded that the seven years he had spent in the Shah's prisons were far more preferable to any five minutes of his recent forty-seven-day ordeal.[50] Again the actual video confession was never shown.

The television recantations had been initially produced as grand theater to praise the regime and damn the opposition. But once the stage preparations had been exposed, the same shows threatened to become counterproductive. Instead of legitimizing those in power, they risked delegitimizing them. Instead of focusing attention on the opposition, they reminded the public of the regime's own horrifying features. Instead of dividing the opposition, they helped to bring it together—if not formally, at least in their common denunciations of forced confessions and horrendous prison conditions. Instead of highlighting the weaknesses of the opposition, they drew attention to the regime itself—especially its methods for producing such shows. Instead of presenting "sensational revelations," they bored the public with a similar cast of characters with similar scripts and similar cast-down faces and expressions. The grand theater had turned into grade-B horror shows—minus the suspense. It was high time to terminate them.

Their disappearance, however, does not mean that they left no mark on Iranian history. On the contrary, many in contemporary Iran—as in the former Soviet Union—have had to ask themselves some fundamental questions: "What sort of regime needs such shows?" "What do these shows reveal about the real nature of the regime?" "Can individual liberties be protected in a state that resorts to such methods?" "What is the moral standing of a regime that is so reliant on prison torture?" The Islamic Republic has survived the last decade. But these shows may well return to haunt it in future decades. Forced confessions have left their imprint on the regime as well as on the opposition—on the torturers as well as on the tortured.

Notes

Introduction

1. Cited in E. Peters, *Torture* (Oxford: Blackwell, 1985), 5.

2. Amnesty International, *Iran* (London, 1987); Amnesty International, *Iran: Imprisonment, Torture, and Execution of Political Prisoners* (New York, 1992); United Nations (Economic and Social Council), *Situation of Human Rights in the Islamic Republic of Iran* (New York, February 1990); United Nations (Economic and Social Council), *Situation of Human Rights in the Islamic Republic of Iran* (New York, January 1994); Human Rights Watch, *World Report: 1990* (New York, 1991).

3. M. Foucault, *Discipline and Punish: The Birth of the Prison* (London: Penguin, 1975).

4. D. Rajali, *Torture and Modernity: Self, Society, and State in Modern Iran* (Boulder: Westview, 1994).

5. E. Scarry, *The Body in Pain* (New York: Oxford University Press, 1985), 27–59.

6. M. Ruthven, *Torture: The Grand Conspiracy* (London: Weidenfeld, 1978), 10.

7. Interview with Bozorg Alavi, Berlin, July 1993.

8. A. Shamideh, *Khaterat-e Zendan* (Prison Memoirs) (Baku, 1980), 9.

9. S. Parsipour, *Khaterat-e Zendan* (Prison Memoirs) (Stockholm, 1996), 300.

10. A. Ladjevardi cited in *Iran Times*, 11 February 1982.

11. R. Briggs, *Witches and Neighbours* (London: Fontana Press, 1996).

12. M. Barber, *The Trial of the Templars* (Cambridge: Canto, 1994), 191–92.

13. R. Medvedev, *Let History Judge* (New York: Vintage, 1973), 236.

14. E. Abrahamian, "The Paranoid Style in Iranian Politics," in *Khomeinism: Essays on the Islamic Republic* (Berkeley: University of California Press, 1993), 111–31; A. Ashraf, "Conspiracy Theories," *Encyclopeaedia Iranica* (Costa Mesa: Mazda, 1992), 6:138–47.

15. A. Kors and E. Peters, *Witchcraft in Europe: A Documentary History* (Philadelphia: University of Pennsylvania Press, 1995), 175.

16. R. Conquest, *The Great Terror* (New York: Macmillan, 1973), 667.

17. H. Lea, *A History of the Inquisition in the Middle Ages* (London: Macmillan, 1922), 1:406.

18. Ibid., vols. 1–4.

19. Kors and Peters, *Witchcraft in Europe*, 168.

20. H. Lea, *A History of the Inquisition in the Middle Ages.*

21. Conquest, *The Great Terror*, 673. See also A. Vaksberg, *Stalin's Prosecutor: The Life of Andrei Vyshinsky* (New York: Weidenfeld, 1990), 122.

22. Vaksberg, *Stalin's Prosecutor*, 123.

23. Ibid., 52.

24. F. Beck and W. Godin, *Russian Purge and the Extraction of Confession* (New York: Viking, 1951), 184.

25. Ibid., 39, 169.

26. T. Asad, *Genealogies of Religion* (Baltimore: Johns Hopkins University Press, 1993), 83–124.

27. I. Deutscher, *The Prophet Outcast* (New York: Oxford University Press, 1962), 370.

28. V. Zafari, *Habsiyeh dar Adab-e Farsi: Az Aghaz-e Sh'er-e Farsi to Payan-e Zandieh* (Confinement in Persian Literature: From the Earliest Persian Poetry until the Zands) (Tehran, 1987).

29. B. Alavi, *Varaqpareh-ha-ye Zendan* (Prison Scrap Papers) (Tehran, 1942), 36–37.

1. Reza Shah

1. For general works on the sharia, see W. Floor, "Changes and Development in the Judicial System of Qajar Iran (1800–1925)," in *Qajar Iran: Political, Social and Cultural Changes*, ed. E. Bosworth and C. Hillenbrand (Edinburgh: Edinburgh University Press, 1993), 113–47; M. Bassiouni, ed., *The Islamic Criminal Justice System* (New York: Oceana, 1982); J. Schacht, *An Introduction to Islamic Law* (Oxford: Oxford University Press, 1964); N. Coulson, *History of Islamic Law* (Edinburgh: Edinburgh University Press, 1964); F. Rosenthal, *The Muslim Concept of Freedom* (Leiden: Brill, 1960).

2. Bassiouni, *The Islamic Criminal Justice System*, 70.

3. M. Rodinson, *Mohammed* (London: Penguin, 1971), 100–111.

4. Bassiouni, *The Islamic Criminal Justice System*, 72.

5. J. Malcolm, *The History of Persia* (London: Longman, 1815), 2:454.

6. J. Shahri, *Tarikh-e Ejtema'i-ye Tehran* (Social History of Tehran) (Tehran, 1990), vol. 5.

7. M. Sheil, *Glimpses of Life and Manners in Persia* (London: Murray, 1856), 276, 279.

8. Ibid., 281.

9. A. Sa'idi-Sirjani, ed., *Vaqay'-e Ettefaqiyeh: Majmu'eh-e Gozaresh-ha-ye Khafiyeh-e Nevesan-e Englesi* (Events that Occurred: The Collected Secret Reports of an English Writer) (Tehran, 1982).

10. Shahri, *Social History of Tehran*, 5:373, 196.

11. Ibid., 384–404.

12. T. Danesh, *Hoquq-e Zendanyan* (The Rights of Prisoners) (Tehran, 1987).

13. A. Ovanessian, *Yaddasht-ha-ye Zendan: Salha-ye 1928–42* (Prison Memoirs: The 1928–42 Years) (Stockholm, 1979), 6–7.

14. A. Dashti, *Ayyam-e Mahbas* (Prison Days) (Tehran, 1954), 15.

15. Firuz Mirza Farmanfarma (Nosrat al-Dawleh), *Majmu'ah-e Mokatibat* (Collected Papers), ed. M. Ettehadieh and S. Sa'dvanian (Tehran, 1987), 2:121–68.

16. For example, Tehran, with a population of over 200,000, had no more than five murders in 1925. British Legation, "Mortality Statistics," *F.O. 371*/Persia 1926/34–11500.

17. J. Pishevari, *Yaddasht-ha-ye Zendan* (Prison Memoirs) (Tehran, 1944), 147.

18. M. Hosseini, "Prisons and Imprisonment in Iran," *Ganjineh* 1, nos. 2–3 (Fall–Winter 1991): 44–58.

19. G. Forutan, *Hezb-e Tudeh dar Sahneh-ye Iran* (The Tudeh Party on the Iranian Scene) (n.p., n.d.), 242.

20. Ovanessian, *Prison Memoirs* (1979), 6–7.

21. Pishevari, *Prison Memoirs*, 147.

22. Ovanessian, *Prison Memoirs* (1979), 34.

23. A. Kambakhsh, "Concerning Stalin's Cult of Personality," *Donya* 5, no. 1 (Spring 1964): 16–38.

24. For later revelations about these convictions, see "The Trials of 1938–39," *Bakhtar*, 26 July 1942.

25. "The Trial of Traitors and Spies," *Ettela'at*, 29 June 1932.

26. G. Agabekov, *OGPU: The Russian Secret Terror* (New York: Brentano's, 1931), 124, 273–74.

27. Agabekov repeats the Iranian Communist party boast that its Second Congress (1927) had been daringly convened in Urmiah (Rezaieh) within Iran (*OGPU,*123). In fact, the congress had been convened safely on the outskirts of Moscow. See A. Shamideh, *Zendeginameh-e Shamideh* (The Life Story of Shamideh) (Cologne, 1994), 36.

28. Y. Eftekhari, *Khaterat-e Dowran-e Separishudeh* (Mem-

oirs of a Bygone Era), ed. K. Bayat and M. Tafreshi (Tehran, 1991), 62; Pishevari, *Prison Memoirs*, 34–37.

29. Pishevari, *Prison Memoirs*, 37.

30. See police interrogations in K. Bayat, ed., *Asnad-e Ahzab-e Siyasi-ye Iran: Fe'aliyat-ha-ye Komunisti dar Dowreh-e Reza Shah* (Documents on Iranian Political Parties: Communist Activities during the Reza Shah Era) (Tehran, 1991), 208.

31. Ovanessian, *Prison Memoirs* (1979), 63.

32. Eftekhari, *Memoirs*, 61.

33. A. Ovanessian, "The Communist University of the Toilers of the East (KUTIV)," *Donya* 9, no.1 (Spring 1969): 103.

34. Similar conclusions can be drawn from 30 communists arrested in Tabriz in 1930. The group included 11 weavers, 6 office employees, 2 apprentices, 2 unemployed workers, 1 teacher, 1 watchmaker, 1 carpenter, 1 tailor, 1 chauffeur, 1 workshop employee, and 1 household servant. Bayat, *Communist Activities*, 98.

35. J. Pishevari, "My Recollections," *Azhir*, 6 December 1943.

36. Eftekhari, *Memoirs*, 29.

37. Foreign Office to the British Legation, 4 May 1929, *F.O. 371*/Persia 1929/34–13783.

38. A. Ovanessian, *Khaterat* (Memoirs) (Cologne, 1990), 21.

39. A. Kobari, "Reminiscences from the Cultural Society and the Communist Party in Gilan," *Donya* 12, no. 4 (Summer 1971): 80–83; E. Tabari, "Concerning the Cultural Society in Rasht," *Donya* 3, no. 2 (June 1980): 173–75.

40. British Vice-Consul in Rasht, "Bolshevik Activity in Rasht," *F.O.371*/Persia 1929/34–13783.

41. British Legation to the Foreign Office, "Bolshevik Activities in Persia," 19 December 1928, *F.O. 371*/Persia 1924/34–13783.

42. R. Rusta, "The Cultural Societies," *Donya* 6, no. 3 (Autumn 1965): 82–88.

43. British Report on the Tudeh Congress, August 1944, *F.O. 371*/Persia 1944/34–40187.

44. "The Trial of Mokhtari," *Parcham*, 28 July 1942; "The

Biggest Trial in Iranian History," *Bakhtar*, 26 July 1942; M. Golban and Y. Sharifi, *Mohakemeh-e Mohakemegan* (The Prosecution of the Prosecutors) (Tehran, 1984), 112–85.

45. Reza Rusta was arrested in 1930 and kept in prison until 1941 but was never brought to trial. See J. Abdoh, *Khaterat-e Chehel Sal dar Sahneh-ye Qaza'i* (Memoirs of Forty Years in the Judiciary), ed. M. Tafreshi (Tehran, 1988), 2:954–60.

46. Ibid., 932–33.

47. Pishevari, *Prison Memoirs*, 105.

48. Ibid., 65.

49. Eftekhari, *Memoirs*, 38, 57.

50. Ovanessian, *Prison Memoirs* (1979), 17–19, 25.

51. Bayat, *Documents*, 112–40, 155–74.

52. Pishevari, *Prison Memoirs*, 42–43, 65.

53. Abdoh, *Memoirs*, 2:932.

54. Ovanessian, *Prison Memoirs*, 22–24.

55. Eftekhari, *Memoirs*, 53; Ovanessian, *Prison Memoirs* (1979), 10; Pishevari, *Prison Memoirs*, 11.

56. Ovanessian, *Prison Memoirs* (1979), 28.

57. Ibid., 9–10.

58. A. Ovanessian, *Yaddasht-ha-ye Zendan* (Prison Memoirs) (Tehran, 1944), 92.

59. Pishevari, *Prison Memoirs*, 125–26.

60. Ovanessian, *Prison Memoirs* (1944), 92.

61. A. Ovanessian, *Memoirs* (1990), 240.

62. B. Alavi, *Varaqpareh-ha-ye Zendan* (Prison Scrap Papers) (Tehran, 1942), 48.

63. Ibid., 74.

64. G. Yeqikian, *Shuwravi va Jonbesh-e Jangal* (The Soviets and the Jangali Movement) (Tehran, 1984), 110.

65. Eftekhari, *Memoirs*, 55.

66. Ovanessian, *Prison Memoirs* (1979), 34–35.

67. In later years he developed these arguments in "What Is a Real Political Party," *Azhir*, 13–22 June 1943. See also "The Justice and the Democratic Parties," *Azhir*, 19 July–27 November 1943.

68. Anonymous (Pishevari), "What Is a Real Political Party" and "The Justice and the Democratic Parties."

69. Shamideh, *The Life Story of Shamideh*, 80.

70. Ovanessian, *Prison Memoirs* (1979), 55.

71. Firuz, *Prison Memoirs*, 34, 70.

72. Pishevari, *Prison Memoirs*, 46–47.

73. Ovanessian, *Prison Memoirs* (1979), 55.

74. Pishevari, *Prison Memoirs*, 50.

75. Dashti, *Prison Days*, 180–220. See J. Knorzer, *Ali Dashti's Prison Days* (Washington, D.C., 1994).

76. Ovanessian, *Prison Memoirs* (1979), 65.

77. Pishevari, *Prison Memoirs*, 110.

78. A. Shamideh, *Katerat-e Zendan* (Prison Memoirs) (Baku, 1980), 52.

79. N. Pesyan, *Vaq'eh-e E'dam-e Jahansouz* (The Incident of Jahansouz's Execution) (Tehran, 1991), 57–62.

80. Ovanessian, *Prison Memoirs* (1979), 39.

81. Pishevari, *Prison Memoirs*, 45.

82. A. Khamehei, *Panjah Nafar va Seh Nafar* (The Fifty and the Three) (Tehran, 1984), 16.

83. T. Arani, "The Persian Language," *Iranshahr* 2, nos. 5–6 (November–December 1923): 355–58; "Heroes in Iranian History," *Iranshahr* 2, no.1 (September 1923): 63–64; "Azerbaijan," *Farangestan* 1, no. 5 (September 1924): 247–54.

84. H. Ahmadi, *Tarikhcheh-e Ferqeh-e Jomhuri-ye Enqelabi-ye Iran* (Short History of the Revolutionary Republican Party of Iran) (Berlin, 1992).

85. H. Farzaneh (Pseudonym), *Parvandeh-e Panjah-u-Seh Nafar* (The File for the Fifty-three) (Tehran, 1993), 237. Arani may have joined the Communist party in 1934 when, on a summer trip to Berlin, he stopped over in Moscow and met the main party leader.

86. Gh. Zakeri, "Interview with Anvar Khamehei Concerning Ehsan Tabari," *Adineh* 36 (May 1989): 11–14.

87. I. Iskandari, "Reminiscences of Dr. Arani and the Journal *Donya*," *Donya* 10, no. 4 (Winter 1969): 10–13.

88. I. Iskandari, *Khaterat-e Siyasi* (Political Memoirs) (Paris, 1986–89), 1:34.

89. A. Khamehei, "Obituary of Taqi Makinezhad," *Kelk*, nos. 76–79 (June–October 1996): 818–26.

90. A. Mahmudi, *Iran Demokrat* (Democratic Iran) (Tehran, 1945), 10.

91. N. Jahanshahlu, *Sarguzasht* (Recollections) (Berlin, 1986), 1:8.

92. Khamehei, *The Fifty and the Three*, 77–78.

93. M. Tafreshi and M. Taher-Ahmadi, *Guzareshha-ye Mahramaneh-e Shahrbani* (Secret Police Reports) (Tehran, 1992), 1:493.

94. "The May Day Manifesto of 1936," *Iran Ma*, 1 May 1946.

95. Khamehei, *The Fifty and the Three*, 45, 191–41.

96. M. Boqrati, "Letter to the Central Committee of the Tudeh Party" (On A. Kambakhsh's Obituary), *Ketab-e Jom'eh* 4 (Spring 1985): 68–88.

97. R. Ibrahimzadeh, *Khaterat-e Yek Zan-e Tudehi* (Memoirs of a Woman Member of the Tudeh Party) (Cologne, 1994), 65–67.

98. I. Iskandari, *Yadmandeh-ha va Yaddasht-ha-ye Parakandeh* (Scattered Memoirs) (Tehran, 1986), 259–62.

99. Khamehei, *The Fifty and the Three*, 105.

100. Jahanshahlu, *Recollections*, 1:42.

101. Iskandari, *Political Memoirs*, 1:13.

102. K. Maleki, *Khaterat-e Siyasi* (Political Memoirs) (Hannover, 1981), 250–51.

103. There has been much debate on whether Arani was actually a member of the Communist party. K. Shakeri argues that he was (*Aresh* 30 [September 1993] and 32 [November 1993]). H. Ahmadi counters that he was not (*Adineh* 88 [February 1993] and 89 [April 1993]). Probably, Arani was close but not a formal member. If he had joined, documentary evidence would have been produced by the Tudeh party, which between the 1960s and 1980s had access to the Comintern archives and liked to link itself to the early Communist party. The lack of evidence indicates that Arani never joined even though he had

communist contacts in Tehran and in Moscow whom he visited briefly in 1934 on his way to Berlin to take a course on forensic medicine. Ironically, the course was organized by the Berlin Police Department and Arani's trip was paid for by the Iranian government. In his police investigation, Arani is intentionally ambiguous, admitting only that on his Moscow trip he had "established contact with the party."

104. Farzaneh, *The File for the Fifty-Three*, 227–58.

105. British Legation to the Foreign Office, 3 November 1938, *F.O. 371/34–21890*.

106. For summaries of the trials, see *Ettela'at*, 2–17 November 1938.

107. "Dr. Arani's Defense at the Trial of the Fifty-three," *Donya* 4, nos.1–2 (Spring–Summer 1963):107–20. See also Farzaneh, *The File for the Fifty-three*, 515–40.

108. British Legation to the Foreign Office, 23 November 1938, *F.O.371/*Persia 1938/34–21890.

109. Alavi, *Prison Scrap Papers*, 71.

110. Alavi, *The Fifty-three*, 95.

111. Khamehei, *The Fifty and the Three*, 149.

112. Jahanshahlu, *Recollections*, 1:65.

113. Khamehei, *The Fifty and the Three*, 148–50.

114. Ibid., 204–7.

115. Jahanshahlu, *Recollections*, 1:31.

116. Interview with Alavi, Berlin, July 1993.

117. Jahanshahlu, *Recollections*, 1:68.

118. Alavi, *The Fifty-three*, 136.

119. Ovanessian, *Prison Memoirs* (1944), 35.

120. D. Raffat, *The Prison Papers of Bozorg Alavi* (Syracuse: Syracuse University Press, 1985), 66.

121. I. Iskandari, trans., *Capital* (n.p., 1966), 1–5.

122. Jahanshahlu, *Recollections*, 1:141.

123. A. Khamehei, "Obituary for Taqi Makinezhad," *Kelk*, no. 76–79 (June–October 1996): 826.

124. Jahanshahlu, *Recollections*, 1:127–28.

125. Khamehei, *The Fifty and the Three*, 185, 198.

126. Maleki, *Political Memoirs*, 292, 320.

127. Eftekhari, *Memoirs*, 60, 80, 89.

128. Anonymous (Pishevari), "Concerning the Book *The Fifty-three*," *Azhir*, 22–29 October 1944.

129. Iskandari, *Political Memoirs*, 2:10–11.

130. Khamehei, *The Fifty and the Three*, 32–33.

131. Maleki, *Political Memoirs*, 337.

132. Iskandari, *Political Memoirs*, 1:84.

133. Ibid., 88.

134. Khamehei, *The Fifty and the Three*, 158.

135. Golbani, *The Prosecution of the Prosecutors*, 110.

136. Khamehei, *The Fifty and the Three*, 145–46.

137. Maleki, *Political Memoirs*, 252.

138. Alavi, *The Fifty-three*, 60.

139. R. Bullard, *Letters from Tehran* (London: Tauris, 1991), 223.

2. Mohammad Reza Shah

1. State Department, *Foreign Relations of the United States* (Washington, D.C.: U.S. Government Printing Office, 1969), 1948, 5:176–77. See also State Department, *Foreign Relations of the United States* (Washington, D.C.: U.S. Government Printing Office, 1970), 1949, 6:583.

2. British Minister, "Annual Report for 1942," *F.O. 371/* Persia 1943/34–35117.

3. A. Ovanessian, *Khaterat* (Memoirs) (Cologne, 1991), 61–62.

4. Tudeh Party, "Party Program," *Rahbar*, 12 February 1943.

5. I. Iskandari, *Khaterat-e Siyasi* (Political Memoirs) (Paris, 1986–89), 2:19–22.

6. A. Qassemi, *Hezb-e Tudeh Cheh Meguyad va Cheh Mekhavhad?* (What Does the Tudeh Party of Iran Say and Want?) (Tehran, 1944), 5.

7. Iskandari, *Political Memoirs*, 2:67–68.

8. Ovanessian, *Memoirs*, 261–62.

9. A. Zibayi, *Komunism dar Iran* (Communism in Iran) (Tehran, n.d.), 2:241.

10. British Labour Attaché to the Foreign Office, "The Tudeh Party and the Iranian Trade Unions," *F.O. 371*/Persia 1947/34–61993.

11. A. Khamehei, *Farsat-e Bozorg az Dast Rafteh* (A Big Opportunity Lost) (Tehran, 1983), 125.

12. M. Kaymaram, *Rafiqha-ye Bala* (Exalted Comrades) (n.p., 1995), 104.

13. R. Namvar, *Shahidan-e Tudehi* (Tudeh Martyrs) (Tehran, 1982), 20–44.

14. A. Shamideh, *Zendeginameh-e Shamideh* (The Life Story of Shamideh) (Cologne, 1994), 273. Another refugee places the figure at 15,000. See A. Shafayi, *Qiyam-e Afsaran-e Khurasan* (The Revolt of the Khurasan Officers) (Tehran, 1986), 170.

15. British Embassy, "Tudeh Activities in the Last Year," *F.O. 371*/Persia 1950/34–1493.

16. State Department, *Foreign Relations of the United States*, 1949, 6:476. See also British Ambassador to the Foreign Office, 28 September 1948, *F.O. 371*/Persia 1948/68708.

17. A. Qassemi, "Escape from Qasr," in Q. Forutan, *Hezb-e Tudeh dar Sahneh-e Iran* (The Tudeh Party on the Iranian Scene) (n.p., n.d.), 244–45.

18. S. Ansari, *Az Zendegi-ye Man* (From My Life) (Los Angeles, 1996), 229.

19. For the trials, see *Ettela'at*, 22 April–4 June 1949.

20. A. Mani, *Darbareh-e Mohakemat-e Siyasi-ye Panjah-u-Seh Nafar* (Concerning the Political Trial of the Fifty-three) (Tehran, 1952).

21. *Ettela'at*, 17 May 1949.

22. Forutan, *The Tudeh Party on the Iranian Scene*, 156.

23. N. Kianuri, *Khaterat-e Nuraldin Kianuri* (The Memoirs of Nuraldin Kianuri) (Tehran, 1992), 336.

24. Ansari, *From My Life*, 416.

25. M. Araqi, *Nagofteh-ha: Khaterat-e Shahed Hajj Mehdi Araqi* (Things Unsaid: Memoirs of the Martyred Hajj Mehdi Araqi) (Tehran, 1981), 217.

26. Ansari, *From My Life*, 392.

27. G. Baqeyi, *Angizeh: Khaterat az Dowreh-e Fe'aliyat-e Hezb-e Tudeh* (The Reasons: Memoirs from the Period of Tudeh Party Activities) (Tehran, 1994), 446.

28. Namvar, *Tudeh Martyrs*, 60–130.

29. Kianuri, *The Memoirs of Nuraldin Kianuri*, 302.

30. T. Haqshenas, ed., *Bazandeh: Dastani az Dastgiri, Shek- anjeh, va Taslim-e Qassem 'Abedeni* (The Loser: The Story of the Capture, Torture, and Capitulation of Qassemi 'Abedeni) (Swe- den, 1985), 3.

31. Zibayi, *Communism in Iran*, 2:785–929. This list was be- ing used even in the late 1970s to screen visa applicants to the United States. See J. Temple, "Memo on Visa Applicants," *Es- nad-e Laneh-e Jasous-ye Amerika* (Documents from the Ameri- can Den of Spies), no. 24 (Tehran, 1982): 102.

32. The occupations have been obtained from "letters of res- ignation" published in *Ettela'at*, 1 September 1953–1 May 1957.

33. Foreign Office Note, 23 October 1953, *F.O. 371/104573*.

34. American Embassy to the State Department, "Estimates of Tudeh Numerical Strength," *F.O. 371/104573*.

35. K. Keshavarz, *Chahardah Mah dar Khark: Yaddasht-ha- ye Ruzaneh-e Zendani* (Fourteen Months on Khark: Daily Prison Memoirs) (Tehran, 1984). See also Kaymaram, *Exalted Com- rades*, 353–85; A. Anjoyi-Shirazi, "Nowruz on Khark," *Adineh*, no. 55 (March 1992); and H. Ahmad, "Video-Interview with Morteza Zarbakht," in *The Iranian Left Oral History Project* (Amsterdam: International Institute of Social History, 1996).

36. Quoted by M. Alamutti, *Iran dar Asr-e Pahlavi* (Iran in the Pahlavi Era) (London, 1991), 9:188.

37. U.S. Embassy to the State Department, "Government Anti-Tudeh Campaign," in *The Declassified Documents: Micro- fiche Retrospective Collection*, 309A.

38. Baqeyi, *The Reasons*, 406. See also R. Abbasi, *Khaterat- e Yek Afsar-e Tudehi* (Memoirs of a Tudeh Officer) (Saar- brücken, 1979), 341.

39. Foreign Office Comment, 3 December 1954, *F.O. 371/ 109987*.

40. Foreign Office Comments, 7 September–13 December 1954, *F.O. 371/109985*.

41. British Ambassador, "Report on Tudeh Activities (21 April 1956)," *F.O. 371/120713*.

42. M. Hashemi, *Davari: Sokhani dar Karnameh-e SAVAK* (Judgment: Remarks about SAVAK's Record) (London, 1994), 584.

43. Zibayi, *Communism in Iran*, 2:431.

44. British Embassy, "Notes on Political Parties (16 August 1957)," *F.O. 371/127075*.

45. Tudeh Party, *Akherin Dafaʿ-e Khosrow Rouzbeh* (Khosrow Rouzbeh's Final Defense) (Strassfurt, 1970).

46. Shamlu disowned his poem after the revolution when he finally saw Rouzbeh's confession about Massoud's assassination.

47. M. Khanbaba-Tehrani, *Negahi az Darun beh Jonbesh-e Chap-e Iran* (An Inside Look at the Leftist Movement in Iran) (Saarbrücken, 1986), 1:57.

48. M. Behazin, *Az Har Dari* (From Every Valley) (Tehran, 1991), 56–59.

49. M. Yazdi, "Letter," in Alamutti, *Iran in the Pahlavi Era*, 9:187.

50. For Yazdi's trial, see *Ettelaʿat*, 16 May–11 October 1955.

51. For his broken arm, see Khanbaba-Tehrani, *An Inside Look at the Leftist Movement in Iran*, 1:51.

52. British Ambassador, "Report on Tudeh Activities (21 April 1956)," *F.O. 371/120713*.

53. Ansari, *From My Life*, 425.

54. M. Bahrami, "Letter of Disgust," *Ettelaʿat*, 6 April 1957.

55. Ansari, *From My Life*, 431.

56. Kaymaram, *Exalted Comrades*, 383.

57. Keshavarz, *Fourteen Months on Khark*, 72.

58. Kaymaram, *Exalted Comrades*, 440, 482, 494, 497.

59. Khanbaba-Tehrani, *An Inside Look at the Leftist Movement in Iran*, 1:65.

60. There is some controversy over whether the leaders

ordered members to sign these letters of regret. Kaymaram and Khanbaba-Tehrani insist they did (*Exalted Comrades*, 342; *An Inside Look at the Leftist Movement in Iran*, 1:65). Kianuri insists they did not—but admits they were divided on the issue (*The Memoirs of Nuraldin Kianuri*, 344). In 1958, the central committee in exile expelled five former leaders, including Yazdi and Bahrami, for signing such letters.

61. Kianuri, *The Memoirs of Nuraldin Kianuri*, 63, 355.

62. Abbasi, *Memoirs of a Tudeh Officer*, 431–34. See also Khanbaba-Tehrani, *An Inside Look at the Leftist Movement in Iran*, 1:44.

63. M. Behazin, *Mehman-e In Aqayan* (The Guests of These Gentlemen) (Tehran, 1970).

64. M. Amoui, "Dard-e Zaman: Khaterat-e Mohammad Ali Amoui" (The Epoch's Pain: Memoirs of Mohammad Ali Amoui) (Tehran, 1993). This is a typed manuscript.

65. P. Novidi, "Interview Concerning the Martydom of Bezhan Jazani," *Aghazi Now*, no. 20 (February 1992): 38–40.

66. Amoui, *The Epoch's Pain*, 76.

67. Mojahedin Organization, *Akherin Defaʿeyat* (Final Testimonies) (n.p., 1972), 7.

68. Information obtained from *Bakhtar-e Emruz*, 1970–78; *Mojahed*, 1972–78, 1979–80; *Khabarnameh*, 1971–79; *Kar*, 1979–80; *Peykar*, 1979–81; *Ettelaʿat*, 1971–81; *Kayhan*, 1978–79; and *Ayandegan*, 1978–79.

69. A. Dehqani, *Hamasah-e Moqavamat* (Heroic Resistance) (Beirut, 1974).

70. "The Trial of Tehrani," *Ettelaʿat*, 21 June 1970.

71. H. Fardoust, "Israel and SAVAK Specialists," *Kayhan-e Havaʾi*, 15 April 1992.

72. Fedayi Organization, *System-e Polisi-ye Siyasi* (The Political Police System) (Beirut, 1974), 28–29, 34; Dehqani, *Heroic Resistance*, 60; Confederation of Iranian Students, *Zendan* (Prison) (n.p., 1973), 36; Mojahedin Organization, *Hushyar-e Enqelabi: Vazifeh-e Yek Mobarez Asir dar Zendan* (Revolutionary Awareness: The Responsibility of a Captured Militant in Prison) (n.p., 1972), 49.

73. Democratic Society of Iranians in France, *Dar Rahruha-ye Khon: Yazdah Gozaresh* (In the Labyrinths of Blood: Eleven Eyewitness Accounts) (Paris, 1984), 37.

74. "SAVAK Executioner Confesses," *Ettela'at*, 22 May 1979.

75. "The Trial of Tehrani," *Ettela'at*, 21 June 1979.

76. Amoui, *The Epoch's Pain*, 138.

77. Araqi, *Things Unsaid*, 239–40.

78. Interview with a former political prisoner, Berlin, December 1996.

79. Anonymous, *Mosahebeh* (Interview) (n.p., n.d), 1–31.

80. "Message from a Confederation Leader to Its Members," *Kayhan Havai'i*, 30 December 1972; Anonymous, *Mosahebeh-e Bahram Malayi Daryani* (Interview with Bahram Malayi Daryani) (n.p., n.d.), 1–24; and "Interview with Five Former Members of the Confederation," *Ettela'at-e Hava'i*, 11 August 1971.

81. "Qalechi-Khani Speaks on His Activities," *Ettela'at-e Hava'i*, 15 March 1972.

82. J. Lordman, "The Iranian Solzhenitzyn" (unpublished paper).

83. "Chitchat with Dr. Ghulam-Hossein Sa'edi," *Kayhan*, 19 June 1975.

84. R. Barahani, *The Crowned Cannibals* (New York: Vintage, 1977).

85. R. Barahani, "Terror in Iran," *New York Review of Books*, 28 October 1976.

86. Barahani, *Crowned Cannibals*, 187.

87. M. Ghanoonparvar and J. Green, eds., *Iranian Drama: An Anthology* (Costa Mesa: Mazda, 1989), 63–132.

88. S. Parsipour, *Khaterat-e Zendan* (Prison Memoirs) (Stockholm, 1996), 26.

89. Lordman, "An Iranian Solzhenityn."

90. Barahani, *Crowned Cannibals*, 196.

91. Gh. Sa'edi, in an interview recorded in 1984 in Paris, *Iranian Oral History Collection*, Harvard University. For the transcript, see "Iranian Oral History, *Alefba* 7 (Spring 1986): 70–139.

92. Gh. Sa'edi, "Thought: Manacled," *New York Times*, 21 July 1978.

93. M. Azimi, "The Big Hunger Strike of Prisoners in Qasr," *Noqteh* 4–5 (Winter–Spring 1996): 12–17.

94. Interview with a former political prisoner, New York, 1995.

3. The Islamic Republic

1. List compiled from *Ettela'at*; *Ayandegan*; and National Movement of the Iranian Resistance, *Iran: In Defence of Human Rights* (Paris, 1983).

2. "The Trial of General Hassan Pakravan," *Ettela'at*, 11 April 1979.

3. "The Trial of General Hossein Rabi'i," *Ettela'at*, 9 April 1979.

4. Cited in *Iran Times*, 25 July 1980.

5. Cited in *Iran Times*, 11 July 1980.

6. "The Trial of General Rabi'i," *Ettela'at*, 9 April 1979.

7. "The Trial of Hoveida," *Ettela'at*, 8 April 1979.

8. Cited in *Iran Times*, 22 February 1980.

9. Babak (Pseudonym), "Evin Prison: The Prison for the Innocent," *Iran Times*, 27 August 1982–25 March 1983.

10. K. Homayun, "Short Study of Prisons in the Ten-Year Period 1979–89," *Fedayi*, nos. 64–68 (July–November 1990).

11. E. Naraghi, *From Palace to Prison* (Chicago: Ivan Dee, 1994).

12. M. Fazel, "Prison Diaries," in *Az Armani Keh Mejushad* (From an Ideal that Erupts) (Sweden, 1984).

13. "The Trial of Amir-Abbas Entezam," *Ettela'at*, 18 March 1981.

14. "The Chief Prosecutor Meets the Press," *Ettela'at*, 8 August 1982.

15. Mojahedin Organization, "The Eternal Martyrs of Freedom: The Names and Specific Information on 12,028 Martyrs of the New Iranian Revolution," *Mojahed*, no. 261 (6 September 1985): 1–182.

16. S. Parsipour, *Khaterat-e Zendan* (Prison Memoirs) (Stockholm, 1996), 83–84.

17. "The Complete Text of the Retribution Law," *Iran Times*, 6 March 1981. See also *Iran Times*, 22 May 1981 and 15 October 1982.

18. "The Retribution Law," *Kar International*, June 1981.

19. Imam Jom'eh of Qom, "The Whip Is Better than Prison," *Iran Times*, 20 November 1987.

20. His reasoning is based on the well-known Koranic ruling that husbands can detain—at home—disobedient wives until they mend their ways.

21. "Interview with Hojjat al-Islam Ansari, the Supervisor of Prisons," *Kayhan Hava'i*, 17–25 March 1987.

22. Society for Political Refugees, *Gozaresh az Zendan* (Prison Report) (Göttingen, 1984). See also Anonymous, "Confinement," *Kar (Aksariyat)*, nos. 46–50 (November 1987–March 1988).

23. Anonymous, "Prison and Imprisonment," *Mojahed*, nos.174–256 (20 October 1983–8 August 1985).

24. Amnesty International, *Ill-Treatment of Prisoners in Iran* (London, 1992).

25. Society for Political Refugees, *Prison Report*, 5.

26. A. Khamenei, "Speech," *Ettela'at*, 5 March 1981.

27. A. Nasim, "No Death Have I Feared," *Noqteh* 6 (Summer 1996): 18.

28. Interview with Akbar, Berlin, July 1991.

29. United Nations, *Situation of Human Rights in the Islamic Republic of Iran* (February 1990), 18.

30. *Ettela'at*, 13 February 1984. See also "Prison Repentances: Real or Phony?" *Iran Times*, 30 December 1986 (reprinted from the *Manchester Guardian*).

31. M. Faraz, "Prison Memoirs," *Ettehad-e Kar* 11 (June 1991).

32. Rah-e Kargar Organization, "Horrific Nightmare: Discussions with Three Survivors of the 1988 Mass Executions," *Rah-e Kargar* 90 (January 1992).

33. P. Alizadeh, *Khob Negah Konid: Rastegi Hast* (Observe Well: It Is Real) (Paris, 1987), 23.

34. Democratic Society of Iranians in France, *Dar Rahruha-ye Khon: Yazdah Gozaresh* (In the Labyrinths of Blood: Eleven Eyewitness Accounts) (Paris, 1984), 38.

35. Ibid., 12.

36. A. Entezam, "Letters," *Hoquq-e Bashar* 31 (Spring 1994): 2–5; "Letter from Evin Prison," *Hoquq-e Bashar* 32 (Summer 1994): 10–18; "Letter to the Society for the Defence of Human Rights," *Hoquq-e Bashar* 37 (Spring 1996): 17–23; "Letter to the UN Commission on Human Rights," in United Nations, *Final Report on the Situation of Human Rights in the Islamic Republic of Iran* (New York, 1993).

37. Anonymous, "Letter from Evin," *Rah-e Tudeh*, 12 March 1984.

38. Mojahedin Organization, "The Eternal Martyrs of Freedom."

39. M. Raha (Pseudonym), *Haqiqat-e Sadeh: Khaterat-e az Zendan-ha-ye Zanan-e Jomhuri-ye Islami* (Plain Truths: Memoirs from Women's Prisons in the Islamic Republic) (Hannover, 1992–94), vols. 1–3.

40. Anonymous, "Prison and Imprisonment."

41. Anonymous (E.A.), "Evin: The University Where I Studied Fear," *'Elma va Jam'eh* 54–63 (July 1987–September 1988).

42. "Interview with the Chief Prosecutor," *Kayhan-e Hava'i*, 21 December 1983.

43. "Roundtable Discussion with Twenty-nine Former Activists from the Mini-Groups," *Ettela'at*, 20 October 1982–21 November 1982.

44. Rah-e Kargar Organization, "Horrific Nightmare."

45. Anonymous (E.A.), "Evin: The University Where I Studied Fear."

46. Raha, *Plain Truths*, 1:57.

47. Parsipour, *Prison Memoirs*, 287–91.

48. Anonymous, "Prison and Imprisonment."

49. M. Faraz, "Prison Memoirs," *Ettehad-e Kar* 16–21 (February–July 1991).

50. Ibid.

51. Ibid.

52. Anonymous, "Imam Ali Spoke of the Monafeqin," *Ettela'at*, 3 September 1981.

53. "A Confession," *Ettela'at*, 12 July 1981; "Conversations with Misled Monafeqs," *Ettela'at*, 25 August 1981–28 September 1981; "I Was Sacrificed to Rajavi's Ambitions," *Ettela'at*, 29 September 1981; "Relatives of Martyrs Meet Monafeqs," *Ettela'at*, 24 July 1982; "Roundtable Discussion with Twenty-nine Former Militants from the Mini-Groups," *Ettela'at*, 20 October 1982–21 November 1982; "Text of Conversations with Former Monafeqs," *Ettela'at*, 31 August 1983–6 September 1983.

54. Raha, *Plain Truths*, 1:77.

55. "Television Interview with Sa'id Shahsavandi," *Kayhan-e Hava'i*, 1 February–18 April 1989; "Sa'id Shahsavandi's Lecture at the Industrial University," *Kayhan-e Hava'i*, 17 May 1989; "Shahsavandi's Open Letter to *Le Monde*," *Kayhan-e Hava'i*, 22 February 1989; "Shahsavandi's Open Letter to Rajavi," *Kayhan-e Hava'i*, 29 August 1990.

56. *Kayhan* (London), 28 March 1994, 23 February 1995.

57. Mojahedin Organization, *Bayanieh-e E'lam-e Mavaze'-e Ideolozhik-e Sazeman-e Mojahedin-e Khalq-e Iran* (Manifesto Explaining the Ideological Position of the People's Mojahedin Organization of Iran) (n.p., 1975).

58. "Interviews with Comrades Torab Haqshenas and Hossein Ruhani," *Peykar* 70–84 (1 September 1980–23 November 1980).

59. "Interview with Hossein Ruhani, the Former Ideological Leader of the Mojahedin," *Ettela'at*, 9 May 1982.

60. Raha, *Plain Truths*, 1:70–71.

61. Anonymous (E. A.), "Evin: The University Where I Studied Fear."

62. "Roundtable Discussion with Twenty-nine Former Activists from the Mini-Groups," *Ettela'at*, 20 October 1981–18 November 1981; "Roundtable Discussion with Militants from Kamuleh and the Union of Militant Communists," *Ettela'at*, 19 April 1983–17 May 1983; "Confession of a Fedayi Guerrilla

from the Ashraf Dehqani Branch," *Ettela'at*, 20 June 1981; "Confessions from Members of the Union of Iranian Communists," *Ettela'at*, 11 January 1983–29 January 1983.

63. "Complete Text of Taher Ahmadzadeh's Presentation at the Roundtable Discussions," *Kayhan-e Hava'i*, 14 December 1983.

64. A. Lahiji, "Public Confessions," *Iranshahr*, 9 September 1983.

65. "Text of Sadeq Qotbzadeh's Shocking Confession," *Ettela'at*, 20 April 1982.

66. "Plots Are Revealed," *Ettela'at*, 20 April 1982.

67. C. Jerome, *The Man in the Mirror* (Toronto: Unwin, 1987), 210.

68. "Text of Qotbzadeh's Trial," *Ettela'at*, 23–28 August 1982.

69. Jerome, *The Man in the Mirror*, 289.

70. "Shariatmadari's Confession," *Ettela'at*, 3 May 1982.

71. Ibid.

72. "Why Shariatmadari Fell," *Ettela'at*, 4 May 1982.

73. Ibid.

74. *Iranshahr*, 5 May 1982.

75. "Text of General Fardoust's Confession," *Kayhan-e Hava'i*, 8 April 1987.

76. Anonymous, "The Memoirs of Retired General Hossein Fardoust," *Kayhan-e Hava'i*, 30 November 1988–14 October 1992. See also *Ettela'at*, February 1998.

77. M. Reyshahri, *Khaterat-e Siyasi* (Political Memoirs) (Tehran, 1990).

78. "Full Text of Mehdi Hashemi's Confession 'I Am Manifest Proof of Deviation,'" *Kayhan-e Hava'i*, 17 December 1987.

79. "Interview with the Minister of Intelligence," *Kayhan-e Hava'i*, 24 December 1986.

80. "The Text of the Chief Prosecutor's Indictment against Mehdi Hashemi," *Kayhan-e Hava'i*, 27 August 1987.

81. "Mehdi Hashemi's Trial," *Kayhan-e Hava'i*, 26 August 1987.

82. Reyshahri, *Political Memoirs*, 136–367.

83. Anonymous, *Ranjnameh-e Hazrat Hojjat al-Islam va al-*

Musleman Aqa-ye Hajj Sayyed Ahmad Khomeini beh Hazrat Aya-tollah Montazeri (The Pained Letter of His Highness Hojjat al-Islam Mr. Hajj Sayyed Ahmad Khomeini to Ayatollah Montazeri) (Tehran, 1990), 21.

84. Ibid., 28.

85. Reyshahri, *Political Memoirs*, 73.

86. Anonymous, "Prison and Imprisonment."

87. Editorial, "The Law for Discretionary Punishments," *Aksariyat*, 18 May 1989.

88. Faraz, "Prison Memoirs," *Ettehad-e Kar* 18 (April 1991).

89. Raha, *Plain Truths*, 1:99–100.

90. Homayoun, "Short Study of Prisons," *Fedayi* 65 (August 1990).

91. Parsipour, *Prison Memoirs*, 139.

92. Raha, *Plain Truths*, 2:74.

93. Homayoun, "Short Study of Prisons," *Fedayi* 66 (September 1990).

94. Anonymous, "Confinement," *Kar* 48 (December 1987).

95. Parsipour, *Prison Memoirs*, 209.

96. Democratic Society of Iranians, *In the Labyrinths of Blood*, 4.

97. Anonymous (E.A.), "Evin: The University Where I Studied Fear."

98. Raha, *Plain Truths*, 1:88.

99. Parsipour, *Prison Memoirs*, 355.

4. Tudeh Recantations

1. *Rah-e Tudeh*, 13 May 1983.

2. S. Parsipour, *Khaterat-e Zendan* (Prison Memoirs) (Stockholm, 1996), 196.

3. Anonymous (E.A.), "Evin: The Prison Where I Studied Fear," *'Elm va Jam'eh* 54–63 (July 1987–September 1988), pt. 12, 54–55.

4. V. Kuzichkin, *Inside the KGB: My Life in Soviet Espionage* (New York: Pantheon, 1990), 2. See also pp. 285, 286, 287. He claims erroneously that Iraj Iskandari had been the leader of the Tudeh party since 1944 (p. 264).

5. "Interview with Kianuri," from *Revolution,* reprinted in *Rah-e Tudeh,* 4 March 1983.

6. "Tudeh Starting to Criticize the Regime," *Iran Times,* 1 October 1982.

7. N. Kianuri, "The Iranian Revolution Is in Danger," reprinted in *Iran Times,* 8–22 April 1983.

8. Kuzichkin, *Inside the KGB,* 356.

9. A. Ettemadzadeh, "Letter to Ayatollah Montazeri," *Rah-e Tudeh,* 19 August 1983.

10. "Tudeh Leaders Confess to Spying for the Soviets and Betraying the Country," *Ettela'at,* 1 May 1983.

11. Kianuri elaborated on these themes in his second television appearance. See "Kianuri Exposes Half-Century of Treachery by the Soviets, the Marxists, and the Tudeh Party," *Ettela'at,* 28 August 1983.

12. *Kayhan-e Hava'i,* 11 May 1983.

13. Ettemadzadeh, "Letter to Ayatollah Montazeri."

14. Prosecutor General, "The Official Dissolution of the Tudeh Party," *Kayhan-e Hava'i,* 11 May 1983.

15. *Iran Times,* 13 May 1983.

16. R. Khomeini, "Undermining the Islamic Republic Is the Same as Undermining Islam," *Ettela'at,* 29 May 1983.

17. Editorial, "Confession," *Ettela'at,* 8–26 May 1983.

18. "Conversation with the Chief Prosecutor," *Ettela'at,* 31 May 1983.

19. "Ayatollah Janati Speaks on the Arrest of the Treacherous Leaders of the Tudeh Party," *Ettela'at,* 17 May 1983.

20. "Ayatollah Taheri's Message," *Ettlela'at,* 7 May 1983.

21. M. Hojjati-Kermani, "Congratulations to the Imam and the Community for Their Ideological Victory," *Ettela'at,* 15 May–5 June 1983.

22. M. Rajavi, "The Lesson to Be Drawn from the Fate of the Tudeh Party," *Mojahed,* 12 May 1983.

23. A. Shams, "Ehsan Tabari's Game," *Kayhan* (London), 14 March 1985.

24. L.M., "Effort to Save the Spies," *Nahzat,* 10 October 1985.

25. Editorial, "The End of Revisionism, " *Kar,* 9 May 1983.

26. Liberation Front, "Announcement Concerning the Treacherous Tudeh Party," *Iranshahr*, 29 July 1983.

27. N. Jahanshahlu, *Sarguzasht* (Recollections) (Berlin, 1986), 2:243.

28. I. Iskandari, "The Medicine of Confession," *Golsorkh* 1 (Summer 1985): 30–43.

29. A. Sayyed-Javadi, "The Memoirs of Dr. Faust," *'Elm va Jam'eh* 57 (December 1987): 18–30.

30. B. Bakhtiari, "The Leftist Challenge: The Mojahedin-e Khalq and the Tudeh Party," *Journal of South Asian and Middle Eastern Studies* 13, nos. 1–2 (Fall–Winter): 29–51.

31. S. Zabih, *The Left in Contemporary Iran* (Stanford: Hoover Institution Press, 1986), 42–45.

32. "Qaempanah Confesses to Working for the KGB," *Ettela'at*, 3 May 1983.

33. "Mohammadzadeh's Confession," *Ettela'at*, 3 May 1983.

34. "Ovanessian's Confession," *Ettela'at*, 3 May 1983.

35. M. Firuz, *Khaterat-e Maryam Firuz* (Memoirs of Maryam Firuz) (Tehran, 1994), 64.

36. "Rasadi's Confession," *Ettela'at*, 3 May 1983.

37. "Zarshenas's Confession," *Ettela'at*, 3 May 1983.

38. "Tudeh Leader Reveals Plan to Overthrow the Islamic Republic," *Ettela'at*, 4 September 1983.

39. "Reza Sheltouki Declares He Has No Choice but to Confess to Treason," *Ettela'at*, 10 May 1983.

40. "Mohammad Ali Amoui's Confession," *Ettela'at*, 7 May 1983.

41. M. Hojjati-Kermani, "Congratulations to the Imam and the Community for Their Ideological Victory," *Ettela'at*, 15 May–6 June 1983.

42. H. Allahi, "The Tudeh Party—the Conspiratorial Instrument of Both East and West," *Ettela'at*, 4 July 1983.

43. "The Text of the Confessions of Eighteen Leaders of the Dissolved Tudeh Party Concerning Subversion, Spying, Separatism, and Forty Years of Treason," *Ettela'at*, 4–8 October 1983; "Leaders of the Dissolved and Treacherous Tudeh Party Describe Their Espionage Activities on Behalf of the Soviets,"

Kayhan-e Hava'i, 19 October–4 November 1983; Islamic Republic, *Jambadi-ye Chehel-u-Dow Sal-e 'Amalkard-e Hezb-e Tudeh* (Summary of Forty-two Years of Tudeh Party Activities) (Rome, 1984), 1–63.

44. Anonymous, "Memorial to the Martyrs," *Donya* 1, no. 2 (February 1986): 138–200.

45. United Nations (Economic and Social Council), *Situation of Human Rights in the Islamic Republic of Iran* (New York, November 1990), 53.

46. N. Kianuri, *Khaterat-e Nuraldin Kianuri* (The Memoirs of Nuraldin Kianuri) (Tehran, 1992), 546–47.

47. For summaries of the court proceedings, see *Ettela'at*, 7 December 1983–17 January 1984; and *Kayhan-e Hava'i*, 14 December 1983–24 January 1984.

48. Anonymous, "In Memory of the Officers Fallen in the 1988 Mass Executions," *Mardom* 513 (26 August 1997).

49. "Interview with the Presiding Judge," *Ettela'at*, 22 February 1984.

50. "Ehsan Tabari Repudiates Marxism, Soviet Policies, and Forty Years of the Tudeh Party," *Ettela'at*, 7–9 May 1984.

51. E. Tabari, "The Crooked Road," *Ettela'at*, 7 February–4 March 1985; "Knowledge and Considerations of Marxism," *Kayhan-e Hava'i*, 28 December 1989–8 August 1990.

52. A. Salek, "An Important Document on the History of Contemporary Iran," *Kayhan-e Hava'i*, 9 December 1987.

53. *Kayhan International*, 21 October 1984.

54. A. Barhan (Pseudonym), *Biraheh: Pasokh Beh Kazh Rahah-e Ehsan Tabari* (The Deviated Road: Answer to Ehsan Tabari's Crooked Road) (Tehran, 1989).

55. E. Tabari, "The Nature of Life and the Soul," *Kayhan International*, 21 October 1984–27 January 1985.

56. M. Faraz, "Prison Memoirs," *Ettehad-e Kar* 20 (June 1991): 16–17.

57. "Ehsan Tabari Passed Away," *Kayhan-e Hava'i*, 10 May 1989.

5. Mass Executions of 1988

1. For eyewitness accounts, see M. Raha (Pseudonym), *Haqiqat-e Sadeh: Khaterat-e az Zendan-ha-ye Zanan-e Jomhuri-ye Islami* (Plain Truths: Memoirs from Women's Prisons in the Islamic Republic) (Hannover, 1992–94), 3:125–48; N. Pakdaman, ed., "Five Eyewitness Accounts of the 1988 Executions," *Cheshmandaz*, no.14 (Winter 1995): 54–74; Rah-e Kargar Organization, "Horrific Nightmare: Discussion with Three Survivors of the 1988 Mass Executions," *Rah-e Kargar* 90–93 (January–March 1992); K. Homayun, "The Slaughter at Gohar Dasht," *Fedayi* 61–62 (March–April 1990); Anonymous, "Reminiscences of the Mass Executions from Family Members," *Ettehad-e Kar* 12 (August 1990); Anonymous, "Clerics Without Mercy: Letter from a Martyr's Mother," *Ettehad-e Kar* 35 (August 1992); Anonymous, "Letter from a Grieving Relative," *Ettehad-e Kar* 12 (August 1990); Anonymous, "Letter from Gohar Dasht," *Mardom* 297 (6 February 1990); Anonymous, "Letter from Prison," *Mardom* 259 (16 May 1989); Anonymous, "I Witnessed the Slaughter of Political Prisoners," *Payam-e Kargar* 64–68 (February–May 1990); Amnesty International, *Iran: Violations of Human Rights, 1987–90* (London, 1990), 1–65; Refugee Committee, *Dar Sal-e 1377 Bar ma Cheh Ghozasht?* (What Happened to Us in 1988?) (Paris, 1994), 1–32; N. Mohajer, "The Mass Killings in Iran," *Aresh* 57 (August 1996): 4–8; "Interview with Two Survivors of the Mass Killings," *Ettehad-e Kar* 41 (August 1997).

2. Raha, *Plain Truths*, 3:129.

3. Anonymous, "Letter from Gohar Dasht," *Mardom* 297 (6 February 1990).

4. "The Mass Executions as Narrated by Eyewitnesses," *Rah-e Tudeh* 64 (September 1997).

5. "Interview with Two Survivors."

6. Editorial, "The Islamic Law of Repentence," *Aksariyat*, 18 May 1989.

7. "Interview with Two Survivors."

8. "The Mass Executions as Narrated by Eyewitnesses."

9. Anonymous, "Examples of Valiant Resistance," *Mardom* 297 (6 February 1990).

10. "Interview with Two Survivors"; "An Introduction to Those Responsible for the Mass Executions," *Rah-e Tudeh* 65 (October 1997).

11. E. Mahbaz (Pseudonym), "The Islamic Republic of Iran—The Hell for Women: Seven Years in Prison" (unpublished paper, 1996).

12. Ibid.

13. H. Mottaqi, "Life after 1988," *Noqteh* 6 (Summer 1966): 20–22.

14. Raha, *Plain Truths*, 2:129. See also Ayatollah Montazeri, "Letter to Imam Khomeini," 31 August 1988.

15. Anonymous, "I Was Witness to the Slaughter of Political Prisoners in Gohar Dasht," *Cheshmandaz*, no. 14 (Winter 1995): 68.

16. K. Homayun, "The Slaughter at Gohar Dasht," *Kar* 62 (April 1992).

17. N. Mohajer, "The Mass Killings in Iran," *Aresh* 57 (August 1996): 7.

18. Amnesty International, *Iran: Violations of Human Rights, 1987–1990* (London, 1991), 12.

19. Central Committee of the Majority Fedayi, "Those Sacrificed in the Mass Political Executions," *Kar* 59–60 (January–February 1990).

20. *Mardom*, 6 January 1989–21 June 1992.

21. "Introduction to Those Responsible for the 1988 Executions."

22. Hojjat al-Islam Ansari, "The Reasons for Ayatollah Montazeri's Resignation," *Kayhan-e Hava'i*, 26 April 1989.

23. "The Mass Executions as Narrated by Eyewitnesses," *Rah-e Tudeh* 64 (September 1997).

24. Editor, "Montazeri's Letters," *Cheshmandaz*, no. 6 (Summer 1989): 35–37.

25. *Iran Times*, 29 March 1989.

26. Anonymous, *Ranjnameh-e Hazrat Hojjat al-Islam va al-*

Musulman Aqa-ye Hajj Sayyed Ahmad Khomeini beh Hazrat Ayatollah Montazeri (The Pained Letters of His Highness Hojjat al-Islam al-Muslim Mr. Hajj Sayyed Ahmad Khomeini to Ayatollah Montazeri) (Tehran, 1990).

27. "The Regime Denounces Ayatollah Montazeri," *Rah-e Tudeh* 68 (January 1998).

28. "Interview with Two Survivors."

29. Anonymous, "The Morning of Freedom for Those Returning to the True Light," *Kayhan-e Hava'i*, 15 March 1989.

30. United Nations, "Report on Human Rights in Iran," *Iran Times*, 18 February 1994.

31. United Nations, "Report on Iran," *Iran Times*, 13 May 1994.

32. Amnesty International, "Report on Iran," *Iran Times*, 26 August 1994.

33. A. Entezam, "Letter to the UN Human Rights Commission on Iran," 18 January 1993.

34. A. Danesh, "Open Letter to Ayatollah Montazeri," *Mardom*, June 1988.

35. United Nations (Economic and Social Council), *Situation of Human Rights in the Islamic Republic of Iran* (New York, February 1990), 32.

36. United Nations (Economic and Social Council), *Situation of Human Rights in the Islamic Republic of Iran* (New York, November 1990), 53.

37. S. Siyasi, "Interview with Nuraldin Kianuri, the Former Chairman of the Dissolved Tudeh Party, on Recent Events in the Soviet Union," *Kayhan-e Hava'i*, 23–30 October 1991; Special Correspondent, "Interview with Kianuri on the Collapse of Communism," *Jomhuri-ye Islam*, 10 December 1992–26 January 1993.

38. Raha, *Plain Truths*, 1:141–43.

39. Ibid., 3:28.

40. Ibid., 1:111.

41. Rah-e Kargar Organization, "Horrific Nightmare . . . ," *Rah-e Kargar* 91 (February 1992): 12.

42. Ibid.

43. Anonymous, "The Repenters," *Kar* 48 (February 1988): 6.

44. Homayun, "The Slaughter at Gohar Dasht," *Fedayi* 65 (July 1990): 33.

45. United Nations (Economic and Social Council), *Situation of Human Rights in the Islamic Republic of Iran* (New York, November 1990), 65.

46. J. Simpson, *Behind Iranian Lines* (London: Robson, 1988), 192.

47. "Behbahani Confesses to Having Links with America," *Kayhan-e Hava'i*, 15 August 1990.

48. Editorial, "Another Show Produced by Torture," *Mardom*, 13 August 1990.

49. "Sa'idi Sirjani Confesses to Working for the CIA," *Kayhan-e Hava'i*, 15 June 1994.

50. F. Sarkouhi, "Open Letter," *Rowshanai*, February 1997.

Bibliography

General Works

Amnesty International. *Torture in Greece*. London: Amnesty International, 1977.

Barber, M. *The Trial of the Templars*. Cambridge: Canto, 1994.

Bassouni, M., ed. *The Islamic Criminal Justice System*. New York: Oceana, 1982.

Beck, F., and W. Godin. *Russian Purge and the Extraction of Confession*. New York: Viking, 1951.

Briggs, R. *Witches and Neighbours*. London: Fontana Press, 1966.

Cheng, N. *Life and Death in Shanghai*. New York: Penguin, 1988.

Christenson, R. *Public Trials*. New Brunswick: Transaction Books, 1986.

Cohn, N. *Europe's Inner Demons*. London: Pimlico, 1993.

Conquest, R. *The Great Terror*. New York: Macmillan, 1973.

Coulson, N. *History of Islamic Law*. Edinburgh: Edinburgh University Press, 1964.

Dassin, J., ed. *Torture in Brazil*. New York: Vintage, 1986.

Davies, I. *Writers in Prison*. Oxford: Blackwell, 1990.

Deutscher, I. "The Moscow Trial." In *Marxism, Wars and Revolution*. London: Verso, 1984.

Dostoevsky, F. *The Brothers Karamazov*. New York: Norton, 1976.

———. *The House of the Dead*. New York: Macmillan, 1915.

Douglas, Mary, ed. *Witchcraft Confessions and Accusations*. London: Tavistock, 1970.

Floor, W. "Changes and Development in the Judicial System of Qajar Iran (1800–1925)." In *Qajar Iran: Political, Social and Cultural Changes*, ed. E. Bosworth and C. Hillebrand, 113–47. Edinburgh: Edinburgh University Press, 1993.

Foucault, M. *Discipline and Punish: The Birth of the Prison*. London: Penguin, 1975.

Ginzburg, C. *Clues, Myths, and the Historical Method*. Baltimore: John Hopkins University Press, 1986.

———. *Night Battles*. New York: Penguin, 1985.

Given, J. "The Inquisitors of Languedoc." *American Historical Review* 94, no. 2 (April 1989): 336–59.

Harlow, B. *Barred: Women, Writing and Political Detention*. Hanover: Wesleyan University Press, 1992.

Hellman, L. *Scoundrel Time*. Boston: Little, Brown, 1976.

Hill, F. *A Delusion of Satan*. New York: Doubleday, 1995.

Hodos, G. *Stalinist Purges in Eastern Europe, 1948–54*. New York: Praeger, 1987.

Ignatieff, M. *A Just Measure of Pain: The Penitentiary in the Industrial Revolution*. New York: Pantheon, 1978.

Kaplan, J. *Report on the Murder of the General Secretary*. London: Tauris, 1991.

Koestler, A. *Darkness at Noon*. London: Cape, 1954.

Kors, A., and E. Peters. *Witchcraft in Europe: A Documentary History*. Philadelphia: University of Pennsylvania Press, 1995.

Kropotkin, P. *Memoirs of a Revolutionist*. New York: Houghton Mifflin, 1899.

Ladurie, E. *Montaillou: The Promised Land of Error*. New York: Vintage, 1979.

Langbein, J. *Torture and the Law of Proof*. Chicago: University of Chicago Press, 1976.

Larina, A. *This I Cannot Forget*. New York: Norton, 1993.

Lea, H. *A History of the Inquisition in the Middle Ages*. 4 vols. London: Macmillan, 1922.

Levak, B. *The Witch-Hunt in Early Modern Europe*. London: Longman, 1993.

Lifton, R. J. *Thought Reform and Psychology of Totalism: A Study of "Brainwashing" in China*. Chapel Hill: University of North Carolina Press, 1989.

Malcolm, J. *The History of Persia*. London: Longman, 1815.

Marshall, B. *Victor Serge*. New York: St. Martin's, 1996.

Medvedev, R. *Let History Judge*. New York: Vintage, 1973.

Millet, K. *The Politics of Cruelty*. New York: Norton, 1994.

Morris, N., and D. Rothman. *The Oxford History of the Prison*. Oxford: Oxford University Press, 1995.

Navasky, V. *Naming Names*. New York: Penguin, 1980.

Orwell, G. *Nineteen Eighty-four*. London: Penguin, 1949.

Peters, E. *Inquisition*. Berkeley: University of California Press, 1989.

——. *Torture*. Oxford: Blackwell, 1985.

Rodinson, M. *Mohammed*. London: Penguin, 1971.

Rosenthal, F. *The Muslim Concept of Freedom*. Leiden: Brill, 1960.

Rusche, G., and O. Kirckheimer. *Punishment and Social Structure*. New York: Russell, 1968.

Ruthven, M. *Torture: The Grand Conspiracy*. London: Weidenfeld, 1978.

Scarry, E. *The Body in Pain*. New York: Oxford University Press, 1985.

Schacht, J. *An Introduction to Islamic Law*. Oxford: Oxford University Press, 1964.

Schrecker, E. *No Ivory Tower: McCarthyism and the Universities*. New York: Oxford University Press, 1986.

Serge, V. *The Case of Comrade Tulayev*. London: Penguin, 1968.

—— *From Lenin to Stalin*. New York: Pathfinder, 1987.

—— *Men in Prison*. London: Penguin, 1972.

Sharp, J. "Last Dying Speeches: Religion, Ideology and Public

Execution in Seventeenth-Century England." *Past and Present*, no.107 (May 1985): 144–67.

Sheil, M. *Glimpses of Life and Manners in Persia*. London: Murray, 1856.

Smith, L. "English Treason Trials and Confessions in the Sixteenth Century." *Journal of the History of Ideas* 15, no. 4 (October 1954): 471–98.

Spierenburg, P. *The Spectacle of Suffering*. Cambridge: Cambridge University Press, 1984.

Stauth, G. "Revolution in Spiritless Times: An Essay on Foucault's Enquiries into the Iranian Revolution." *International Sociology* 6, no. 3 (September 1991): 159–80.

Suedfeld, P., ed. *Psychology and Torture*. New York: Hemisphere, 1990.

Thomas, K. *Religion and the Decline of Magic*. New York: Scribners, 1971.

Trevor-Roper, H. R. *The European Witch-Craze*. New York: Harper, 1965.

Tucker, R., and S. Cohen. *The Great Purge Trial*. New York: Dunlop, 1965.

Vaksberg, A. *Stalin's Prosecutor: The Life of Andrei Vyshinsky*. New York: Weidenfeld, 1990.

Waterbury, J. "Kingdom-building and the Control of the Opposition in Morocco: The Monarchical Uses of Justice." *Government and Opposition* 5, no. 1 (Winter 1969): 54–72.

Wilde, O. *De Profundis*. London: Penguin, 1986.

Works on Iranian Prisons

Abbasi, R. *Khaterat-e Yek Afsar-e Tudehi* (Memoirs of a Tudeh Army Officer). Saarbrücken, 1979.

Abdoh, J. *Khaterat-e Chehel Sal dar Sahneh-ye Qaza'i* (Memoirs of Forty Years in the Judiciary). 2 vols. Ed. M. Tafreshi. Tehran, 1988–89.

Ahmadi, H. *Khaterat-e Bozorg Alavi* (Memoirs of Bozorg Alavi). Stockholm, 1997.

———. *Tarikhcheh-e Ferqeh-e Jomhuri-ye Enqelabi-ye Iran* (Short History of the Revolutionary Republican Party of Iran). Berlin, 1992.

———. "Video Interview with Morteza Zarbakht." In *The Iranian Left Oral History Project*. Amsterdam: International Institute of Social History, 1996.

Ahmadi-Eskouyi, M. *Khaterati az Yek Rafiq* (Memoirs from a Comrade). Aden, 1974.

Alamutti, M. *Iran dar Asr-e Pahlavi* (Iran in the Pahlavi Era). Vol. 9. London, 1991.

Alamutti, Z. *Fasuli az Tarikh* (Chapter from History). Tehran, 1991.

Alavi, B. *Panjah-u-Seh Nafar* (The Fifty-three). Tehran, 1944.

———. *Varaqpareh-ha-ye Zendan* (Prison Scrap Papers). Tehran, 1942.

Alizadeh, P. *Khob Negah Konid: Rastegi Hast* (Observe Well: It Is Real). Paris, 1987.

Amnesty International. *Evidence of Torture in Iran*. London, 1984.

———. *Human Rights Violations in Iran*. London, 1982.

———. *Ill-Treatment of Prisoners in Iran*. London, 1992.

———. *Iran*. London, 1987.

———. *Iran: Executions of Prisoners Continue Unabated*. London, 1992.

———. *Iran: Imprisonment, Torture, and Execution of Political Prisoners*. New York, 1992.

———. *Iran: Victims of Human Rights Violations*. London, 1993.

———. *Iran: Violations of Human Rights, 1987–90*. London, 1991.

———. *Iran: Violations of Human Rights, 1989–90*. New York, 1990.

Amoui, M. "Dard-e Zaman: Khaterat-e Mohammad Ali Amoui" (The Epoch's Pain: Memoirs of Mohammad Ali Amoui). Tehran, 1993.

Anjoyi-Shirazi, A. "Nowruz on Khark." *Adineh* 55 (March 1992).

Anonymous. "Confinement." *Kar (Aksariyat)* 46–50 (November 1987–March 1988).

Anonymous (E.A.). "Evin: The University Where I Studied Fear." *'Elm va Jam'eh* 54–63 (July 1987–September 1988).

Anonymous. "The Guerrilla Movement and the Prisons" *Mojahed* 4 (November 1974): 75–93.

Anonymous. "In Memory of the Officers Fallen in the 1988 Mass Executions." *Mardom* 513 (26 August 1997).

Anonymous. "Interview with Two Survivors of the 1988 Mass Executions." *Ettehad-e Kar* 41 (August 1987).

Anonymous. "Introduce to the Public Those Responsible for the Mass Executions." *Rah-e Tudeh* 65 (October 1997).

Anonymous. "I Witnessed the Slaughter of Political Prisoners." *Payam-e Kargar* 64–68 (February–May 1990).

Anonymous. "The Mass Executions as Narrated by Eyewitnesses." *Rah-e Tudeh* 64 (September 1997).

Anonymous. "Memorial to the Martyrs." *Donya* 1, no. 2 (February 1986): 138–200.

Anonymous. "Prison and Imprisonment." *Mojahed* 174–256 (20 October 1983–8 August 1985).

Anonymous. "Prisons and Executions." *Cheshmandaz*, no. 6 (Winter 1989): 28–42.

Anonymous. "Prison Experiences." *Ettehad-e Kar* 9–11 (April–July 1990).

Ansari, S. *Az Zendegi-ye Man* (From My Life). Los Angeles, 1996.

Aramesh, A. *Haft Sal dar Zendan-e Aryamehr* (Seven Years in Aryamehr's Prison). Tehran, 1979.

Araqi, M. *Nagofteh-ha: Khaterat-e Shahed Hajj Mehdi Araqi* (Things Unsaid: Memoirs of the Martyred Hajj Mehdi Araqi). Tehran, 1981.

Azad, M. (Pseudonym). "The Shiraz Prison." *Noqteh* 6 (Summer 1996): 9–13.

———. *Yad-ha-ye Zendan* (Prison Reminiscences). Paris, 1997.

Azadi, H. *Dar-ha va Divar-ha: Khaterati az Zendan-e Evin* (Doors and Walls: Memoirs from Evin Prison). Paris, 1997.

Azimi, M. "The Big Hunger Strike of Prisoners in Qasr." *Noqteh* 4–5 (Winter–Spring 1996): 12–17.

Azod, A. *Baznegri dar Tarikh* (A Review of History). Bethesda, 1996.

Babak (Pseudonym). "Evin Prison: The Prison for the Innocent." *Iran Times*, 27 August 1982–25 March 1983.

Bahai International Community. *The Bahai Question.* New York: Bahai International Community, 1993.

Bakhtiyar, T. *Evolution of Communism in Iran.* Tehran, 1959.

———. *Ketab-e Siyah* (The Black Book). Tehran, 1955.

Baqeyi, G. *Angizeh: Khaterat az Dowreh-e Fe'aliyat-e Hezb-e Tudeh* (The Reasons: Memoirs from the Period of Tudeh Party Activities). Tehran, 1994.

Barahani, R. *The Crowned Cannibals.* New York: Vintage, 1977.

———. *God's Shadow.* Bloomington: Indiana University Press, 1976.

Barhan, A. (Pseudonym). *Biraheh: Pasokh Beh Kazh Rahah-e Ehsan Tabari* (The Deviated Road: Answer to Ehsan Tabari's Crooked Road). Tehran, 1989.

Bayat, K. *Asnad-e Ahzab-e Siyasi-ye Iran: Fe'aliat-ha-ye Komunisti dar Dowreh-e Reza Shah* (Documents on Iranian Political Parties: Communist Activities during Reza Shah's Era). Tehran, 1991.

Behazin, M. (M. Ettemadzadeh). *Az Har Dari* (From Every Valley). Tehran, 1991.

———. *Mehman-e In Aqayan* (The Guests of These Gentlemen). Tehran, 1970.

Boqrati, M. "Letter to the Central Committee of the Tudeh Party" (On A. Kambakhsh's Obituary). *Ketab-e Jom'eh* 4 (Fall 1985): 67–88.

Butler, W. *Human Rights and the Legal System in Iran.* Geneva, 1976.

Confederation of Iranian Students. *Asnad-ye darbareh Mobarezeh bar'aleh-e Polis-e Siyasi* (Documents on the Struggle against the Political Police). New York, 1973.

————. *Darbareh SAVAK* (Concerning SAVAK). Frankfurt, 1969.

————. *Zendan* (Prison). N.p., 1973.

Cooper, R. *Death Plus Ten Years*. London: HarperCollins, 1993.

Danesh, T. *Hoquq-e Zendanyan* (The Rights of Prisoners). Tehran, 1987.

Darvish, H. *Va Hanouz Qaseh bar Yad Ast* (And Still Lives Our Story). Berkeley, 1998.

Dashti, A. *Ayyam-e Mahbas* (Prison Days). Tehran, 1954.

Dehqani, A. *Hamasah-e Moqavamat* (Heroic Resistance). Beirut, 1974.

Dehqani, M. *Zendan Khatreh Larindeh* (Prison Memoirs). Baku, 1987.

Democratic Society of Iranians in France. *Dar Rahruha-ye Khon: Yazdah Gozaresh* (In the Labyrinths of Blood: Eleven Eyewitness Accounts). Paris, 1984.

Derakhsani, F. "Evin's Gate." Unpublished manuscript, 1986.

Eftekhari, Y. *Khaterat-e Dowran-e Separishudeh* (Memoirs of a Bygone Era). Ed. K. Bayat and M. Tafreshi. Tehran, 1991.

Fakheteh, N. *Dastanha-ye Dehkadeh-e Evin* (Stories from the Hamlet of Evin). Sweden, 1992.

Faraz, M. "Prison Memoirs." *Ettehad-e Kar* 16–21 (February–July 1991).

————. "Prison Memoirs." *Ettehad-e Kar* 17 (June 1991).

Farzaneh, H. (Pseudonym). *Parvandeh-e Panjah-u-Seh Nafar* (The File for the Fifty-three). Tehran, 1993.

Fazel, M. "Prison Diaries." In *Az Armani Keh Mejushad* (From an Ideal that Erupts). Sweden, 1984.

Fedayi Organization. *Shekanjeh va Koshtar-e Mehanparastan* (The Torture and Killing of Patriots). N.p., 1984.

————. *System-e Polisi-ye Siyasi* (The Political Police System). Beirut, 1974.

————. *Tojareb-e Bazjoyi va Shanjeh* (Torture and the Interrogation Experience). Beirut, 1974.

Firuz Mirza Farmanfarma (Nosrat al-Dawleh). *Khaterat-e Mahbas* (Prison Memoirs). Ed. M. Ettehadieh and S. Sa'dvanian. Tehran, 1986.

———. *Majmuʿah-e Mokatibat* (Collected Papers). 2 vols. Ed. M. Ettehadieh and S. Saʿdvanian. Tehran, 1987.

Fischer, M. "Legal Postulates in Flux: Justice, Wit, and Hierarchy in Iran." In *Law and Islam in the Middle East*, ed. D. Dwyer, 115–42. New York, 1990.

Forutan, Q. *Afsaneh-e Ma* (Our Myth). N.p., n.d.

———. *Hezb-e Tudeh dar Mahajerat* (The Tudeh Party in Exile). N.p., n.d.

———. *Hezb-e Tudeh dar Sahneh-e Iran* (The Tudeh Party on the Iranian Scene). N.p., n.d.

Ghanoonparvar, M., and J. Green, eds. *Iranian Drama: An Anthology*. Costa Mesa: Mazda, 1989.

Golban, M., and Y. Sharifi, *Mohakemeh-e Mohakemegan* (The Prosecution of the Prosecutors). Tehran, 1984.

Gorgani, F. "Commemorating the Martyrdom of Dr. Taqi Arani." *Donya* (March 1980): 118–64.

Haqshenas, T., ed. *Bazandeh: Dastani az Dastgiri, Shekanjeh, va Taslim-e Qassem ʿAbedini* (The Loser: The Story of the Capture, Torture, and Capitulation of Qassem ʿAbedini). Sweden, 1985.

Hashemi, M. *Davari: Sokhani dar Karnameh-e Savak* (Judgment: Remarks about SAVAK's Record). London, 1994.

Homayun, K. "Short Study of Prisons in the Ten-Year Period 1979–89." *Fedayi* 64–68 (July–November 1990).

Hosseini, M. "Prisons and Imprisonment in Iran." *Ganjineh* 1, nos. 2–3 (Fall–Winter 1991): 44–58.

Human Rights Watch. *Guardians of Thought: Limits of Freedom of Expression in Iran*. New York, 1993.

———. *The Justice System of the Islamic Republic of Iran*. New York, 1993.

———. *World Report: 1990*. New York, 1991.

Ibrahimoff, I. (T. Shahin). *Paydayesh-e Hezb-e Komunist-e Iran* (Formation of the Iranian Communist Party). Baku, 1963.

Ibrahimzadeh, R. *Khaterat-e Yek Zan-e Tudehi* (Memoirs of a Woman Member of the Tudeh Party). Ed. B. Chubineh. Cologne, 1994.

International Federation on Human Rights. "Report on Violations of Human Rights in Iranian Kurdestan." *Alefba* 4 (Fall 1983): 157–76.

International Solidarity Front for the Defense of the Iranian People's Democratic Rights. *The Crimes of Khomeini's Regime.* New York, 1982.

Irani, M. (Pseudonym). *King of the Benighted.* Washington, D.C.: Mazda, 1995.

Iskandari, A. *Ketab-e Arzu* (Book of Aspirations). Tehran, 1982.

Iskandari, I. *Khaterat-e Siyasi* (Political Memoirs). 4 vols. Paris, 1986–89.

———. "The Medicine of Confession." *Golsorkh* 1 (Summer 1985): 30–43.

———. "Reminiscences of Dr. Arani and the Journal *Donya.*" *Donya* 10, no. 4 (Winter 1969): 10–13.

———. *Yadmandeh-ha va Yaddasht-ha-ye Parakandeh* (Scattered Memoirs). Tehran, 1986.

Islamic Republic. *Jambadi-ye Chehel-u-Dow Sal-e 'Amalkard-e Hezb-e Tudeh* (Summary of Forty-two Years of Tudeh Party Activities). Rome, 1984.

Jahanshahlu, N. *Sarguzasht* (Recollections). 2 vols. Berlin, 1986.

Kaymaram, M. *Rafiqha-ye Bala* (Exalted Comrades). N.p, 1995.

Keshavarz, F. *Afkar va Aqayed-e Siyasi-ye Doktor Fereydun Keshavarz* (The Thoughts and Political Ideas of Dr. Fereydun Keshavarz). Bethlehem, Pa., 1992.

———. *Man Motahem Mekonam* (I Accuse). Tehran, 1978.

Keshavarz, K. *Chahardah Mah dar Khark: Yaddasht-ha-ye Ruzaneh-e Zendani* (Fourteen Months on Khark: Daily Prison Diaries). Tehran, 1984.

Khaksar, N. *Dirouzha* (Yesterdays). N.p., 1987.

Khalili, M. *Tarikh-e Shekanjeh: Az Qademtarin Ayam to Payan-e Sassanyan* (History of Torture: From the Earliest Times to the End of the Sassanids). Tehran, 1980.

Khamehei, A. *Farsat-e Bozorg az Dast Rafteh* (A Big Opportunity Lost). Tehran, 1983.

———. *Panjah Nafar va Seh Nafar* (The Fifty and the Three). Tehran, 1984.

———. *Pasokh beh Muda'ye* (Answer to the Plaintiff). Tehran, 1989.

Khanbaba-Tehrani, M. *Negahi az Darun beh Jonbesh-e Chap-e Iran* (An Inside Look at the Leftist Movement in Iran). 2 vols. Saarbrücken, 1986.

Knorzer, J. *Ali Dashti's Prison Days*. Washington, D.C.: Mazda, 1994.

Kobari, A. "Reminiscences from the Cultural Society and the Communist Party in Gilan." *Donya* 12, no. 4 (Summer 1971): 80–83.

Kotayun (Pseudonym). "Prison Memoirs." *Mizegerd* 2, nos. 3–8 (July 1991–July 1992).

Lawyers Committee for Human Rights. *The Justice System of the Islamic Republic of Iran*. Washington, D.C., 1993.

League for the Defence of Human Rights in Iran. *Hoquqeh Beshar* (Human Rights). Occasional Reports. Berlin, 1982–95.

MacEoin, D. *A People Apart: The Bahai Community of Iran in the Twentieth Century*. London: School of Oriental and African Studies, 1989.

Mahmud, A. *Dastan-e Yek Shahr* (Tale of a City). Tehran, 1985.

———. *Hamsayeh-ha* (Neighbors). Tehran, 1984.

———. *Zamin-e Sukhteh* (Burnt Land). Tehran, 1982.

Makinezhad, T. "Khalel Maleki, Taqi Arani, and the Tudeh Party." In *Yadnameh-e Khalel Maleki* (Memorial to Khalel Maleki), ed. A. Pishdad and H. Katouzian, 271–76. Tehran, 1991.

Maleki, Kh. *Khaterat-e Siyasi* (Poltical Memoirs). Hannover, 1982.

Mani, A. *Darbareh Mohakemat-e Siyasi-ye Panjah-u-Seh Nafar* (Concerning the Political Trials of the Fifty-three). Tehran, 1952.

Martin, D. *The Persecution of the Bahais of Iran, 1944–1984*. Ottawa: Association of Bahai Studies, 1985.

Milani, A. *Tales of Two Cities: A Persian Memoir*. Washington, D.C.: Mazda, 1996.

Mobaser, M. *Parvahesh* (Investigation). Bethesda, 1994.

Mohajer, N. "The Mass Killings in Iran." *Aresh* 57 (August 1996): 4–8.

Mojahedin Organization. *Akherin Defa'eyat* (Final Testimonies). N.p., 1972.

———. "The Eternal Martyrs of Freedom: The Names and Specific Information on 12,028 Martyrs of the New Iranian Revolution." *Mojahed* 261 (6 September 1985).

———. *Hushyar-e Enqelabi: Vazifeh-e Yek Mobarez Asir dar Zendan* (Revolutionary Awareness: The Responsibility of a Captured Militant in Prison). N.p., 1972.

———. *List of Names and Particulars of 14,028 Victims of the Khomeini Regime's Executions.* N.p., 1987.

———. *Yaddasht-ha-ye az Zendan-e Evin* (Notes from Evin Prison). Memphis, 1972.

———. *Zendan* (Prison). Berlin, n.d.

Momeni, B. "The Tragedy of Our Generation." *Noqteh* 7 (Spring 1997): 128–33.

Mottaqi, H. "Life after 1988." *Noqteh* 6 (Summer 1996): 20–22.

Nafisi, M. "Letters from Prison." *Aresh* 52 (October–November 1995): 26–28.

Namvar, R. *Shahidan-e Tudehi* (Tudeh Martyrs). Tehran, 1982.

———. *Yadnameh-e Shahidan* (Martyr's Memorial). N.p., 1964.

Naraghi, E. *From Palace to Prison.* Chicago: Ivan Dee, 1994.

Nash, G. *Iran's Secret Pogrom: The Conspiracy to Wipe Out the Baha'is.* Suffolk: Spearman, 1982.

Nasim, A. "No Death Have I Feared." *Noqteh* 6 (Summer 1996): 18–19.

National Front. *Iran: Chronique de la Repression, 1963–75.* Paris, 1975.

National Movement of the Iranian Resistance. *Iran: In Defence of Human Rights.* Paris, 1983.

Novidi, P. "Interview Concerning the Martyrdom of Bezhan Jazani." *Aghaze-e Now* 29 (March 1992): 50–56.

Ovanessian, A. "The Communist Party in Khurasan." *Donya* 6, no. 3 (Fall 1965): 76–86.

——. "The Communist University of the Toilers of the East (KUTIV)." *Donya* 9, no. 1 (Spring 1969): 96–103.

——. *Khaterat* (Memoirs). Cologne, 1990.

——. "Reminiscences of the Communist Party." *Donya* 3, no. 1 (Spring 1962): 33–39.

——. "Reminiscences of the Communist Party in Gilan." *Donya* 10, no. 3 (Fall 1969): 85–90.

——. "Reminiscences of the Communist Party in Tehran." *Donya* 7, no. 3 (Spring 1966): 107–13.

——. *Safhat-e Chand az Jonbesh-e Kargari va Komunisti-ye Iran* (Some Notes on the Workers and Communist Movement in Iran). Stockholm, 1979.

——. *Yaddasht-ha-ye Zendan* (Prison Memoirs). Tehran, 1944.

——. *Yaddasht-ha-ye Zendan: Salha-ye 1928–42* (Prison Memoirs: The 1928–42 Years). Stockholm, 1979.

Paknezhad, S. "Keramat Daneshyan in Prison." *Azadi* 1 (September 1987): 52–57.

Parsipour, S. *Khaterat-e Zendan* (Prison Memoirs). Stockholm, 1996.

Parvaresh, Nima. *Dar Sal-e 1367 bar Ma Cheh Gozasht?* (What Happened to Us in 1988?). Paris, 1994.

Paya, A. (Pseudonym for P. Ousiya). *Zendan-e Towhidi* (Monotheistic Prison). Paris, 1987.

Pesyan, N. *Vaq'eh-e E'dam-e Jahansouz* (The Incident of Jahansouz's Execution). Tehran, 1991.

Peykar Organization. *Az Armani Keh Mejusht* (From an Ideal that Erupts). Sweden, 1984.

Pishevari, J. "My Recollections." *Azhir*, 6 December 1943.

——. *Yaddasht-ha-ye Zendan* (Prison Memoirs). Tehran, 1944.

Pourpirar, N. *Chand Begumegu darbareh Hezbi Tudeh* (Some Words Concerning the Tudeh Party). Tehran, 1995.

Qassemi, A. "Escape from Qasr." In Q. Forutan, *Hezb-e Tudeh dar Sahneh-e Iran* (The Tudeh Party on the Iranian Scene). N.p. n.d.

Raffat, D. *The Prison Papers of Bozorg Alavi.* Syracuse: Syracuse University Press, 1985.

Raha, M. (Pseudonym). *Haqiqat-e Sadeh: Khaterat-e az Zendanha-ye Zanan-e Jomhuri-ye Islami* (Plain Truths: Memoirs from Women's Prisons in the Islamic Republic). 3 vols. Hannover, 1992–94.

Rah-e Kargar Organization. "Horrific Nightmare: Discussion with Three Survivors of the1988 Mass Executions." *Rah-e Kargar* 90–93 (January–March 1992).

———. *Shahidan-e Ma* (Our Martyrs). Berlin, 1988.

Rajavi, M. "Paknezhad in Prison." *Showra* 15 (January 1984): 3–12.

Rejali, D. *Torture and Modernity: Self, Society, and State in Modern Iran.* Boulder: Westview, 1994.

Reyshahri, M. *Khaterat-e Siyasi* (Political Memoirs). Tehran, 1990.

Roohizadegan, O. *Olya's Story: A Survivor's Dramatic Account of the Persecution of Bahais in Revolutionary Iran.* Oxford: Oneworld, 1993.

Russell, B. "Inside the Shah's Prison" Unpublished report issued by the Bertrand Russell Office. London, 1965.

Rusta, R. "The Cultural Societies." *Donya* 6, no. 3 (Autumn 1965): 82–88.

Sa'edi, A. "The Incident of My Television Interview." *'Elm va Jam'eh* 57 (November 1987): 66–69.

Sa'idi-Sirjani, A., ed. *Vaqay'-e Ettefaqiyeh: Majmu'eh-e Gozaresh-ha-ye Khafiyeh-e Nevesan-e Englesi* (Events that Occurred: The Collected Secret Reports of an English Writer). Tehran, 1982.

Sayyed-Javadi, A. "The Memoirs of Dr. Faust." *'Elm va Jam'eh* 57 (December 1987): 18–30.

Shafayi, A. *Qiyam-e Afsaran-e Khurasan* (The Revolt of the Khurasan Officers). Tehran, 1986.

Shahri, J. *Tarikh-e Ejtema'i-e Tehran* (Social History of Tehran). 5 vols. Tehran, 1990.

Shamideh, A. *Khaterat-e Zendan* (Prison Memoirs). Baku, 1980.

————. *Zendeginameh-e Shamideh* (The Life Story of Shamideh). Ed. B. Chubineh. Cologne, 1994.

Shirazi, A. "New Year on Khark." *Adineh* 55–56 (March 1991): 6–10.

Shirazi, A. (Pseudonym). *Baba Bia Berim Khaneh* (Daddy Let's Go Home). The Netherlands, 1996.

Shukat, H. *Negah-ye az Darun deh Jonbesh-e Chap-e Iran* (An Inside Look at the Leftist Movement in Iran). 2 vols. Saarbrücken, 1989.

Society for Political Refugees. *Gozaresh az Zendan* (Prison Report). Göttingen, 1984.

Tabari, E. "Concerning the Cultural Society in Rasht." *Donya* 3, no. 2 (June 1980): 173–75.

Tafreshi, M., and M. Taher-Ahmadi. *Guzaresh-ha-ye Mahramaneh-e Shahrbani* (Secret Police Reports). Tehran, 1992.

Tafreshian, A. *Qiyam-e Afsaran-e Khurasan* (The Revolt of the Khurasan Officers). Tehran, 1985.

Tangestani, A. "I Was in Khomeini's Prison: A Woman's Testimony." *Azadi* 2 (March–May 1987): 46–56.

Tudeh Party. *Akherin Dafa ̔-e Khosrow Rouzbeh* (Khosrow Rouzbeh's Last Defense). Strassfurt, 1970.

————. "Examples of Valiant Resistance." *Mardom* 297 (February 1990).

————. "In Memory of Military Officers Fallen in the 1988 Mass Executions." *Mardom* 513 (August 1997).

United Nations (Economic and Social Council). *Situation of Human Rights in the Islamic Republic of Iran.* New York, February 1990.

————. *Situation of Human Rights in the Islamic Republic of Iran.* New York, November 1990.

————. *Situation of Human Rights in the Islamic Republic of Iran.* New York, January 1993.

————. *Situation of Human Rights in the Islamic Republic of Iran.* New York, January 1994.

Vatani, M. "Mothers and Children in Khomeini's Prisons." *Azadi* 2–3 (March–May 1987): 132–36, 93–98.

Zafari, V. *Habsiyeh dar Adab-e Farsi: Az Aghaz-e Sh ̔er Farsi ta*

Payan-e Zandieh (Confinement in Persian Literature: From the Earliest Persian Poetry until the Zands). Tehran, 1987.

Zarkar, Y. *Khaterat-e Yek Cherik dar Zendan* (Memoirs of a Guerrilla in Prison). N.p., 1977.

Zibayi, A. *Komunism dar Iran* (Communism in Iran). 2 vols. Tehran, n.d.

Texts of Public Recantations

Ettela'at, 1970–95.
Jomhuri-ye Islami, 1981–95.
Kayhan, 1981–95.
Kayhan-e Hava'i, 1981–95.

Books Written in Prison

Fardoust, H. *Khaterat-e Hossein Fardoust* (The Memoirs of Hossein Fardoust). Tehran, 1989.

Firuz, M. *Khaterat-e Maryam Firuz* (The Memoirs of Maryam Firuz). Tehran, 1994.

Kianuri, N. *Khaterat-e Nuraldin Kianuri* (The Memoirs of Nuraldin Kianuri). Tehran, 1992.

Tabari, E. *Kuzh Raheh* (The Crooked Road). Tehran, 1984.

———. *Shenakht va Sanjesh-e Marksism* (Epistemololgy and Evaluation of Marxism). Tehran, 1989.

Obituaries of Those Killed Under Torture

Aksariyat, 1984–89
Donya, 1979–95
Ettehad-e Kar, 1985–92.
Fedayi, 1988–94.
Gozareh, 1994–95.
Jahan, 1982–87.
Kar, 1979–98.
Mardom, 1979–98.
Mojahed, 1979–95.
Peykar, 1979–82.
Rah-e Kargar, 1983–98.
Rah-e Tudeh, 1982–98.

Index

Page numbers in italics denote tables.

Text: 10/13 Aster
Display: Aster
Composition: Binghamton Valley Composition
Printing and binding: Maple-Vail Manufacturing Group